D0561381

WITHDRAWN

JAMES I AND HENRI IV

JAMES I
and
HENRI IV

❋ ❋ ❋ ❋ ❋ ❋ ❋ ❋ ❋ ❋ ❋ ❋ ❋ ❋ ❋ ❋ ❋ ❋ ❋ ❋

An Essay in English Foreign Policy

1603-1610

Maurice Lee, Jr.

UNIVERSITY OF ILLINOIS PRESS

Urbana   Chicago   London

FOR MAURI AND BLAIR

CONTENTS

❖ ❖

I.	*King James VI and I*	3
II.	*The Peace with Spain*	17
III.	*Aftermath of Peace*	41
IV.	*Spain and the Dutch: Peace or War?*	71
V.	*Spain and the Dutch: The Treaties of Guarantee*	97
VI.	*Spain and the Dutch: The Truce of Antwerp*	118
VII.	*The Cleves–Julich Succession*	142
VIII.	*After Henri IV*	168
	Index	187

ILLUSTRATIONS

❖ ❖

Following page 82

Anglo-Spanish peace conference, 1604

James I

Henri IV

Archduke Albert

Sir Ralph Winwood

Johan van Oldenbarnevelt

Nicolas de Neufville, Seigneur de Villeroy

Pierre Jeannin

Map, page 145

The Rhineland in 1609: the Cleves-Julich Succession

Abbreviations used in the footnotes

B.M.—British Museum, London

P.R.O.—Public Record Office, London

Beaumont—P. Laffleur de Kermaingant, *Mission de Christophe de Harlay, Comte de Beaumont,* 2 vols. (Paris, 1895)

Boderie—*Ambassades de M. de la Boderie en Angleterre sous le regne d'Henri IV et la minorité de Louis XIII,* 5 vols. (Paris, 1750)

De L'Isle—W. A. Shaw and G. D. Owen, eds., *Report on the Manuscripts of Lord De L'Isle and Dudley,* vols. III–V, Historical Manuscripts Commission publication (London, 1936–1962)

Downshire—E. K. Purnell and A. B. Hinds, eds., *Report on Manuscripts of the Marquess of Downshire,* vols. II–IV, Historical Manuscripts Commission publication (London, 1936–1940)

Jeannin—M. Petitot, ed., *Négociations du Président Jeannin,* in *Collection des Memoires relatifs à l'histoire de France,* 2nd ser., vols. XI–XV (Paris, 1821–1822)

Pays-Bas—H. Lonchay, J. Cuvelier, and J. Lefèvre, eds., *Correspondance de la Cour d'Espagne sur les affaires des Pays-Bas au XVIIe siècle,* 6 vols. (Brussels, 1923–1937)

Prinsterer—G. Groen van Prinsterer, ed., *Archives ou correspondance inédite de la maison d'Orange-Nassau,* 2nd ser., vol. II (Utrecht, 1858)

Salisbury—M. S. Giuseppi and D. McN. Lockie, eds., *Report on the Manuscripts of the Marquess of Salisbury,* vols. XV–XIX, Historical Manuscripts Commission publication (London, 1930–1965)

C.S.P. Venetian—H. F. Brown, ed., *Calendar of State Papers, Venetian, 1603–1613,* 3 vols. (London, 1900–1905)

Winwood—E. Sawyer, ed., *Memorials of Affairs of State in the Reigns of Q. Elizabeth and K. James I. Collected chiefly from the original papers of . . . Sir Ralph Winwood,* 3 vols. (London, 1725)

FOREWORD

❋ ❋

A REVIEWER of the second edition of Conyers Read's *Bibliography of British History, Tudor Period* described the amount of writing dealing with the Tudors that had seen the light in the twenty-five years or so since the appearance of the first edition as a "publication explosion." The same phrase is equally apt for the period of the early Stuarts and the civil war. Gallons of ink have been spilled over the gentry, and Professor Lawrence Stone's work on the aristocracy is a kind of explosion all by itself. Tudor scholars have devoted a good deal of attention to foreign policy as well as to domestic affairs—Read's own work on Walsingham and Burghley comes readily to mind. The historians of the early seventeenth century have not imitated their Tudor colleagues in this respect, however. They have been concerned primarily with the civil war, its causes and course and consequences, and so they have focussed on Puritanism and social change and constitutional conflicts and economic developments and the history of ideas. Even S. R. Gardiner did not devote many pages of his magisterial history to English relations with the outside world until he arrived at the period of the Thirty Years War, at which point James I's foreign policy became a matter of serious domestic controversy and Parliamentary attack upon the government.

This study represents an attempt to remedy that neglect in some small part, by providing a detailed account of the diplomatic relations between England and France in the period between the accession of James I to the English throne in 1603 and the assassination of Henri IV in 1610. It is a strictly diplomatic narrative. I have not attempted to give any account of those domestic developments, such as the Gunpowder Plot or the increasingly grave financial circumstances of the government, which affected Anglo-French relations, though of course they are mentioned where necessary in order to explain the course of English foreign policy. What I have tried to do is to explain the principles upon which the government of James I acted in foreign affairs, and to provide an account from the sources of how those principles, such as they were, were implemented in English relations with France during the lifetime of Henri IV. I have chosen to focus upon this particular aspect of English foreign policy because it seems to me that the spectacular disaster which overtook that policy after the outbreak of the Thirty Years War stems very largely from James's failure to come to a solid understanding with France when such an agreement was possible, i.e., while Henri IV stood forth as the leader of anti-Habsburg Europe.

The bulk of the primary source material for this study is to be found in the Public Record Office and the British Museum, whose overworked staffs were both courteous and helpful. My grateful thanks are also owing to the following: the University of Illinois Library, the Princeton University Library, the Folger Shakespeare Library, the New York Public Library, and the London Library; the University of Illinois and the John Simon Guggenheim Memorial Foundation for providing both time and money to do the research for this work; my former student Joseph Bernard for his diligence during his year as my research assistant; Mrs. Joseph H. D. Allen of Champaign, Illinois, for her translation of various Spanish documents; Mrs. Maurice Weber and Miss Anita Tammara for their typing of various drafts which required them to read my abominable handwriting; and finally my wife, who endured a great deal of churlishness during the writing of this book and complained far less than could be expected.

The dates used in this work are Old Style, save that the year is taken to begin on January 1. For letters dated New Style both dates are given. The spelling and punctuation of quotations from contemporary sources have been modernized.

JAMES I AND HENRI IV

CHAPTER I

❖ ❖

King James VI and I

"TRULY ALL other princes sought unto us and desired the help of King James. He was the occasion of much peace in the Christian world, and certainly held very good correspondence with all the princes of Christendom. . . . While all the Christian world was in wars, he alone governed his people in peace. He was a most just and good king."[1]

So wrote Godfrey Goodman, bishop of Gloucester, appointed to his benefice by James I, and the king's admirer and defender. Historians have found much less to admire and defend in James's conduct of his office. The whole Whig school has weighed him in the balance and found him wanting; he seems no less incompetent to the latter-day courtiers of Gloriana. In S. R. Gardiner's opinion James "sowed the seeds of revolution and disaster"; to Sir John Neale he was "a weak sovereign who had neither the character nor the political skill to maintain the discipline of the past."[2] James's most recent scholarly biographer, while not altogether unsympathetic, on the whole arrives at an unfavorable verdict on the king, both as a ruler

[1] Godfrey Goodman, *The Court of King James the First* (London, 1839) I, 249–50.

[2] S. R. Gardiner, *History of England from the Accession of James I to the Outbreak of the Civil War* (new ed., London, 1890–91) V, 316. J. E. Neale, *Essays in Elizabethan History* (New York, 1958), p. 84.

and as a man.[3] Historians of Scotland have been much more favorable, and, indeed, James's successes in his northern kingdom are not seriously in question. But these scholars have for the most part not become involved in a discussion of James's policy south of the border; they have usually contented themselves with pointing out that Elizabeth left things in a rather messy condition.[4] It is all summed up in the famous phrase from *1066 and All That*: "King James I slobbered at the mouth and had favorites; he was, thus, a Bad King."

All of the historians of Jacobean England, the king's few defenders and his many critics, agree that James's experiences as king of Scotland determined his conduct of English domestic affairs. His numerous quarrels with a group of outspoken Calvinist Presbyterian ministers helped to lead him to espouse the doctrine of the divine right of kings. The insolence of some of his factious aristocrats led him to detest rebels of all sorts. The ease with which he controlled the subservient Scottish Parliament caused him to neglect the arts of management which were so necessary to good relations with a Parliament which had given Elizabeth, with all her tact and skill, a good many difficulties. His hand-to-mouth existence in a poverty-stricken and economically backward realm hardly prepared him either for the complexities of the English economic and financial structure or for the fact that the resources of the English crown were not limitless and had to be husbanded. His lonely and unnatural childhood and youth, growing up, always a king, amid dour Calvinist intellectuals and bloody-minded aristocratic politicians who treated him as a kind of political tennis-ball, taught him dissimulation and gave him a craving for affection and deference so great that more often than not he was unable to distinguish between the genuine article and the postures of the sycophant. Sycophancy, in turn, led him to exaggerate his genuine talent, to believe that he

[3] D. H. Willson, *King James VI and I* (London, 1956).
[4] See, for instance, G. Donaldson, *Scotland: James V–James VII* (Edinburgh, 1965), pp. 236–37.

could govern successfully in the intervals which bad weather or some other cause created in his endless hunting. In short, James was lazy, extravagant, conceited, imbued with an inflated sense of his power as a king, unwilling to learn or to distinguish good advice from bad—hence the errors which reaped the whirlwind for his son.

It is less often realized that James's conduct of foreign policy after 1603 was also conditioned by his Scottish experience. As king of Scotland James had two objectives in his foreign policy. The first was to persuade other powers not to interfere in Scottish domestic affairs, so that he could go about the business of gaining control of the dissident elements in his kingdom, the turbulent aristocracy and those stiff-necked and interfering clerics who followed Andrew Melville in his advocacy of the doctrine of the two kingdoms. Given the feebleness of France in the last years of Henri III, the power most likely to intervene was England, and, after England, Spain. The Anglo-Scottish treaty of 1586 amounted to a tacit pledge of nonintervention on Elizabeth's part, a pledge which for the most part was kept, save in those periods, notably the early 1590s, when James appeared to the English government to be too lax in his treatment of the Catholic, pro-Spanish element in the Scottish aristocracy. The Queen had made it clear in 1590 and thereafter, when James suggested the possibility of a Protestant league, that she welcomed no initiatives from him in foreign policy. So James adopted a passive policy. By doing nothing to offend Elizabeth, he kept English interference in his affairs to a minimum, made it probable that England would help him if a serious Spanish threat materialized, and achieved considerable success in gaining control of his kingdom.

James's second great objective in foreign policy, in fact the great objective of his life, was to succeed to the English throne. Here, once again, Elizabeth's attitude determined the policy he had to pursue. The Queen would not acknowledge him as her successor; she would go no further than to do nothing to prejudice his claim. By the rules of primogeniture James's claim was certainly the best, after the execution of his mother, but it was open to question in certain respects. Henry VIII had prescribed that the heirs of his younger sister Mary should be preferred to those of his older sister Margaret, James's great-grandmother. Some held that the crown could pass only to a native-born Englishman. Above all there was the specter raised by the famous *Conference about the next Succession to the Crown of England*, a tract usually attributed to the Jesuit Robert Persons, which argued that the next ruler must be a member of the true church. It behooved James, therefore, to obtain as much support from as many different sources as he could. Given Elizabeth's attitude, he could not openly canvass. So he had to approach people secretly and unofficially, at the same time remaining on good terms with everybody. James misread the English political situation and came very near to overcommitting himself to the earl of Essex, but in the end his intrigue with Essex did him no harm. The Queen chose to overlook it, and Robert Cecil decided that it was in his and the nation's interest that James should succeed quietly and unopposed. Cecil saw to it that it happened just this way—possibly the most significant act of his career.

It was not only within England that James looked for support, but on the continent as well. He approached everybody—Spain, France, the Protestant powers, Tuscany, even the Pope. His maneuvering was complicated, obscure, sometimes faintly silly, and not particularly effective. The Protestant states had no reason to oppose James, though there was but little any of them could do to help him had they been so inclined. The Catholic states might well have opposed him, but their opposition would be effective only if they could agree on a rival candidate, and they could not. James was saved from a serious Catholic challenge, not by the effectiveness of his own diplomacy, but by circumstances over which he had no control. His diplomacy, says his biographer, did not

> enhance his personal prestige, for he was considered a kind of irrepressible and erratic bounder whose bizarre diplomacy was crass and uncivilized and whose words and actions offered no basis of confidence.

"He practices in Rome, in Spain, and everywhere else as he does with me," wrote Henry IV, "without attaching himself to anyone, and is easily carried away by the hopes of those about him without regard for truth or merit. Hence I foresee that he will allow himself to be surprised on all occasions."[5]

The general situation in Europe in the last years of Elizabeth's reign was indeed favorable to James. His greatest asset lay in the difficult situation of the Spanish monarchy, disliked by the Protestant states of Europe and by many Catholic ones as well, still at war with England and with the rebels in the Netherlands, wars which Spain was able neither to win nor to end. The government of Philip III was slow-moving and unimaginative, and singularly unwilling to strike out on a new line. From Spain's point of view there was no point in continuing the war with England, particularly after the fiasco at Kinsale, in Ireland, in 1601, and every reason to make peace before Elizabeth died if Philip seriously expected a Catholic candidate, any Catholic, to succeed her. The possibility of such a peace alarmed James. The rulers of the Low Countries were anxious for peace; it was they who took the initiative in bringing about the abortive negotiations with England at Boulogne in the summer of 1600. These rulers were Philip's cousin, Archduke Albert of Austria, who was the younger brother of the Holy Roman Emperor Rudolf II and who had become governor-general in 1596, and Albert's wife, Philip's sister Isabella. They were in theory independent sovereigns by grant of Philip II, though it was provided that sovereignty over the Low Countries would revert to the Spanish crown should they die without issue, which was, in fact, what eventually happened. The Spanish candidate to succeed Elizabeth on the English throne was this same Isabella, who did not want to become involved. She was convinced that Philip was putting her forward in order to recover Spanish sovereignty in the Low

[5] Willson, *King James VI and I*, p. 148. The best account of James's maneuvering is contained in H. G. Stafford, *James VI of Scotland and the Throne of England* (New York, 1940), esp. chaps. IV and VIII.

Countries immediately. Her candidacy was bound to alienate Henri IV, who would never support a Habsburg for obvious reasons. Pope Clement VIII was also cool to the proposal, as he was not anxious to see such a considerable expansion of Habsburg power. James's own devious and unofficial negotiations with Clement led the Pope to believe that James's conversion, while unlikely, was not outside the realm of possibility.

Only if Philip abandoned the Habsburg claim would it be possible to get the other Catholic states even to discuss an alternative to James. Philip did not do so until early in 1603, just before Elizabeth's death, and by then it was too late. Spanish inertia and lethargy, Philip's refusal to make a serious effort to make peace with Elizabeth, largely because he insisted that toleration for English Catholics be a part of any settlement, his support of a hopeless candidate who firmly refused to consider herself as such—all this made James's path to his heart's desire far smoother than it might otherwise have been. James's own direct contribution to this happy result was almost negligible. His one positive and useful step was to remain on friendly terms with the government of the Archduke, who sent an agent to Edinburgh chiefly to put a stop, if he could, to Dutch recruiting there.[6]

As for Henri IV, his attitude was rather complicated; it was based on a combination of his delicate relations with the government of Elizabeth and his appreciation of the advantages to France inherent in the continued separation of England and Scotland. English aid in men and money had been enormously useful to Henri in the first years of his reign, but even then there had been disagreements as to how that aid should be used. England was preoccupied with the dangerous possibility that Spain might get control of an area, such

[6] This account of Spanish policy is based mostly on A. J. Loomie, "Philip III and the Stuart Succession in England," *Revue belge de Philologie et d' Histoire* XLIII (1965), 492–514. See also A. J. Loomie, *Toleration and Diplomacy: The Religious Issue in Anglo-Spanish Relations 1603–1605* (Transactions of the American Philosophical Society, New Series, vol. 53, pt. 6, Philadelphia, 1963), pp. 5–9.

as Brittany, which might be used as a base for a renewed attempt at invasion. Brittany was a peripheral area to Henri, who wanted to employ English troops wherever they would be most useful in defeating his enemies of the Holy League. After Henri's conversion the friction increased. Elizabeth insisted that Henri turn over a seaport to her, either for use as a military base or as a pledge that Henri would repay his substantial debt. Henri flatly refused to do this; he regarded the English request as a Machiavellian attempt to beggar and dismember his kingdom.

After the peace of Vervins between France and Spain, signed in 1598, French need for English aid ceased, but the disagreements did not. There was the problem of French trade with Spain, which, in the English view, aided the Spanish war effort. English ships took to searching French vessels and often seizing them. An agreement was eventually reached: France promised not to ship war material to Spain, and England agreed to leave French ships alone. This agreement did not work very well, partly because Spanish ships took advantage of it to sail under French colors. There was the problem of the English export of cloth to France; Henri's advisers felt that the English had too large a share of the cloth market, and that a good deal of what they sent into France was defective. Henri's edict of April, 1600, ordering the confiscation of defective cloth provoked a bitter and hostile reaction in England. And there was the problem of the debt. Now that France was at peace, England thought she ought to arrange to repay it. Henri's government pleaded poverty, but went on sending money to the Dutch. Some effort was made to come to an agreement on these issues, but nothing was really settled, in part because Henri believed that England's principal purpose, after the failure of the Boulogne peace conference, was to smooth over the points of difficulty in order to lure France back into the war.[7]

Henri found very little to admire in his brother of Scotland, either

[7] For Anglo-French relations in this period see J. B. Black, *Elizabeth and Henry IV* (Oxford, 1914).

before or after 1603, an opinion which James cordially reciprocated. Henri found James's diplomacy in the 1590s both ridiculous and untrustworthy, and he never forgot that James's grandmother was a Guise. James's habits of business astonished him. In July, 1605, the Venetian representative in France reported to his government that the English ambassador had asked Henri for an audience in a great hurry; it turned out that what he wanted was to deliver his master's request that Henri send over a particular huntsman. Henri agreed, and after the ambassador had left "he remarked to his suite that he was amazed that in such troublous times his Majesty of England should think of nothing but the chase."[8] As for James, Henri's apostasy, as he viewed it, indicated weakness of character and a fundamental untrustworthiness, and he never forgave Henri's famous gibe that he was properly called the Scottish Solomon since he was the son of David. The deep and bitter personal dislike between the two men contributed greatly to the sense of mutual mistrust which was so heavily to color the diplomatic relations between their kingdoms after 1603.

James seemed to Henri, therefore, somewhat less than desirable as a successor to Elizabeth; furthermore, France had good reason not to want to see a union of the two kingdoms. The existence of an independent Scotland had always been of use to France in her dealings with England, as the sturdiness and duration of the "auld alliance" demonstrates, though since the Reformation and the subsequent friendship between England and Scotland the usefulness of the Franco-Scottish connection had markedly diminished. Nevertheless there was nothing France would gain from a union of the crowns, and such a union might lead to demands that the great commercial privileges enjoyed by Scottish merchants in France be extended to English merchants as well. Partly for this reason Henri followed very closely the development of James's proposals for genuine unification of the two kingdoms after 1603, and was delighted when they came to nothing. For a long time, however, Henri

[8] C. S. P. Venetian 1603–1607, p. 261.

was prepared to accept James as Elizabeth's successor, since there seemed to be no viable alternative and nothing much for him to do about it in any case. It was not until the summer of 1602 that he began to indicate an active interest in supporting a Catholic candidate, who, of course, must not be a Habsburg. It was necessary to proceed cautiously and indirectly since the odds against success were great, and if James should discover what Henri was about, he would be hopelessly alienated—a serious matter if he should succeed to the English crown. It took time, therefore, for Henri's new attitude to be taken seriously at the Spanish court—too much time. Only in March, 1603, did Philip let it be known that he was willing to consider a non-Habsburg candidate, and in that month Elizabeth died.[9] James achieved his heart's desire peacefully, without bloodshed, without opposition.

As King James rode south in the spring of 1603 to take his place on Elizabeth's throne, therefore, he came equipped with a stock of ideas with respect to foreign policy which had developed from his experiences as king of Scotland. He also came with no concrete policy objectives in mind—those he had had while king of Scotland had now been achieved. He regarded his conduct of Scottish foreign policy as highly successful, and so, indeed, it was. He had reached his goals, though he failed to see that his accomplishment was due less to his own abilities than to a set of fortunate circumstances. In his opinion his own skill, the principles he had worked out for his foreign policy, and the methods he had employed to implement those principles were responsible for his success. James's views were to be very costly to England in the long run, because as circumstances changed he failed to change his diplomatic strategy and tactics to meet the altered conditions. In fact in both foreign and domestic affairs James's very success in Scotland, given his character, militated against his making an equally successful king of England. James was nothing if not self-confident, and he was con-

[9] For the shift in Henri's attitude see Loomie, "Philip III and the Stuart Succession," *Revue belge* XLIII, 509–13.

vinced that he knew all the answers. It seems not to have occurred to him that the methods which had been so successful in Scotland would not work in England, that a point of view with respect to government developed in Scotland might not fit the vastly different circumstances to be found south of the Tweed.

In place of specific objectives in foreign affairs, James came south with a generalized but very firm conviction of the advantages of peace and friendship with as many states as possible. Peace had given him the opportunity to concentrate on domestic problems, and to achieve greater power in his kingdom than any of his predecessors. Peace, and the fact that he had no real enemies abroad, had smoothed his path to the English throne. James never lost his belief in the advantages of peace. His first major action after 1603 was to put an end to the Anglo-Spanish war, and throughout his life he was always most reluctant to embrace any policy which threatened to lead to war. More than that, he strove to stop other people's wars, by offering his services as a mediator, and sometimes with considerable success, especially in the Baltic area. He recognized, of course, that certain of other people's wars, notably that between Spain and the Dutch, were beneficial to England, but even in the case of this war his attitude was cautious and deliberately ambiguous, lest he find himself compelled to spend money to keep it going, or, worse still, become involved.

James believed that the way to remain at peace was to stay on good terms with all the world, with the Pope, even—though reluctantly—with the Turk. This, in turn, depended upon pursuing an essentially passive foreign policy. Taking the initiative would only lead to trouble, because initiatives were bound to annoy someone, as Elizabeth had been annoyed by James's proposal for a Protestant league in 1590. It became James's settled practice, therefore, to wait upon events. Then, if trouble arose, no one could blame him for having caused it, and he would be free to adopt whatever policy seemed most likely to preserve the peace and the reservoir of goodwill which James imagined he had accumulated. Indeed, the only occasions on which James was anxious to take the initiative were those which involved English mediation in a dispute, or his theological or monarchical convictions. If he found a book published abroad to be theologically offensive, he was always tempted to pick up his pen and reply. If a book attacked his beliefs on the question of the prerogative of kings, he would pelt his ambassador in the country where the book was published with letters demanding that the government in question suppress the offensive volume immediately. "I would wish" wrote Robert Cecil wearily to the English ambassador in France, "my master read fewer [books] than he doth."[10]

This policy of unadventurous and inoffensive goodfellowship was perfectly appropriate to the king of a powerless state such as Scotland. England was anything but a powerless state, however, and such a policy could succeed only in impairing English influence and reducing her to a cipher in international affairs except under very special circumstances. It might have worked, for instance, in a Europe in which England was one of several states of roughly equal strength with no major causes of dispute between them—a Utopian Europe, in fact, which obviously did not exist in 1603. What did exist in that year was a situation which offered, on the surface at least, some chance for James's policy, because it gave England the apparent opportunity to hold the balance of power. Spain was still the greatest state in Europe, though clearly less powerful than she had been in the palmy days of Philip II. The recovery of France under the gifted rule of Henri IV and his talented associates had been remarkably rapid; Henri was the avowed enemy of Spain; and Spain's wasting war with the Dutch dragged on, as did her war with England until James put an end to it. James was also the ruler of the wealthiest Protestant state in Europe. Given the hostility between France and Spain, and the French links with Protestant Europe,

[10] Sept. 20, 1611, Cecil to Sir Thomas Edmondes, P.R.O., State Papers (henceforth S.P.) 78/58, ff. 175–76. Throughout this work, for convenience's sake, Robert Cecil will be called that instead of by his later titles, first Cranborne, then Salisbury.

James, once he had ended the Anglo-Spanish war, believed that he was in a position to balance between the two major parties on the Continent, to be friendly with both sides, to follow a policy of peaceful coexistence. As long as France remained hostile to Spain, ideological complications could be minimized, a minimization which was essential for England, since it was clear enough that if France and Spain were ever to be sufficiently united to embark on an ideological crusade, the Protestant powers would be in very grave difficulties. Franco-Spanish enmity was the cornerstone upon which James's pacific diplomatic edifice had to be built.

It was easy, perhaps too easy, to take the permanence of this enmity for granted. To be sure, France and Spain had been hostile for a very long time, and as long as Henri IV lived the situation was unlikely to change, despite Henri's steadily improving relations with the Papacy, despite the occasional tentative suggestion for collaboration such as that which involved the possibility of a neutral Catholic candidate for Elizabeth's crown. Still, it was important for England to be sure that there was always a solid bone of contention between the two rivals. The current bone of contention was the Dutch. France could not afford to see Spain conquer her rebels—no more could England, for that matter. As long as the war between Spain and the Dutch went on, France would support the Dutch, and Franco-Spanish friendship would be impossible. In such circumstances, England, too, had to support the Dutch to some extent; if she did not, French influence would become paramount at The Hague. It would be very dangerous if the United Provinces became a client state of France, only slightly less dangerous than their reconquest by Spain or a Franco-Spanish rapprochement. It was, therefore, a vital interest for England that this war should continue, even though it might cost England something in terms of money at least, and perhaps even of men, to keep it going, and thus to help neutralize French influence with the Dutch. The end of the war would seriously weaken England's bargaining power, and create economic difficulties as well, since peace would make the Dutch commercial challenge, already serious enough, more formidable still.

In his pacifism James failed to understand this. He imagined that, in peace or war, he would always have the choice of allies. And yet James had no real choice of allies. Given Spain's great power, and the differing religious attitudes of Spain and France—the government of Philip III burned Protestants, while that of the ex-Huguenot tolerated them by law—there could be no genuine friendship between England and Spain. They had no significant common interest in 1603, and a great many points of friction, to which a new one was soon to be added, in the persons of the English colonists in Virginia. Spain was a menace to England; France was not. Spain was a menace to France; England was not. Here lay the great common interest between the two countries.

There existed, therefore, a very solid foundation for friendship between England and France, in spite of the points of disagreement between them, in spite of Henri's mistrust of James as a politician, in spite of James's dislike of a man who had abjured the true faith and was immoral to boot. Each king saw the usefulness of the other's friendship. For Henri it was highly necessary that England be kept in the anti-Spanish camp. For James, friendship with a reviving France would render England immune to the Spanish danger, but the friendship must not be too close, lest France drag England into a renewed war with the Habsburg colossus. It was a delicate tightrope which English statesmanship had to walk.

The issue, then, of the success or failure of English foreign policy in James's reign hinged upon English relations with France. In the resolution of this issue the seven years between James's accession and the death of Henri IV were crucial. It was during those years that the opportunity existed to put Anglo-French friendship on a firm enough basis to survive any change of rulers, to establish the kind of alliance which would provide security for both sides, and which would be strong enough to discourage the Spanish government from reverting to the aggressive policies of Philip II. The fact that the opportunity was wasted contributed mightily to the disaster which was to overtake England, James's policy of peace, and James himself in his last years, which were also the opening years of the Thirty Years War. The first years of James's reign were for Jacobean England what, in Sir Winston Churchill's view, the decade of the 1930s was to be for the England of his day: the years that the locust hath eaten.

CHAPTER II

❉ ❉

The Peace with Spain

THE CHANGE of monarchs in England was atypical in one respect at least: the new king was not an unknown quantity. James's love of peace and his dislike of rebels were well known. He had never been at war with Spain, and did not so regard himself now; one of his first steps was to recall the letters of marque which Elizabeth's government had issued to English privateers to prey on Spanish shipping. It was clear to both the late Queen's ministers and to foreign governments that there would be changes in English policy; the question was how abrupt and extensive these changes would be.

As it turned out, the change was not great, in part because James inherited his predecessor's chief minister as well as her crown. Historians have usually described Robert Cecil as "anti-Spanish"; this is one of those half-truths which tend to confuse rather than enlighten. Cecil was anti-Spanish only in the sense that his father was. He believed in peace; he had none of the romantic longing for military glory which had helped to ruin his rival Essex. Continental entanglements were dangerous but unfortunately necessary; isolation was a luxury England could not afford in an age of ideological warfare. Spain was the enemy because only Spain represented a threat to the English position, but it was a threat which by 1603 was far less serious than it once had been, with the military stalemate in the Low Countries and the end of the Irish rebellion. Spain was untrustworthy and had to be watched—but then, so was everybody else, including France and the Dutch. Cecil was cynical and suspicious of everyone, as befitted one who had made his way to power in the Byzantine atmosphere of the last decade of the Elizabethan court. If he was anti-Spanish in the sense that he did not believe in the possibility of permanent good relations with Spain, he could by the same token be described as anti-French. His outlook was essentially a cautious and negative one; like his new master, he preferred to wait upon events.

Cecil may have had little to offer James in the way of new ideas in foreign affairs, but he did have a willingness to work, to assume the day-to-day burden of affairs, and so he became indispensable. The king gladly left the implementation of policy in his hands. He conducted virtually all of the negotiations with the representatives of foreign powers in London, and he was an excellent negotiator, tactful, supple, and patient. He also kept a tight grip on other aspects of the conduct of foreign policy. Almost all of the men employed as diplomatic agents abroad had risen under the aegis of his father or himself, or had not been sufficiently prominent in the Essex faction to make a transfer of allegiance difficult; they were, for the most part, a group of conscientious, hard-working professionals. During Cecil's tenure of power there was none of the factionalism and discord over foreign policy in the king's inner circle which characterized the years after his death. There were some differences of opinion between him and the king, but the differences were not great and were resolved without difficulty, since they were firmly agreed on the desirability of peace, though for rather different reasons. James believed in peace as such; *beati pacifici* was his motto in foreign affairs. Cecil believed in it because it was necessary for the economic well-being of the country and the solvency of the treasury. Given this similarity of outlook, there was nothing, really, for him and his master to quarrel over.

To Cecil and his political allies there was nothing now to be gained by a continuation of the Spanish war, especially in view of the steadily worsening financial situation. Public opinion, said Giovanni Scaramelli, the Venetian representative in London, desired peace for commercial reasons; the savage outbreak of plague in 1603, which seriously if temporarily disrupted English overseas trade, strengthened this sentiment. Peace, however, must not be bought at the sacrifice of the objectives for which England had been fighting, which, at this point, meant the position of the United Provinces. James must be made to see that their interests must be safeguarded. This turned out not to be difficult; James might disapprove of the Dutch because they were rebels, but they were also Protestants, and James had no love for Spain, who, after all, had trafficked in rebellion in Scotland. Thomas Lake, the clerk of the signet, whom Cecil sent to Edinburgh to discuss these questions with James, was able to report that James had promised not to abandon the Dutch, especially as this would mean a throwing away of the benefits of their bargains with Elizabeth's government and would infallibly increase French influence at The Hague. James wanted the Dutch to send a commission to London to discuss the situation with him.[1]

The Dutch commission duly arrived; so, too, did one from France, headed by Henri IV's chief adviser, Maximilien de Béthune, the marquis of Rosny, better known under his later title of duke of Sully.[2] The new situation in England was not altogether palatable to Henri, who was afraid of the possibility of a revival of Anglo-Spanish friendship; James seemed to be more ready to be friendly to Archduke Albert than to him. Rumors circulated in France that James had refused to continue English aid to the Dutch on the ground that Elizabeth's quarrels were not his.[3] Henri's policy now

---

[1] April 4, 1603, Lake to Cecil, *Salisbury* XV, 30–31. See also the memorandum in P.R.O., S.P. 103/64, ff. 12–13. Apr. 21/May 1, Scaramelli to the Doge and Senate of Venice, *C.S.P. Venetian 1603–1607*, pp. 17–18.

[2] For convenience's sake he will be referred to as Sully.

[3] Apr. 26/May 6, 1603, Sir Thomas Parry to Cecil, P.R.O., S.P. 78/49, ff.

was the same as it had been since the peace of Vervins. France needed peace; everything possible must be done to keep both England and the Dutch embroiled with Spain. The Dutch were determined to fight on; if England could not be persuaded to do so too, then at least she should help the Dutch *sub rosa*, as France had been doing since Vervins. To this end the French ambassador in England, Christophe de Harlay, count of Beaumont, suggested that the Dutch might tell James that if he ceased to help them, they would have no other choice than to throw themselves into the arms of France.[4]

Cecil made it clear enough that England had no intention of abandoning the Dutch; his attitude was such that Charles de Ligne, count of Aremberg, the Archduke's envoy, believed that he really favored war and had been bought by the Dutch.[5] The Archduke sent Aremberg to London ostensibly to congratulate James on his accession, but actually to find out if the peace which the Archduke so badly needed was possible. The reports of the agent the Archduke had sent to Scotland as to James's pacifism and dislike of the Dutch were encouraging; he now gave evidence of his own intentions by ordering an end to attacks on English shipping, save for those ships taking food or munitions to the Dutch.[6] Aremberg was not an effective envoy, owing to a combination of bad health, English suspicion of his possible involvement in the abortive plotting of the summer of 1603, and their conviction that the Archduke could do nothing by himself: all depended on Spain. And the Spanish government acted in its usual leisurely fashion; its envoy, Don Juan de Tassis, count of Villa Mediana, did not arrive in England till late in September. For once Spanish delays made little difference; be-

---

71–72. Apr. 28/May 8, Henri to Beaumont, *Beaumont* II, 110–12. Parry was the English ambassador in France.

[4] May 5/15, May 27/June 6, 1603, Beaumont to Henri, *Prinsterer*, pp. 191–93.

[5] June 8/18, June 17/27, 1603, Aremberg to the Archduke, *Pays-Bas* I, 146, 149–50. Aremberg believed that everyone in England could be bought. *Ibid.*, p. 151.

[6] *Ibid.*, pp. 139–40, 141–42. Apr. 11, 1603, Sir Robert Mansell to Cecil, *Salisbury* XV, 42–43. Mansell was the English admiral in the Channel.

fore any serious peace negotiation could begin, it was essential for England to discuss matters with the French and the Dutch.

The immediate problem was the situation of Ostend, which had been under siege by the Archduke's forces since 1601 and was now in extremities. The Dutch were clamoring for immediate help, and a great deal of it: 10,000 foot and 2,500 horse. The English Council was "at a stand" to know what to do, in the period before James's arrival in London, but it permitted the Dutch to go on recruiting in view of the peril to the town.[7] James's first reaction was unsympathetic: "Was not Ostend originally the King of Spain's, and therefore now the Archduke's?" he reportedly said.[8] It soon became clear that England would make no special effort to relieve Ostend, which Cecil apparently believed was not in as grave danger as the Dutch made out.[9] The crucial interview between Cecil and the Dutch delegation, headed by Johan van Oldenbarnevelt, the most important Dutch politician, took place on May 27. Cecil talked obliquely, as was his habit, but the English line was clear: England was going to make peace. If the Dutch wished, they could be a party to the negotiations, and at all events England would not abandon them. The Dutch deputies were upset; they even thought that James was attempting to frighten them into offering him a protectorate over them. They were also alarmed by the specter of close Anglo-Danish cooperation—James was the brother-in-law of King Christian IV of Denmark—directed against their trade in the Baltic.[10] There was nothing for it, however, but to await Sully and hope that he could alter the king's resolution.

[7] Apr. 8, 1603, the Privy Council to James, *Salisbury* XV, 38–40. Apr. 24, Sir Francis Vere to Cecil, P.R.O., S.P. 84/64, ff. 13–14. Vere was the English commander at Brill, one of the two English cautionary towns, the other being Flushing.

[8] Apr. 28/May 8, 1603, Scaramelli to the Doge and Senate, *C.S.P. Venetian 1603–1607*, pp. 20–23.

[9] May 25, 1603, Cecil to Parry, P.R.O., S.P. 78/49, f. 131.

[10] May 18/28, June 2/12, 1603, Scaramelli to the Doge and Senate, *C.S.P. Venetian 1603–1607*, pp. 39–42, 48–50. May 27/June 6, Beaumont to Henri, *Prinsterer* pp. 192–93. June 9, Cecil to Parry, P.R.O., S.P. 78/49, f. 151.

Sully arrived in England in June, in a diplomatic atmosphere which was rather chilly. The continual French stalling on the matter of the debt owed to Elizabeth was an irritant. So, too, was the conduct of Beaumont, who, James believed, favored the claims of his cousin Arabella Stuart to the English throne, apparently because Beaumont had said that all good Catholics ought to protect ladies. Equally annoying to the sensitive James was Henri's joking threat to give one of his bastards permission to see if he could make himself a new William the Conqueror.[11] The purposes of Sully's mission were well known; as early as April the English ambassador in France, Sir Thomas Parry, had informed Cecil that the French would do their best to keep England in the war and would propose a formal treaty to guarantee protection to the Dutch, a treaty which might well be cemented by a marriage alliance. These matters, said Parry, had been thoroughly discussed with the Dutch agent in Paris.[12] In later dispatches Parry was able to add more. Henri talked expansively of a military alliance, the details of which, he said, Sully would spell out. Parry added that Sully would also raise the vexatious question of English depredations on French shipping, and perhaps also the even more delicate matter of tolerance for English Catholics. There was much alarm in France at the prospect of an Anglo-Spanish peace, Parry reported, especially in Huguenot circles; he urged Cecil to take a public stand in the current quarrel between the city of Geneva and the duke of Savoy in order to reassure not merely the Huguenots, but all continental Protestants.[13]

Given the obvious attitude of the English government (Aremberg reported in late June his conviction that James wanted peace; Henry

[11] May 15/25, 1603, Marin Cavalli (Venetian representative in France) to the Doge and Senate; June 2/12, Scaramelli to the Doge and Senate, *C.S.P. Venetian 1603–1607*, pp. 37–38, 48–50.
[12] P.R.O., S.P. 78/49, ff. 41, 56–57.
[13] Apr. 14, Apr. 26/May 6, May 12/22, May 23, May 31, 1603, Parry to Cecil, P.R.O., S.P. 78/49, ff. 56–57, 71–72, 90–91, 119–20, 135–36. Henri had in fact already instructed Beaumont to raise the Catholic question if he judged the atmosphere favorable. Apr. 4/14, Henri to Beaumont, *Beaumont* II, 104–10.

Howard, earl of Northampton, who stood high in the king's confidence, had assured him that James would not listen to French blandishments on this score)[14] it was surprising that Sully got as much as he did. His problem was a very simple one, so simple as to be completely insoluble. It was, as the Venetian agent put it, "to give a satisfactory answer to a question which the Council advised the King to address to his most Christian Majesty, namely, 'How can you ask me to live at war in order that you may live in peace?' "[15]

There was, in fact, no answer to this question, and Sully and Oldenbarnevelt, who were in close contact throughout Sully's stay, never did find one, despite all their best efforts. The English discounted Sully's argument that Spain wanted peace with England only to have her hands free to crush the Dutch; once that was done, said Sully, Spain would attack England again. Oldenbarnevelt tried his eloquence on the king personally. He could not obtain a formal audience, but got himself smuggled into a gallery in the palace at Greenwich, where, probably by design, he met with James. There he rehearsed to the king the long list of Spanish aggressions and iniquities, and pointed out how dangerous it would be for England to abandon the Dutch. James was sufficiently impressed to ask Oldenbarnevelt if he would repeat his arguments at the proper time before the ambassadors of Spain and the Archduke, but the king's mind was in effect made up: he would have peace. The size of the Dutch requests for aid was a further inducement in this direction. Small wonder that Sully was anxious to get home as quickly as possible.[16]

Henri's instructions to Sully reflected the French dilemma. The one way in which France might have overcome the English inclination to peace was to resume fighting herself, and this Henri was not yet prepared to do. So Sully was instructed to talk of an

[14] June 12/22, June 22/July 2, 1603, Aremberg to the Archduke, *Pays-Bas* I, 148, 152.

[15] June 16/26, 1603, Scaramelli to the Doge and Senate, *C.S.P. Venetian 1603–1607*, pp. 54–56.

[16] *Ibid*. See also B.M., Cottonian Mss., Galba E 1, ff. 101–104.

offensive-defensive league and a marriage alliance if England showed any inclination to go on fighting, but to make no precise commitments. The most the French king could reasonably expect was that England, after a peace, would help the Dutch in the same underhand way as he had been doing for the past five years, but this prospect was clouded by the difficulty, which kept cropping up in the negotiations, of the French debt to England, which Henri had no intention of paying if he could help it. France was also concerned to renegotiate the trade treaty of 1572, which, the French felt, was unfair in that it gave English merchants in France privileges not possessed by French merchants in England; but Sully was told not to touch this question and that of the treatment of English Catholics, if raising them would complicate a solution of the larger issue. Sully was to harp on the dangers of the growth of Habsburg power and the disasters which would result if the Dutch went under.[17]

Sully was not a good negotiator. He did not like the English, whom he regarded as haughty and unstable.[18] He was tactless with the king; when James, in talking of the Pope, objected to the use of the title "Holy Father," Sully replied that some kings took the title of kingdoms to which they had no right—an obvious allusion to the inclusion of "King of France" in the English king's style.[19] Perhaps in retaliation, James addressed Henri in a letter as "mon très cher frère" instead of "Monsieur mon frère"; Sully was annoyed.[20]

Sully's problem was further complicated by Henri's serious illness in the summer of 1603. Sully made light of it in conversation with James, but Parry reported that it was grave enough for Henri to be instructing his wife in affairs of state, and emphasized the chaos

---

[17] Maximilien de Béthune, duc de Sully, *Memoires des sages et royalles Oeconomies d'Estat de Henry le Grand* (Paris, 1820) IV, 261–90.

[18] *Ibid.*, p. 305.

[19] *Ibid.*, pp. 327, 348.

[20] June 27, 1603, Sir Lewis Lewkenor to Cecil, *Salisbury* XV, 152–53. J. Cuvelier, "Les préliminaires du traité de Londres (29 août 1604)," *Revue Belge de Philologie et d'Histoire* II (1923), 303. Lewkenor held a position comparable to that of a chief of protocol nowadays.

which would ensue in France if the king should die.[21] The memory of the French civil wars was still green; Henri's heir was a boy of three whose legitimacy was not beyond question. France's ability to fulfill any long-range commitments, and her willingness to do so, hung on the thread of the life of one man, a middle-aged rake who had had a very hard life. This consideration was to weigh very heavily in the minds of English statesmen over the next seven years, and goes far to explain their caution about committing themselves to France. Nowhere in history is there a better example of the pitfalls of hindsight than the condemnation which historians have meted out to James for what appears in retrospect to be an error of judgment respecting the relative strength of Spain and France. James did not regard Spain as a colossus; throughout his reign his diplomatic agents in Spain kept him well informed of the weaknesses of the Spanish government and the Spanish system. But France in the opening decades of the seventeenth century appeared in no better light. The France of Henri IV was not the France of Louis XIV, or even of Richelieu. Her strength and her future looked highly uncertain; the great destiny which lay ahead of her was no more visible in 1603 than was the disaster which overtook the Stuart dynasty.

James cannot be reasonably blamed for his failure to anticipate the long-range future of the French monarchy; but Henri's illness should have made James and his ministers acutely aware that the French king was mortal, and that his foreign policy might die with him, especially if he died while his heir was still a child. The permanence of France's anti-Spanish posture should not have been taken for granted. James and Cecil were wise not to commit themselves to France at this stage, before the signing of the peace with Spain. Once the peace was made, and gave evidence of being more or less permanent, then the time would have been ripe for a bargain with France which might have prevented or at least minimized the

[21] Sully, *Oeconomies* IV, 345–46. June 9, June 30, 1603, Parry to Cecil, P.R.O., S.P. 78/49, ff. 143, 171–72.

reversal of French policy which occurred during the minority of Louis XIII.

Because James and Cecil were unwilling to commit themselves to France in 1603, Sully's negotiations turned into a kind of shadow game. In his meetings with Cecil, sometimes with the Dutch deputies present, each side tried to get a positive statement from the other; each elaborately expressed willingness to follow the other's lead in the matter of helping the Dutch. Neither side wished to make a precise commitment, lest the other reveal it to Spain and leave the committed party out on a limb. Each side tried to throw on the other the major financial and military burden of the defense of the Dutch, but not the entire burden, lest the Dutch become clients of their sole supporter. It was taken for granted that the Dutch would go under if outside aid were cut off, and this could not be allowed to happen. In the discussions Sully kept harping on the dangers of negotiating with Spain: Spain would string out the negotiations so that England would relax her efforts on behalf of the Dutch. Ostend would fall, and Spain would throw off the mask. To the king he raised the specter of a Catholic league, and suggested a huge counter-league of the Protestant states and France.

Sully could not persuade the king to alter his resolution, but both he and James were aware that it would be dangerous if the negotiations came to no result. England could not afford a rupture with France till peace with Spain was made; her bargaining position would be too greatly weakened. France could not afford to allow an Anglo-Spanish peace to be the forerunner of a revival of the old Anglo-Burgundian connection which had proved so difficult for France to cope with in the age of Charles V; reports of Queen Anne's pro-Spanish proclivities were numerous.[22] The upshot was the treaty signed at Hampton Court. It was agreed that a defensive league would be negotiated, which would include the allies of the two

[22] See, e.g., May 5/15, 1603, Beaumont to Henri, *Prinsterer*, p. 191; May 25/June 4, Scaramelli to the Doge and Senate, *C.S.P. Venetian 1603–1607*, p. 44; June 2/12, Henri to Sully, Sully, *Oeconomies* IV, 318–19.

powers, notably the United Provinces. They also agreed to help the Dutch to reach a satisfactory settlement with Spain; in the meantime, military aid would continue. Troops were to be raised in England and paid for by France; one third of the French outlay was to be credited as payment on the French debt to England. This aid was to be provided as secretly as possible, so as not to provoke Spain into attacking France or disrupt the contemplated Anglo-Spanish peace negotiations. Should war nevertheless ensue, either from a Spanish attack on one or both of the two powers or because the latter felt constrained "par raison d'état et pour la sureté, repos et utilité de leur personnes, royaumes, et sujets" to begin war themselves, the military contributions of each party were specified. Significantly, the French acknowledged that they did owe the English government money, by agreeing to pay off the debt in three years if England alone were attacked; if France were at war, England was not to ask for payment as long as the fighting lasted.[23] The agreement was in many respects a highly conditional sort of thing, but Henri professed himself satisfied, and ratified it promptly, as did James.[24] James had accepted the commitment to the Dutch; even if an Anglo-Spanish peace could not be avoided, James's neutrality would be pro-Dutch rather than pro-Spanish.

Almost a year elapsed between the signing of the Anglo-French agreement and the formal opening in May, 1604, of peace talks between England and Spain. During that period relations between England and France were formal and rather chilly. Inside the French government there was a good deal of speculation, and some disagreement, as to the impact of such a peace on France's position. Nicolas de Neufville, seigneur de Villeroy, the French secretary of state, was inclined to believe that France should fight, if necessary, in order to keep England in the war. It could not be done otherwise,

[23] J. Dumont, *Corps Universel Diplomatique du Droit des Gens* (Amsterdam, 1728) V, pt. ii, 30–31, where the agreement is dated July 20/30, 1603.
[24] *Beaumont* II, 117–21. Sully, *Oeconomies* V, 50–51. For the French reaction see July 10, July 16, 1603, Parry to Cecil, P.R.O., S.P. 78/49, ff. 182–83, 195–96.

thought Villeroy, because of James's feeble and peaceloving spirit. Henri was more cautious. He was afraid that any obvious indication on the part of the French that they wanted the war to go on would simply drive England and Spain together. The best line was to try to sow suspicion of Spain in James's mind at every turn, and to point out to him that, even if England did make peace, it was essential that the Dutch be supported, so that the war between Spain and the Dutch would go on. If ever that thorn was removed from the Spaniard's foot, in Villeroy's opinion, there would be no restraining his insolence.

On the matter of resuming the war, however, Henri, after some wavering, decided that it was too soon for France to take up arms again.[25] On this point the English had correctly assessed French policy even before Sully's evasiveness respecting an offensive alliance during his mission to England confirmed their judgment. France would not fight at this stage, and therefore it was neither necessary nor desirable for England to go on doing so, merely to keep the Dutch from throwing themselves into the arms of France. The warnings on this score from English officials in the United Provinces, most of whom were very much afraid of peace, could be discounted.[26]

As the time of the conference drew near, and the indications of England's determination to make peace multiplied, so did Henri's worry about the outcome. He was bothered by what he regarded as the pro-Spanish attitude of James's envoys to other courts, by James's failure to send him a special mission in return for Sully's visit, and by James's refusal to make anything out of Aremberg's

[25] Aug. 28/Sept. 7, 1603, Villeroy to Sully, Oct. 13/23, Henri to Beaumont, Oct. 20/30, Villeroy to Henri, *Prinsterer*, pp. 221–22, 230–32. Sept. 7/17, Henri to Beaumont, *Beaumont* II, 145–51; Nov. 27/Dec. 7, Villeroy to Beaumont, *Beaumont* I, 171–72.

[26] May 22, 1603, Scaramelli to the Doge and Senate, *C.S.P. Venetian 1603–1607*, pp. 32–34. For the reaction from the Netherlands see, e.g., June 13, June 18, 1603, Sir William Browne to Sir Robert Sidney, *De L'Isle* III, 33–35, 36–37. Sidney, later Viscount Lisle, was governor of Flushing; Browne was his deputy.

alleged complicity in the plots of the summer of 1603, a story which the French government diligently spread. Henri did not doubt James's good faith, he said, but he was suspicious of James's feebleness and levity, and of the malice of his entourage. "Il faut craindre qu'à la longue il ne se laisse emporter au torrent de la haine extraordinaire que les Anglais nous portent." He did what he could, by continuing to harp on Spanish treachery and iniquity to Parry, and by instructing Beaumont to do the same.[27]

Henri's efforts to create a more favorable climate of opinion in England—he even went so far at one point as to send over an agent, M. de Vitry, who was supposed to ingratiate himself with James by talking about hunting[28]—were hindered by a number of commercial problems and disputes. The merchants of each country were continuous and clamorous in their complaints of ill treatment by the officials of the other. If, as frequently happened, an ambassador complained in the merchants' behalf, he was met by a long list of countercomplaints, or, occasionally, by vague promises which usually came to nothing.[29] The French were particularly aggrieved about English pirates. Each side threatened seizure of the other's goods in order to compensate its own merchants. At the end of January, 1604, Parry, thoroughly disgusted by the French tactics, wrote a long letter to Cecil about his latest unsatisfactory talks with Villeroy. Henri, he said, had promised justice in various specific instances; Villeroy, as usual, produced generalities and countercomplaints. Parry was convinced that the French had no intention of satisfying any English or Scottish subject, and felt that they were

[27] Jan. 23/Feb. 2, Mar. 11/21, 1604, Henri to Beaumont, *Beaumont* II, 184–89, 199–202. Jan. 31, Parry to Cecil, P.R.O., S.P. 78/51, ff. 24–27. Parry wrote that he believed that Henri was preparing to do some moderate bribing in England.

[28] Aug. 16/26, 1603, Henri to Beaumont, *Beaumont* II, 137–41. Vitry was the huntsman whose presence James urgently requested in 1605; see above, p. 10. For a brilliant analysis of how James's hunting affected the conduct of government, see D. H. Willson, *King James VI and I*, ch. 11.

[29] See, e.g., June 16, Nov. 12, Nov. 20, 1603, Parry to Cecil, P.R.O., S.P. 78/49, f. 202; S.P. 78/50, ff. 103–106, 113–14.

indulging in a form of political blackmail: follow our political lead, and we will satisfy your merchants. "This be wonted fruits of French conferences," he gloomily concluded.[30]

Apart from the merchants' complaints there were two more specific problems which muddied the waters. English pirates were particularly active in the Mediterranean, where they preyed heavily on Turkish shipping. The French agent in Constantinople attempted to take advantage of this situation to bring about a rupture between England and Turkey to the advantage of France. He told the Turks that the English government secretly countenanced these pirates, did nothing to prevent their depredations, and actually welcomed them when they returned to England with their ill-gotten gains. Another problem was that other pirates, some of them French, sailed under English colors and the Turks, "these blockish people," could not tell the difference.[31] The accession of James gave the French agent new opportunity for mischief; he spread lies about domestic troubles in England so that the sultan would not send a congratulatory embassy to the new king.[32]

The French representations made an impression on the sultan, who in August, 1603, wrote to Henri that he would inform James that English piracy must cease, or reprisals and a rupture of relations would follow.[33] When a Turkish agent arrived in France on his way to England, reported Thomas Wilson, one of Cecil's agents in Paris, the French attempted to prevent his going there, lest he should discover the falsity of the French insinuations. If he did not go, English trade in the Levant, "the best we have in the world," would inevitably decay.[34] Parry echoed these views; he was incensed at Henri's double-dealing, but he thought there might be another mo-

[30] P.R.O., S.P. 78/51, ff. 30–34.

[31] Apr. 9, May 7, 1603, Henry Lello to Cecil, P.R.O., S.P. 97/4, ff. 220, 222–23. Nov. 12, Parry to Cecil, P.R.O., S.P. 78/50, ff. 103–6. Lello was the English agent in Turkey.

[32] July 2, 1603, Lello to Cecil, P.R.O., S.P. 97/4, f. 226.

[33] *Salisbury* XV, 225–26.

[34] Nov. 7, 1603, Wilson to Cecil, P.R.O., S.P. 78/50, ff. 98–99.

tive behind the attitude of the Turks. They were no more anxious for peace between England and Spain than were the French; this might well be their way of applying pressure to keep the war going.[35] There was a good deal of discussion of the Turkish problem in the English Privy Council; King James, as a good Christian, wanted to have nothing to do with the Turks, but many of the Council, "where everything is weighed in the scales of material interests," disagreed.[36] In January, 1604, Cecil was finally able to inform Parry that the king had been persuaded to write to the sultan in order to establish friendly relations, and that he had complained sharply to Beaumont about French troublemaking.[37] Anglo-French rivalry in the Levant was to persist throughout James's reign; it continued to be a disruptive factor in the diplomatic relations of the two countries.

The second problem was a new Spanish duty of 30 percent levied in June, 1603, clearly directed against France. From the beginning the French had been suspicious of some such maneuver in the event of an Anglo-Spanish peace: Spain would do her best to bring about commercial disagreements between England and France.[38] Henri promptly retaliated with a 30 percent levy against goods going to or from Spain, and eventually embargoed trade with Spain and Flanders altogether; he was sure that this new duty was a Spanish trap, which both England and France must be careful to avoid.[39] If trap it was, James was careful not to fall into it. He informed the French government that he would work to eliminate the new duty for others as well as for himself. Henri was skeptical,[40] but James

[35] Nov. 12, 1603, Parry to Cecil, *ibid.*, ff. 103–106. See also Nov. 7/17, Nicolo Molin to the Doge and Senate, *C.S.P. Venetian 1603–1607*, pp. 112–13. Molin replaced Scaramelli in England late in 1603.
[36] Dec. 15/25, 1603, Molin to the Doge and Senate, *C.S.P. Venetian 1603–1607*, pp. 125–26.
[37] P.R.O., S.P. 78/51, ff. 12–17. By May the *contretemps* had ended; May 8, 1604, Lello to Cecil, P.R.O., S.P. 97/4, f. 256.
[38] Aug. 28/Sept. 7, 1603, Villeroy to Sully, *Prinsterer* pp. 221–22.
[39] Nov. 7, 1603, Wilson to Cecil, P.R.O., S.P. 78/50, ff. 98–99. Nov. 27/Dec. 7, Henri to Beaumont, *Beaumont* II, 164–71. Feb. 13, 1604, Parry to Cecil, P.R.O., S.P. 78/51, ff. 41–45.
[40] Mar. 11/21, 1604, Henri to Beaumont, *Beaumont* II, 199–202.

was as good as his word. During the peace negotiations he stipulated for its removal from English goods, Spanish goods carried by English ships to England or the Archduke's territories, and German goods carried by English ships to Spain, and, after the peace was signed, he helped to arrange a settlement between France and Spain.

Religious questions also complicated relations between England and France, far more than they had in the days of Queen Elizabeth. This was in part because James, the expert controversialist, cared far more deeply about theological nuances than his predecessor, took his position as Defender of the Faith more seriously, and occasionally allowed this position to influence his conduct of policy. Henri, after his second marriage and the birth of his heir, felt it necessary to remain on good terms with Rome lest the legitimacy of that heir be called in question. His Huguenot subjects were suspicious and restless. They disliked especially the growing influence of the Jesuit Pierre Coton; the king's ears, they said, were stuffed with cotton.[41] Parry, who saw the corrupting influence of the Jesuits everywhere, was also alarmed, and reported that he would ask Henri to prevent his clergy from financing Jesuit missionaries in England.[42] Henri, in his turn, did not want James to enter into relations with his Huguenots, especially with Henri de la Tour d'Auvergne, duke of Bouillon, who, owing to his geographical position on the eastern borders of France, was hopeful of maintaining a quasi-independent position with the aid of his coreligionists in the Rhineland. Bouillon had many friends in English government circles. For the time being James's attitude toward him was noncommittal; he reprimanded Sir Stephen Lesieur, a Huguenot now in English service, for urging various German princes to support Bouillon without any authorization to do so.[43]

[41] P.R.O., S.P. 78/50, f. 129.
[42] Sept. 15, Sept. 29, 1603, Parry to Cecil, *ibid.*, ff. 9–11, 21–24.
[43] Jan. 26/Feb. 5, 1604, Molin to the Doge and Senate, *C.S.P. Venetian 1603–1607*, pp. 131–32.

At the moment, however, the major religious question affecting Anglo-French relations was that of James's attitude to his Catholic subjects. In 1603 this was shrouded in ambiguity owing to the feelers James had previously put out in all directions, including Rome, in order to insure that there would be no opposition to his succession to Elizabeth. Henri would have preferred not to get involved in this question, but the pressure from Rome was considerable; he finally suggested to James that leniency to his loyal Catholic subjects would help prevent conspiracies against him, and that he should deal directly with the Pope. At the same time he urged the Pope not to put pressure on James.[44] It was clearly to Henri's advantage that that there should be no real rupture between James and the Pope, which would force him into the uncomfortable position of having to take sides; so his policy was consistently to urge both parties to be moderate.[45]

Even before Henri made his tentative suggestions to James, Parry was approached by the bishop of Camerino, the Papal nuncio in Paris. His line was that it was the Pope's policy to get troublemaking priests out of England, to allow no turbulence, and to act by persuasion. In September the nuncio wrote a fulsome letter to the king, pointing out that the Pope was kindly disposed toward him; proof of this could be seen in the fact that he had levelled no ecclesiastical censures against James.[46] James, whose policy was one of calculated deference to the Pope, in order to avoid an excommunication and the trouble which might result from it, sent a polite but rather cool reply via Parry. Cecil at the same time instructed Parry to be very cautious, not to meet the nuncio personally, and to remain aloof from the English Catholic colony in Paris.[47] The nuncio was osten-

[44] *Beaumont* I, 135–40, II, 130–36, 181–84.
[45] See his letter of Feb. 25/Mar. 6, 1604, to Beaumont, *Beaumont* II, 193–99.
[46] Aug. 20, 1603, Parry to Cecil, P.R.O., S.P. 78/49, ff. 247–48. Sept. 19/29, Camerino to James, *Salisbury* XV, 249–50.
[47] Nov. 6, 1603, Cecil to Parry, P.R.O., S.P. 78/50, ff. 82–83. James's letter to the nuncio is in *Salisbury* XV, 299–302.

sibly content with this slender return for his efforts.[48] Parry, in reporting this reaction, commented that Henri knew that James's reply to the nuncio was on its way a week before the letters reached the ambassador.[49] The French king was well informed.

The nuncio's efforts had no real result; nor did those of his colleague in Flanders. This was in part because of a clumsy attempt by the Jesuit Robert Persons, one of James's particular bêtes noires, to obtain influence over Queen Anne.[50] James's dislike of Jesuits continued unabated. He urged Henri to expel them from France, and Parry became so zealous in pressing this on the king that the French complained and Cecil had to rebuke him. Henri would not accommodate James on this point, but he did his best to assure James that the presence of Jesuits in France would do England no harm.[51]

The great problem for France, of course, was none of these things, but rather the sort of settlement James would make with Spain. In spite of Sully's treaty the French still feared that it might be made at the expense of the Dutch. Even if James's intentions continued good, Spain, as soon as peace was made, would, France believed, foment domestic discord in England in order to prevent England from further helping the Dutch. Still worse, to the French king, was the prospect that the Dutch might be driven to a truce with Spain; this would cause the war-forged unity of the United Provinces to dissolve, and in time Spain would be able to re-absorb them piecemeal.

The very chilly state of relations between France and Spain did not improve Henri's state of mind. He was afraid of an Anglo-Spanish marriage alliance, and dangled the bait of a French princess before James in an effort to prevent it. Throughout late 1603 and the first half of 1604 his letters to Beaumont reveals his depression. He was suspicious of James's courage, of Cecil's good faith, of the pro-

[48] Dec. 7/17, 1603, Camerino to Parry, P.R.O., S.P. 78/50, f. 137.
[49] Jan. 5, 1604, Parry to Cecil, P.R.O., S.P. 78/51, ff. 3–8.
[50] Jan. 21, 1604, Cecil to Parry, *ibid.*, ff. 12–17.
[51] Jan. 31, 1604, Parry to Cecil, *ibid.*, ff. 30–34. Dec. 9/19, 1603, Henri to Beaumont, *Beaumont* II, 173–81.

Spanish element in James's entourage; he was afraid that James would recall the Englishmen in Dutch service, that there might be an Anglo-Spanish league, and an Anglo-Spanish commercial bargain at French expense, or, alternatively, a Protestant coalition which would attract his disgruntled Huguenot subjects. In the spring of 1604 Lord Hay came to Paris, officially to condole with Henri on the death of his sister; he took the opportunity to recommend that Henri treat his Protestant subjects well, to Henri's irritation. The reports of English sales of artillery in Spain bothered Henri. He warned Parry that ever since the French peace with Spain, Spain had been plotting against him, and that he hoped this would not happen to James. The gloomiest of all his letters to Beaumont was that of May 30/June 9, 1604, in which he wrote that he did not see how England could make peace without consenting to something damaging to the Dutch, since that was Spain's whole purpose in making peace; there could be no other result.[52]

Yet England did make a peace which did no damage to the Dutch; Henri's fears turned out to be groundless. James was as keenly aware as the French that the only real menace to England came from the Habsburgs. He brushed aside the efforts of Spanish partisans to give his policy an anti-French cast,[53] as emphatically as he did the arguments of those who believed that an Anglo-Spanish peace would cause Dutch resistance to collapse, a situation which in turn would compel England either to fight later on much less advantageous ground or acquiesce in the aggrandizement of Spain.[54] He also paid no heed to the argument that peace would turn the Dutch into clients

[52] Sept. 22/Oct. 2, 1603, Mar. 20/30, Apr. 3/13, 1604, Angelo Badoer (Venetian representative in France) to the Doge and Senate, *C.S.P. Venetian 1603–1607*, pp. 99, 140, 143. *Prinsterer*, p. 222. *Beaumont* II, 151. July 10/20, 1604, Wilson to Cecil, P.R.O., S.P. 94/10, ff. 73–75. July 21, Parry to Cecil, P.R.O., S.P. 78/51, ff. 214–16.

[53] May 9, 1603, Sir Anthony Sherley to James, *Salisbury* XV, 77–80. *Prinsterer*, pp. 224–26. Sherley was an adventurer who drifted in and out of the service of several governments, including that of Spain.

[54] For a forceful statement of this line of reasoning see July 10, 1603, Parry to Cecil, P.R.O., S.P. 78/49, ff. 182–83.

of France and would hurt English trade;[55] he believed that peace was good for business, as he told Parliament. He repeatedly informed the Dutch that if they wished to do so, he would be happy to include them in the negotiations; but he made it very clear, to them and to Aremberg, that he would negotiate bilaterally with Spain if they refused.[56]

James assured the French that he would not make peace at their expense either, and that he was aware of the dangers of any cessation in the fighting between Spain and her rebels.[57] His instructions to his commissioners made it clear that he would make no significant concessions in order to secure peace. There was to be no league with Spain. Trade with the Dutch would go on; the most that James would agree to was that English merchants would not attempt to pass off Dutch goods as English, or to ship English goods on Dutch ships. Otherwise there would be no restriction on English merchants—a stipulation which meant, of course, that they could trade with the Archduke's territories as well as with the United Provinces. Flushing and Brill, the cautionary towns held by England as security for the Dutch debt, were not to be turned over to Spain. Englishmen in Dutch service would not be recalled, nor would Dutch recruiting be stopped; but the Archduke could recruit too. On the ticklish business of trade with the Indies, James instructed his commissioners to claim that earlier Anglo-Spanish treaties permitted England to trade anywhere in the Spanish dominions; but, since Spain was unlikely to accept that, England would agree not to deal in areas occupied by Spain. In addition, Spain must make some stipulation concerning the Inquisition's behavior toward English merchants in Spain.[58]

[55] For these arguments see the pamphlet of 1603, Folger Library Mss. G.a.l, ff. 17–57.
[56] Aug. 9, 1603, James to the States-General, P.R.O., S.P. 78/49, ff. 99–100. *Beaumont* I, 126–28.
[57] Oct. 5/15, 1603, Beaumont to Henri, *Prinsterer*, pp. 229–30.
[58] These instructions, dated May 22, 1604, are in P.R.O., S.P. 94/10, ff. 17–23.

In the end the English got most of what they wanted. In the negotiations Cecil used the technique of sliding over the hard questions in order to reach agreement on the easy ones, and, since Spain needed peace more than England did, this worked very well, though it meant that in the final treaty the really insoluble problems, like the Indies trade, were not directly dealt with at all. Throughout the meetings the Dutch were kept carefully informed of how solicitous of their interests England was being; Cecil sent a spate of dispatches to Ralph Winwood, the English representative at The Hague, to this end. Parry was also kept informed, and the most flattering language was used to keep the French happy. For instance, on July 8 Cecil instructed Parry to tell Henri about the treaty, even though it was not yet in final form, because James knows "that he speaketh to himself whensoever he speaketh to the king his brother."[59]

Trade questions and the matter of the cautionary towns worried French and Dutch alike. Respecting the towns, James did make one concession: if, when the time came, the Dutch refused to accept a reasonable peace offer from Spain, James would feel free to dispose of the towns as he liked, i.e., sell them to Spain. This committed James to nothing, Cecil pointed out, since he was the judge of what constituted a reasonable offer. As for trade, England refused the lure of the vague intimations Spain held out in the matter of the 30 percent duty. English trade with Flanders would resume, but England flatly rejected the Spanish proposal that she take steps to prevent Dutch interference with it; it was up to the Archduke to keep the trading lanes clear and make conditions attractive for English merchants. The English government officially promised not to aid the enemies of Spain, but, Cecil explained, unofficial help in the form of allowing volunteers to take service with the Dutch would go on.[60]

The treaty was a victory for English diplomacy; it put an end to a

[59] P.R.O., S.P. 78/51, ff. 210–13.
[60] June 20, 1604, Cecil to Parry, *ibid.*, ff. 191–94. Cecil's commentary on the peace terms is in P.R.O., S.P. 103/64, ff. 134–36.

war which was becoming increasingly costly and increasingly meaningless. Not everyone thought so; the duke of Ossuna, the future viceroy of Naples, remarked that there would have been no peace if James had been less of a pedant and more of a politician.[61] And, predictably, Henri IV was both gloomy and sharp-tongued. "Little Beaumont sticks to the court like a burr" wrote Dudley Carleton to his friend John Chamberlain on September 21, "and yet the king is half out of conceit both with him and his master for certain jests and scorns they have made at our peace."[62]

The Dutch, also predictably, were gloomiest of all. It was freely declared by some of the English soldiers there—but not by Winwood, though he was far from happy about the peace—that a Franco-Dutch alliance would result which would be harmful to England.[63] The Dutch government, however, put a good face on matters to Winwood, and told him they were sure James would continue to help them, out of both generosity and self-interest.[64] There were some gloomy reactions in England, too, where the peace was far from universally popular, chiefly owing to anti-Spanish feeling.[65] Tobie Matthew, the son of the future archbishop of York, put it this way in a letter to Carleton: "I hope it be no treason to say, that either our commissioners were overmatched, or else that we should have perished within three months if we had wanted peace, for otherwise these conditions would never have been accorded to."[66] James, however, was obviously pleased at the skill with which Cecil had con-

[61] J. S. Corbett, *England in the Mediterranean* (London, 1904) I, 20.

[62] P.R.O., S.P. 14/9, no. 42. Carleton was an aspiring diplomatist who was to become ambassador to Venice in 1610 and have an important diplomatic career.

[63] See, e.g., June 21, 1604, John Throckmorton to Sidney, *De L'Isle* III, 123–24. Winwood did not minimize the adverse reaction of the Dutch, however. See his letters of June 15, P.R.O., S.P. 84/64, f. 165, and of Nov. 20, *Salisbury* XVI, 360–61. Throckmorton was a senior officer of the Flushing garrison, and later deputy governor.

[64] June 27, 1604, Winwood to Cecil, P.R.O., S.P. 84/64, ff. 170–71.

[65] For a sample of the arguments see *C.S.P. Venetian 1603–1607*, pp. 102–103. See also *Salisbury* XVI, 136–37.

[66] P.R.O., S.P. 78/51, f. 300.

ducted the negotiations; in August he named his indispensable minister Viscount Cranborne; less than a year later he would become
earl of Salisbury.

In his opening speech to his first Parliament, in March, 1604,
James indicated that he regarded himself as already at peace with
Spain. He acted promptly and intelligently, and with what was for
him an unusual amount of firmness and decision, to implement this
belief. His unswerving determination to put an end to the war was
clear from the beginning, and many historians have treated his policy
as a reversal of that of the late Queen. It was not that; England had
been moving in the direction of peace in the last years of Elizabeth,
and most of his predecessor's advisers, especially Robert Cecil, were
as anxious for peace as was James. A continuation of the war could
not profit England; it could only serve the ends of France.[67] The
only conceivable way in which Henri could have kept England
in the war was to resume fighting himself, and this he was not prepared to do. In fact he held out no real inducement to England,
not even payment of part of the French debt, on which he kept
stalling in the obvious hope of not having to pay anything at all.
He doubtless calculated that concessions on the debt would not
suffice to keep James in the war; but he made no effort to find out.

The Anglo-Spanish peace marked the end of an era in Anglo-
French relations. Both countries were now at peace with all the
world; both were delivered in some part from their fear of the Habsburg colossus, the decay of whose strength was becoming more and
more apparent. Both were determined to keep the war in the Low
Countries alive; James, by making peace, had neatly transferred the
chief responsibility for supporting the Dutch onto Henri's shoulders. England would not turn her back on the Dutch—she could not
afford to—but in James's view her role from now on would be that
of a *tertius gaudens*, at peace and doing business with all parties im-

---

[67] For a discussion of some of the points made in this paragraph see J. D.
Mackie, "James VI and I and the Peace with Spain, 1604," *Scottish Historical
Review* XXIII (1925–26), 241–49.

partially, restoring her prosperity through peace, and holding the balance between France and Spain—the role, in fact, which England had played in the 1570s, before the progressive internal decay of France and the growing power of Spain in the 1580s forced Queen Elizabeth to intervene openly in the Netherlands. It was a policy which the French government was to find most exasperating.

CHAPTER III

❋ ❋

Aftermath of Peace

AFTER THE SIGNING of the peace between England and Spain the dominant consideration which shaped the foreign policies of England and France, and therefore their relations with each other, was the continuing war between Spain and the Dutch. This involved many questions besides the obvious one of aid to the Dutch, which was the major subject of discussion between the two powers. There was, for example, the matter of the nature of English relations with Spain and Flanders, especially in questions of trade, which the Dutch naval blockade of the Archduke's ports complicated considerably. The Archduke was naturally anxious to take advantage of the peace to increase the trade between Flanders and England, as were the English, but he did not have the power to keep the sea lanes open. The Dutch faced an awkward dilemma. They did not dare to risk antagonizing England by acting too vigorously against English merchantmen, which might lead to an English effort to break the blockade by force, but they also could not afford to allow the Archduke to achieve economic recovery through trade with England. English merchants thus found themselves caught, as neutrals so often are, between the conflicting necessities of the belligerents. Indeed, Cecil at one point felt that the difficulties thrown in the way of English merchants trading to Spain were designed to persuade English merchants to deal in Flanders instead, in the hope of embroiling them with the Dutch. As early as November, 1604, Jean Richardot, the Archduke's principal adviser in matters of foreign policy, was commiserating with Cecil over the difficulties of English merchants in Spain and assuring him that they would be "grandement chéris" in Flanders.[1]

As for Spain, the general opinion in England was that she was feeble, prevaricating, and full of hatred for England. The earl of Northampton wrote in his usual hyperbolical way to Sir Charles Cornwallis, the English ambassador there, "though it be true, that by war we are as poor as they, that the realm would give no more, the revenue could afford no more, and that the Queen sold her land by lumps, yet all are now persuaded, that without a peace the King of Spain would have resigned up into the King's hands his whole dominions."[2] Cornwallis believed that two more years of war would have brought about Spain's collapse. Yet, he said, God perhaps had arranged everything for the best: such a collapse might have brought still graver dangers in its wake.[3] An agent of Cecil's summed up very well the typical Englishman's opinion of Spain: "this ill-pleasing country, where a virtuous mind takes small delight, unless it be by learning to abhor vice by continually beholding the hideous face thereof, which here shows itself in every corner and place. Infidelity in men, immodesty in women, hypocrisy in age, ungraciousness in youth, ungodliness in all."[4]

Cornwallis, who was a rather ineffective ambassador, had to spend most of his time dealing with the problems raised by the resumption of trade, problems which helped to bring about considerable disenchantment with the peace. English expectations were high, and doomed to disappointment. "It was generally thought that our peace with Spain would bring in mountains of gold," wrote Richard

[1] P.R.O., S.P. 77/7, f. 55. Aug. 17, 1606, Cecil to Cornwallis, B. M. Cott. Mss. Vesp. C IX, ff. 479–89.

[2] *Winwood* II, 91–95.

[3] June 2, 1605, Cornwallis to Cecil, B.M. Cott. Mss. Vesp. C IX, ff. 33–38.

[4] Oct. 19/29, 1604, Thomas Wilson to Cecil, P.R.O., S.P. 94/10, f. 124.

Locks, an English merchant in Spain in September, 1606, "but now it proveth molehills of earth."[5] The war had caused a brief revival of the Spanish cloth industry.[6] Spanish merchants were poor, and many English were not disposed to advance credit. The Inquisition was a nuisance, sometimes a dangerous nuisance; its officials occasionally searched English ships in violation of the treaty. The Spanish authorities were prone to confiscation of goods which they suspected of being Dutch, and not only the questionable goods but also the entire ship and cargo. They were very slow to implement the agreement to remove the 30 percent levy. There was disagreement over the meaning of the peace treaty with respect to tariffs: the English claimed that Spain had promised to remove all duties laid on since the beginning of the war, Spain, that she had promised to remove only the 30 percent and all taxes imposed subsequent to that levy. The Spaniards confiscated the goods of deceased Englishmen and seized English sailors to serve in Spanish ships. Sometimes English ships themselves were seized for use against the Dutch.

It was almost impossible to get any redress from Spain. Threats to issue letters of marque made very little impression; when Cornwallis brought up the merchants' grievances, he usually got no more than a "shrink of the shoulders," as he put it.[7] The Spanish government was lavish enough with oral promises and even written memoranda,[8] but compliance with these by local officials was another matter. In the autumn of 1605 Cornwallis suggested that the government arrange an attack on Spain in Parliament. In the summer of 1606 he was driven to the point of proposing that James might prohibit the trade altogether; by that autumn he was writing to one of

[5] P.R.O., S.P. 94/13, ff. 97–99.
[6] *Winwood* II, 37–39.
[7] B.M. Cott. Mss. Vesp. C IX, ff. 364–74. Sept. 4, 1605, Cornwallis to Cecil; Oct. 24, Cecil to Cornwallis, P.R.O., S.P. 94/12, 13–15, 94–98. June 18, 1606, Cecil to Sir Thomas Edmondes, P.R.O., S.P. 77/8, ff. 220–21. Edmondes was the English ambassador to the Archduke.
[8] See, e.g., P.R.O., S.P. 94/12, f. 190, S.P. 14/16, nos. 118, 119.

his colleagues that if Spain did not mend her ways peace would be worse than war for England.[9] The suspension of trade would no doubt have pleased him in one respect; Cornwallis had a very low opinion of the English merchants in Spain, "an unbridled and evil-tempered company."[10] "If there were in this estate censors of manners as there are Inquisitors for religion," he wrote in February, 1606, "I imagine that the greater part of our traders hither would fall into their hands, being people disordered, uncharitable and unfriendly amongst themselves and scandalous to this people."[11]

Whenever relations between the two countries became particularly strained, as they were in 1606 in the wake of the Gunpowder Plot, the duke of Lerma, Philip's principal minister, revived what was to be his favorite pacifying device, the suggestion of a marriage treaty. This idea always intrigued Cornwallis, who saw some of the difficulties involved, especially the religious ones, but remained optimistic nevertheless. In a dynastic age it was an article of faith among most diplomatists, especially the more conventionally minded—and Cornwallis was certainly that—that a marriage alliance would automatically lead to better relations and greater diplomatic cooperation. The bait Lerma dangled was artfully chosen; Prince Henry would marry an Infanta and be given the Low Countries, or some part of them, as dowry. Lerma also talked of a large annual pension for James and of Spain's guaranteeing payment of the Dutch debt, and flattered the king's well-known penchant for being a peacemaker by suggesting that he might mediate between Spain and her rebels.[12] The sensibilities, and the allegedly independent position, of the Archduke were conveniently ignored. From the Spanish point of view the plan would have the added advantage of driving a wedge between England and the Dutch, and might even lead England to abandon the Dutch altogether. The plan was so transparent

[9] B.M. Cott. Mss. Vesp. C IX, ff. 177–78, 435–38, 493–95.
[10] Nov. 12, 1605, Cornwallis to Cecil, P.R.O., S.P. 94/12, f. 116.
[11] P.R.O., S.P. 94/13, ff. 44–45.
[12] July 28, 1605, Cornwallis to Cecil, P.R.O., S.P. 94/11, ff. 196–97. See also B.M. Cott. Mss. Vesp. C IX, ff. 254–55.

that men far less astute than Cecil and his master would have seen through it, and England, though never formally rejecting it, remained cautiously aloof, in spite of Cornwallis's occasional fits of enthusiasm.[13] Relations with Spain were formally correct, but no more. In the opinion of the Venetian ambassador, James's desire for peace and Spain's need of English friendship were all that kept the war from breaking out again.[14]

English dealings with the Archduke were considerably more friendly, and at the same time more complex. Here the major problem was whether any trade at all could be conducted without running afoul of the Dutch. The Dutch, although they carried on a sizeable if surreptitious trade in Flanders themselves, insisted on maintaining their blockade of Flemish ports, which, involving as it did what Winwood called the "daily" seizure of English ships, would sooner or later cause a rupture, which, said Winwood, "is the mischief the Spaniard aims at."[15] James's policy at first was to wink at the Dutch depredations, in the hope that the merchants involved would voluntarily divert their trade elsewhere; but as early as October, 1604, the failure of this device was apparent.[16] Any English attempt to break the blockade by force, which the Archduke claimed the peace treaty obligated them to do, would obviously cause real trouble with the Dutch. Various schemes were proposed to get around this difficulty, the most elaborate of which was a plan to demilitarize the Channel altogether, from Cornwall to the North Sea, or, alternatively, to persuade the Dutch to allow English ships to trade via Antwerp, where the Dutch, from their stronghold downstream at Lillo, could check to be sure that no war material or

[13] See, e.g., his memorial of May 29, 1606, B.M. Cott. Mss. Vesp. C IX, ff. 390–93.

[14] Apr. 10/20, 1606, Georgio Giustinian to the Doge and Senate, *C.S.P. Venetian 1603–1607*, pp. 338–39. Giustinian replaced Molin in England at the beginning of 1606.

[15] P.R.O., S.P. 84/64, ff. 214–15. Oct. 23, 1604, Cecil to Winwood, *Winwood* II, 34.

[16] P.R.O., S.P. 84/64, ff. 197–99.

foodstuffs were being carried to their enemies.[17] It proved to be impossible to reach any formal agreements. No one liked the proposal to demilitarize the Channel, and the Dutch would not hear of the reopening of Antwerp to English ships, which would mean reopening it to other countries' traders as well, in spite of the prospect of being able to collect tolls from the ships landing at Lillo—this last an aspect of the plan which did not commend itself to the Archduke. So the trade went on at the risk of the merchants involved, with frequent incidents and the usual battery of complaints.

The Archduke was eager for as much trade with England as possible; on other matters, however, there was much more difficulty. As might be expected, recruiting for his armies went slowly in England, and he accused the English government of discouraging it, while encouraging people to take service with the Dutch. But by far the worst strain resulted from the Gunpowder Plot. The English demanded the surrender of Hugh Owen and the Jesuit Father Baldwin in connection with the plot; the Archduke, after consulting Spain, refused, on grounds which the English considered frivolous.[18] It seems likely that if the Archduke had been a truly free agent the two would have been handed over; certainly he was anxious to do all he could to promote good relations with King James and wean him away from the Dutch. But his hands were tied by the attitude and orders of Madrid, whose opinions, in Cornwallis's view, were shaped on this question by the Jesuits rather than by the king.[19]

The Dutch blockade of the Archduke's ports was only one of several delicate issues in Anglo-Dutch relations after the peace between England and Spain. There was, for example, the constant danger to the Dutch involved in English possession of the cautionary towns. The English government had repeatedly promised that

[17] P.R.O., S.P. 7/2, ff. 77–78.

[18] The correspondence of the months after November 1605 is full of the plot and its ramifications. Cecil's letter to Edmondes on Dec. 2, and Edmondes's report of Dec. 20, pretty well summarize the positions of the two sides. P.R.O., S.P. 77/7, ff. 312–18, S.P. 77/8, ff. 212–13.

[19] Mar. 12/22, 1606, Cornwallis to Edmondes, B.M. Stowe Mss. 168, f. 383.

the towns would not be turned over to Spain, but governments had been known to break promises before. Then too there was the question of the Dutch debt, which, James and Cecil believed, the Dutch could do more about repaying, especially as England after the peace with Spain had to take over the payment of the garrisons of the cautionary towns. In June, 1604, Cecil informed Winwood that a new financial arrangement would have to be negotiated.[20] The Spanish ambassador in England was hopeful of fishing in these waters: if the Dutch refused to pay the debt, Spain might be able to buy back the cautionary towns after all.[21]

Both sides made a serious effort to avoid real difficulty over these questions. In September, 1604, Winwood suggested to Oldenbarnevelt that the Dutch send commissioners to London to discuss the matter of trade before Dutch depredations on English shipping became serious enough to alienate James, and Oldenbarnevelt agreed.[22] The meetings were not very fruitful. The English commissioners agreed that completely free trade would be very harmful to the Dutch, but none of the various compromises suggested was satisfactory. The Dutch disliked the demilitarization plan and the Antwerp scheme; Winwood himself felt that the Antwerp idea was dangerous, since it might lead to the funnelling of all English trade to western Germany through Antwerp, to the serious detriment of the Merchant Adventurers, who had their staple at Middleburg.[23] Diversion of the Flanders trade through Calais, a plan to which the Dutch had no great objection, was not a very satisfactory alternative, since it increased costs.[24]

[20] *Winwood* II, 23–24. See also Cecil's memorandum on this point, P.R.O., S.P. 84/64, ff. 236–37.
[21] Oct. 24/Nov. 3, 1604, Molin to the Doge and Senate, *C.S.P. Venetian 1603–1607*, pp. 190–91.
[22] P.R.O., S.P. 84/64, ff. 184–85.
[23] Feb. 10, 1605, Winwood to Cecil, P.R.O., S.P. 84/65, ff. 7–8.
[24] Nov. 1, 1605, Winwood to Cecil, *ibid.*, ff. 106–107. The French profited from this situation and therefore supported the Dutch in their refusal to lift the blockade. June 3, Winwood to Cecil, B.M. Cott. Mss. Galba E 1, ff. 237–38.

In the end no formal agreement was reached, but the complaints diminished as time went on, which argues that the Dutch showed sufficient discretion to satisfy the English merchants. The Dutch suggestion that the English admiralty court act as judge in maritime cases as between themselves on the one hand and Spain and the Archduke on the other, and their readiness to offer surety for restitution if Spain was willing to do the same, to say nothing of the Gunpowder Plot, inclined James to their side, and throughout 1606 his support of the Dutch became more and more open.[25] It was a support which was largely verbal, and was offset by such things as the proclamation of 1605 recalling all Englishmen serving on foreign ships, an action which was partly owing to fear that if it were not done England might be embroiled with Spain. The Dutch found this most distasteful; they feared that it presaged a recall of the English regiments in their service. This was not likely to happen, however, since Cecil knew well enough that the immediate result of such an action would be the preponderance of French influence in the councils of the United Provinces.[26] In the opinion of the Venetian ambassador James's policy fell between two stools: he did nothing useful for the Dutch, and his open support of them annoyed Spain. Cecil, for his part, was cultivating the Spanish ambassador; king and minister, in partnership, were trying to retain the goodwill of both parties.[27]

The question of the Dutch debt was even more difficult to settle than that of trade. By the terms of the agreement of 1598 the Dutch were to pay the debt, which then stood at £800,000, at the rate of £30,000 a year until half of it was paid; if England made peace, the

[25] Jan. 1, 1606, Cecil to Edmondes, *Salisbury* XVIII, 1–3. Jan. 30, Cecil to Cornwallis, *Winwood* II, 189–91. Aug. 27/Sept. 6, Giustinian to the Doge and Senate, *C.S.P. Venetian 1603–1607*, pp. 397–99.

[26] Mar. 31, 1605, Winwood to Cecil, P.R.O., S.P. 84/65, f. 27. May 28, Sir John Ogle to Cecil, *ibid.*, ff. 42–43. See also *ibid.*, f. 132. Ogle was one of the officers of the Flushing garrison.

[27] June 28, 1606, Giustinian to the Doge and Senate, *C.S.P. Venetian 1603–1607*, pp. 365–66. For Cecil's behavior see A. J. Loomie, "Sir Robert Cecil and the Spanish Embassy," *Bulletin of the Institute of Historical Research* XLII (1969), 34–35.

payment was to drop to £20,000. In 1604, by Cecil's calculation, the Dutch still owed £280,000 of that first £400,000, plus £132,000 for the upkeep of the garrisons of the cautionary towns for the past six years; thus, the total indebtedness now stood at £812,000.[28] Whenever the English government applied pressure for payment, the Dutch replied by talking about the magnitude of their war effort and asking for help against Spain. What the Dutch wanted was either postponement of paying, or else that a lump-sum payment be negotiated, which, presumably, would mean a very considerable reduction in the amount to be paid.[29] Winwood suggested that James might be willing to remit some of the debt if the rest were paid; Oldenbarnevelt replied that his country was living from hand to mouth as it was.[30] Yet the Dutch would not consider the proposal to reopen Antwerp, which would have allowed them to collect tolls at Lillo and thus, as the English pointed out, supply themselves with funds to help pay their obligations. The Dutch attitude was hardly satisfactory to the English; the conversations dragged on intermittently without positive result.

At one point in the discussions over the debt the Dutch agent in England, Noel Caron, attempted to link the question of the French debt to England to theirs: if England would forgive Henri his debts, France would have more money available to send to the Dutch, and they would then pay England. This was a curiously illogical red herring, which appealed neither to England nor to Oldenbarnevelt,[31] but it does indicate what would eventually become a sensitive issue between France and England.

James's desire to live at peace with everyone and be courted on all sides made him particularly anxious to be on better terms with both France and Spain than they were with each other. This particular tightrope was not always easy to walk: as Parry rather

---

[28] P.R.O., S.P. 84/64, ff. 236–37.
[29] June 6, 1606, Cecil to Winwood, P.R.O., S.P. 84/65, ff. 212–15.
[30] June 28, 1606, Winwood to Cecil, *ibid.*, ff. 222–24.
[31] *Ibid.*

wearily wrote to Edmondes, his colleague in Brussels, each of them
had to deal with a government which believed King James did not
love it enough, because they did not love each other.[32] James did
not want to enter into a comprehensive political agreement with
anyone, or even to discuss such a possibility, lest the very discussions themselves precipitate some sort of reaction which would
change the highly favorable situation which presently existed. He
therefore turned aside the occasional French suggestions that such
discussions might profitably take place.[33] Any sign of a Franco-
Spanish rapprochement made English statesmen very nervous. In
Paris, Parry and then Sir George Carew, who succeeded him in 1606,
were usually fairly calm; they were convinced that, as long as Henri
was king, no real reconciliation was possible. Cornwallis was a good
deal more jittery. He eagerly reported evidence that Spanish opinion
was more sympathetic to England than to France; he favored negotiations for an alliance, in spite of the coolness of Cecil and the
Council on this score, and he drew up memoranda for King Philip
pointing out the advantages to Spain of a connection with England.[34]
Spain, he kept repeating, needed English friendship.[35] France also
needed English friendship, but Henri and his advisers saw signs of
instability in English domestic affairs and were not going to be over-
eager. Let England find out about Spanish duplicity and the dis-
advantages of neutrality for herself; then, perhaps, a profitable
bargain could be struck.[36]

English policy toward France was equally cautious. Cecil and

[32] June 1, 1605, Parry to Edmondes, B.M. Stowe Mss. 168, f. 40.
[33] See, e.g., Oct. 17, 1604, Parry to Cecil, P.R.O., S.P. 78/51, ff. 288–89; Nov. 21/Dec. 1, Molin to the Doge and Senate, C.S.P. Venetian 1603–1607, pp. 195–96.
[34] Dec. 5, 1605, Cornwallis to Cecil, P.R.O., S.P. 94/12, ff. 136–37. Apr. 1606, Cecil to Cornwallis; Nov. 16, Cornwallis to the Council, B.M. Cott. Mss. Vesp. C IX, ff. 358–61, 576–85.
[35] See, e.g., his letter of Dec. 31, 1606/Jan. 10, 1607, P.R.O., S.P. 94/13, ff. 127–28.
[36] Feb. 9/19, 1605, Henri to Beaumont, Beaumont II, 293–97. C.S.P. Venetian 1603–1607, pp. 218–20.

James were unwilling to commit themselves to France and equally unwilling to antagonize her. The Venetian ambassador described the English policy, which he attributed to Cecil, as one of deliberate balancing between France and Spain, since alliance with one meant enmity with the other.[37] The English disliked what they regarded as Henri's coddling of Jesuits, and James occasionally gave public expression to his hope that France would expel them.[38] But in view of the uncertain state of relations with Spain, especially after the discovery of the Gunpowder Plot, James and Cecil were not prepared to take any initiative which might drive France and Spain together. This seems to afford the best explanation of England's unwillingness at this stage to put pressure on France to come to a settlement of the French debt to England.

From the beginning of James's reign there had been talk in England of forcing this issue.[39] France admitted that such a debt existed; by the terms of Sully's treaty one-third of the French subvention to the Dutch was to be deducted from it. The French payment for the first year was 450,000 crowns (£135,000); on January 24, 1604, Cecil duly sent Parry an acknowledgement that the debt was thereby reduced by 150,000.[40] But by March, 1604, with peace negotiations with Spain imminent, England began to show signs of unwillingness to continue this arrangement. Henri instructed his ambassador to get James to consent to the same terms for 1604, and in the following month the States-General made the same request.[41] Cecil was not willing to risk the success of the peace treaty in this way, however, and when he heard from Beaumont that Parry had given assurances to the French government that James

[37] *C.S.P. Venetian 1603–1607*, p. 518.

[38] July 16/26, 1606, Giustinian to the Doge and Senate, *ibid.*, pp. 379–80. See also May 2/12, 1606, Henry Wotton to Cecil, P.R.O., S.P. 99/3, ff. 76–77. Wotton was the English ambassador in Venice.

[39] May 12/22, 1603, Scaramelli to the Doge and Senate, *C.S.P. Venetian 1603–1607*, pp. 32–34.

[40] P.R.O., S.P. 78/51, ff. 12–17. A pound sterling was worth approximately 3 1/3 crowns.

[41] *Beaumont* II, 199–202. *Salisbury* XVI, 67–68.

would consent to a defalcation again, he instructed Parry to retract, if he had, indeed, made such a commitment.[42]

Once the peace treaty was signed, England definitively backed out: financial help of this sort to the Dutch, they argued, would be a violation of the treaty.[43] The French were not pleased, but were hardly surprised; from the beginning the tone of the correspondence between Henri and Beaumont indicates that they expected James to take this attitude.[44] Henri tried to pretend that nothing had happened: in November, 1604, he instructed Beaumont to tell James that he was going to continue to help the Dutch on the same terms as before; he was sure, he said, that James would not desert them. He could not carry the load all by himself; if James did back out, then the great effort which Spain was planning for 1605 might overwhelm the Dutch. He also told James to beware of any Spanish marriage offer involving the Low Countries as dowry; it would be a delusive snare.[45] In fact the French had resolved to go on helping the Dutch regardless of England's attitude; the cash of the year before had all come from France, after all, and the bookkeeping could be dealt with when—and if—the time ever came.

By January, 1605, James's attitude on the debt and Sully's treaty was known in both Paris and The Hague. Henri regarded the English argument that the peace with Spain had superseded Sully's treaty as feeble, another example of England's perennial bad faith. He took some consolation from the fact that England had behaved equally treacherously to Spain. As long as James allowed his subjects to take service with the Dutch, made no effort to break the blockade of the Flemish coast, and did not press the Dutch respecting

[42] Apr. 14, 1604, Cecil to Parry, P.R.O., S.P. 78/51, ff. 141–42.
[43] Jan. 29, 1605, Winwood to Cecil, P.R.O., S.P. 84/65, ff. 5–6.
[44] See, e.g., the king's letters of Mar. 11/21 and July 27/Aug. 6, 1604, *Beaumont* II, 199–202, 246–53.
[45] *Beaumont* II, 272–80. Henri persisted in maintaining the fiction of the English contribution. See June 30, 1606, Carew to Cecil, P.R.O., S.P. 78/53, ff. 125–28.

their debt to England, Spain would have gotten little enough from the peace.[46] Henri did his best to increase the pressure on England by constantly telling the Dutch that what he could do for them depended on what England was willing to do, and by complaining to the Dutch that he was bearing the burden of their war while others profited from it.[47] He also told the Spanish ambassador in Paris that it was with money originally obtained from England that he was financing the Dutch; this would not improve James's standing in Madrid.[48]

Among the reasons for England's hesitancy about raising the question of repayment of the French debt was a serious commercial controversy with France which Cecil thought might well have been precipitated because the French wished to avoid discussing the debt.[49] The secretary may well have been right, but there was no way of verifying his suspicions, and the dispute was genuine enough. English merchants had become much more aggressively competitive in recent years; as the Venetian agent in London put it in 1605, "Formerly foreign merchants were willingly admitted in England, and very few English traveled abroad; now they apply all their attention to traffic, and all trade and all gain is concentrated in their hands."[50] These merchants had been flooding France, the French claimed, with shoddy cloth which met neither their standards nor those of the English themselves. In 1600 the French began a policy of intermittent confiscation of this defective merchandise; as a consequence there had already been some desultory discussion of a new trade treaty. Then, after the English had successfully mediated the trade dispute between France and Spain—a far from disinterested action,

[46] Jan. 6/16, 1605, Henri to Beaumont, *Beaumont* II, 290–93.
[47] Jan. 16, 1605, Winwood to Cecil, *Salisbury* XVII, 17–19. Dec. 17/27, François Van Aerssens to Winwood, *Winwood* II, 181–82. Aerssens was the Dutch agent in Paris.
[48] Jan. 21, 1606, Carew to Cecil, P.R.O., S.P. 78/53, ff. 7–8.
[49] Jan. 21, 1605, Cecil to Lake, *Salisbury* XVII, 26–28.
[50] *C.S.P. Venetian 1603–1607*, pp. 276–77.

since the blockage of trade between the two countries hampered the English carrying trade in French goods to Spain[51]—the confiscations resumed.

In November, 1604, English cloth worth 250,000 crowns (£75,-000) was seized at Rouen. This produced an immediate reaction; the Privy Council instructed Parry to tell the French government that political reprisals would follow if the cloth was not released and such practices stopped in the future.[52] Parry went to work at once; on December 7 he reported that he had raised the question three separate times. The king assured him that it would be dealt with quickly; it turned out that what Henri wanted was that James should ask that the cloth be released, not as a matter of right, but as a favor.[53] The English government tried to avoid making such a request. The French position was that the confiscations had been made in accordance with ancient ordinances, not new ones; their purpose, they said, was to punish fraud rather than to hamper trade. Beaumont made it clear from the beginning that a special request from James would procure the speedy release of the goods, and Henri repeated this to the duke of Lennox, who had been sent to Paris as ambassador extraordinary to return the courtesy of Sully's visit.[54]

The English attempted to bluster. James threatened that if their merchants were treated like this, it would mean an end to trade, and Parry made a great show of demanding justice for them. Even Cecil became very impatient, particularly with Beaumont.[55] But in the end the English gave in, as it became apparent to them that the

[51] Sept. 12/22, 1604, Molin to the Doge and Senate, *ibid.*, pp. 182–83. See also P.R.O., S.P. 94/10, ff. 134–35. Henri recognized that the English had interested motives, but he was genuinely pleased at James's helpful attitude. Sept. 13/23, 1604, Henri to Beaumont, *Beaumont* II, 259–64.

[52] Nov. 9, 1604, Parry to Cecil; Nov. 10, the Privy Council to Parry, P.R.O., S.P. 78/51, ff. 303–307.

[53] *Ibid.*, ff. 309–11. *Beaumont* I, 267–69. Dec. 24, 1604, James to Henri, P.R.O., S.P. 78/49, ff. 111–12.

[54] Jan. 9, 1605, Parry to Cecil; Jan. 25, Cecil to Parry; Feb. 13, Lennox to Cecil, P.R.O., S.P. 78/52, ff. 7–8, 15–17, 35.

[55] Feb. 15, 1605, James to Henri; Feb. 20, Cecil to Parry; Mar. 4, Parry to Cecil, *ibid.*, ff. 39, 41–42, 54–55.

French purpose was not the punishment of the offending merchants, but rather the negotiation of a comprehensive agreement. Once James asked for the favor, Henri at once released the goods. He even permitted the merchants to try to sell them, and announced that negotiations for a new agreement would begin as soon as James's commission arrived. But, added the king, the English merchants must meet French standards in future—a threat which, it was hoped, would prod the English government into opening negotiations at once. Parry, in reporting this, urged that his government lose no time: the French still believed that English friendship was necessary to them, but, said Parry, this was being questioned more and more frequently.[56] There was some delay owing to disagreement as to the site of the negotiations. The French insisted on Paris, and James and Cecil, who had no stomach for dealing further with Beaumont, finally agreed. On June 20 Parry was commissioned to negotiate in Paris.[57]

While the site of the negotiations was under discussion the English merchants trading in France drew up a list of their demands. Above all they wanted the withdrawal of the French decree of 1600 which laid down the specifications English cloth was supposed to meet: these specifications were impossible. They also wanted a separate hall in which to sell their cloth in Rouen, Dieppe, and La Rochelle, and the right, after three days and payment of the duty, to take the cloth anywhere they thought they could sell it, as French merchants could do in England. Customs duties should be as they were in 1550; the king should be notified of the table of rates, and no increases should be made. If a merchant was accused of selling faulty cloth, the merchandise should be tested by a mixed commission. And the *droit d'aubaine*, the seizure of the goods of a foreigner dying in France, should be abolished: it caused great trouble and confusion

[56] Mar. 17, 1605, Parry to Cecil, *ibid.*, ff. 66–68. See also Mar. 14/24, Henri to James, *Beaumont* II, 299–300.

[57] Thomas Rymer, *Foedera* (London, 1704–1732) XVI, 630–31. See also *Beaumont* I, 267–69; May 14/24, 1605, Badoer to the Doge and Senate, *C.S.P. Venetian 1603–1607*, p. 242.

and hindered trade, since it made English merchants wary of staying in France and the Dutch and Scots were exempt.[58]

In the end the English merchants got much of what they wanted, at the cost of some equivalent concessions to French traders in England. But it took some time. Parry kept urging the need for haste; consequently he was charged with the conduct of the negotiations even though he was due to be replaced; Cecil explained that there would be no time to brief a successor. Cecil added that he, too, wanted the job done quickly, since the Council had ordered a cessation of trade during the negotiations so that they would not be disturbed by any further incidents.[59] He promised Parry that Sir George Carew would take over the Paris embassy by Michaelmas. Parry was delighted; exile and prison, he wrote his colleague in Brussels, were preferable to the vexations he had suffered in Paris. King Henri was friendly enough, he added, "but the wheels that carry the affairs of the state under him are subject to as many countercourses as the celestial spheres."[60]

Both sides agreed that this was to be a strictly commercial negotiation; the question of a general political league was not to be involved. English merchants were appointed to help Parry with technical questions. In his instructions Parry was told that the principal English demand was the withdrawal of the edict of 1600. He was also to ask for the end of letters of marque and reprisal on land, and to raise once again the everlasting question of justice for English merchants in France. The elimination of the *droit d'aubaine* would be very desirable too, but this was to be asked as a courtesy rather than demanded as a *sine qua non* of the agreement. It might be

---

[58] P.R.O., S.P. 78/52, ff. 85–89. Parry felt that the *droit d'aubaine* benefitted officials and lawyers rather than the French government. Mar. 17, 1605, Parry to Cecil, *ibid.*, ff. 66–68. There was also some sentiment for the creation of a monopolistic trading company for the French trade. *Ibid.*, f. 91; P.R.O., S.P. 14/21, no. 1.

[59] Apr. 17, May 27, 1605, Cecil to Parry, P.R.O., S.P. 78/52, ff. 121–24, 146–47.

[60] June 20, 1605, Cecil to Parry, *ibid.*, f. 150. June 30, Parry to Edmondes, B.M. Stowe Mss. 168, f. 58.

argued, as Carew later did argue, that its elimination would bring so many English men and goods to France as to provide hostages and guarantees for future good relations.[61] Parry was to add, as a bit of gamesmanship, that a history written by the French king's historiographer had scandalized official circles in England.[62]

The negotiations moved slowly. Parry began by asking for removal of all the prejudicial French edicts, especially that of 1600, and met immediate resistance. A good deal of the preliminary discussion was left to the merchant commissioners on either side. The French merchants exhibited the worst piece of English kersey they could find as a horrible example; the English merchants replied in kind, and demonstrated, to their own satisfaction at least, that French-made cloth did not meet the specifications of the decree of 1600 either.[63] The French made a similar charge, that English-made cloth was confiscable by England's own regulations, and Beaumont asked Cecil to send Parry a summary of the English law on this subject.[64] Each side's case was apparently reasonably convincing to the other, and by mid-October the French had conditionally agreed to a withdrawal of the obnoxious decree, if they got equivalent concessions from England.[65]

In Dudley Carleton's view, Parry conducted the negotiations very badly, maundering on about the *jus gentium* and worrying about individual pieces of cloth.[66] But in fact by the end of the year Parry had got most of what he wanted, in spite of his troubles with the merchants, whom he stigmatized as greedy and not very honest, in spite of the replacement of the principal French negotiator in midstream, an action which Cecil regarded as an attempt to stall.[67] The

---

[61] Oct. 4, 1606, Carew to Cecil, P.R.O., S.P. 78/53, ff. 176–79.

[62] P.R.O., S.P. 78/52, ff. 179–81.

[63] Sept. 2, Sept. 10, Sept. 22, 1605, Parry to Cecil, *ibid.*, ff. 218–21, 224–25, 246–247.

[64] *Ibid.*, f. 254.

[65] Oct. 16, 1605, Parry to Cecil, *ibid.*, f. 304.

[66] Nov. 10/20, 1605, Carleton to John Chamberlain, *ibid.*, ff. 342–43.

[67] Oct. 16, 1605, Cecil to Parry, Oct. 16, Parry to Cecil, *ibid.*, ff. 302–304.

French agreed to withdraw the decree of 1600, to abolish local taxes in Normandy, Brittany and Guienne, and the *droit d'aubaine* for ten years. In return they wanted reciprocity: their merchants should have the same treatment in England as English merchants had in France, which by the existing treaties they did not have. Cecil's first reaction was that this was asking too much, and would open the door to similar demands from other countries. Beaumont's return to France in November—the English were delighted to see him leave—was not helpful; Parry reported that he had told his government that the English government was not as concerned for an agreement as it pretended to be, that all it really wanted was the release of the confiscated goods. "I fear me these lenitives will make the mischief incurable in the end," he wrote.[68] But by December, 1605, both sides were more anxious for an accommodation than before, owing to the extremely tense relations which each country had with Spain, in the wake of the Gunpowder Plot and the uncovering of a conspiracy to betray the city of Marseilles to the Spanish; at the end it was the French who were driving for a prompt conclusion to the treaty.[69] So by February, 1606, agreement was reached.

The French met the principal English demands: they withdrew the decree of 1600 and abolished the *droit d'aubaine*. Henceforth faulty cloth brought in by English merchants would not be confiscated, but would be simply sent back to England. Mixed commissions were to be set up in Rouen and London; two merchants of each nationality were to hear complaints against officials. If they divided evenly, a fifth merchant—a Frenchman in Rouen, an Englishman in London—would be co-opted to decide the question. It was contemplated that this arrangement would be extended to other towns in the future. There was to be no immediate change in present tariff levels, subject to discussions and possible modification in future. Existing letters of marque were suspended, and no more were to be

---

[68] Dec. 10, 1605, Parry to Cecil, *ibid.*, f. 365.
[69] Nov. 19, 1605, Parry to Cecil; Dec. 31, Carew to Cecil, *ibid.*, ff. 347–48, 381–82. For the Marseilles episode see *Prinsterer*, pp. 357–66.

issued without prior warning. In return the English went a long way toward conceding the equality the French wanted, with respect to the treatment of ships, various sorts of fees to which merchants were liable, and the removal of restrictions on the sale of French goods by Frenchmen.[70]

The treaty was equitable and beneficial to both sides. Not that the merchants' grievances ceased: they did not. There were the usual complaints of slow implementation and new impositions, and the usual stalling over ratification, complicated in this instance by France's insistence on ratifying only the French text. Carew, who had replaced Parry by this time, regarded this as insulting—it would look like a grant from a superior to an inferior—and wrote a letter to Villeroy in Latin about it. [71] This matter, too, was eventually smoothed over, and when Henri sent his ratification to London, he invited King James to stand godfather to his eldest daughter, and to come to France in person for the occasion. There would be a lot of hunting, he added.[72] Relations between England and France were very cordial on the surface in the summer of 1606.

With the signing of the commercial treaty the exchanges between the English and French reverted chiefly to the problems of the Dutch. By the summer of 1606 the Dutch, whose military expenses had risen since the Anglo-Spanish peace, were showing signs of strain, and demanding greater help from their friends. The commercial agreement had not altered the lack of faith in each other of those "friends." The English attitude to France with respect to the Dutch problem was ambivalent and to some extent contradictory. On the one hand, they were still afraid that if they followed France's urging and committed themselves too heavily to the Dutch, France

[70] Rymer, *Foedera* XVI, 645–57, has the text, in Latin and French.
[71] May 17/27, 1606, Villeroy to Boderie, *Boderie* I, 50–55. May 27, Dec. 7, Carew to Cecil, P.R.O., S.P. 78/53, ff. 96–98, 200–201.
[72] June 2/12, 1606, Henri to Boderie, *Boderie* I, 97–101. James declined the invitation, as the Dauphin was to be christened at the same time. The Pope was the boy's principal sponsor, and the eternal question of precedence would arise.

would find a way of withdrawing and leaving them to bear the burden alone. Jesuit influence in France was increasing, they felt, and was directed to the promotion of a Franco-Spanish alliance.[73] Henri's successful activity as a mediator in the fierce quarrel between the Pope and the Venetian Republic in 1606 was both puzzling and distasteful to the English, who were wholeheartedly on the Venetian side and offered them verbal support aplenty.[74] On the other hand, there continued to be considerable fear, especially among English officials and commanders in the cautionary towns, that Henri by his ostentatious patronage of the Dutch was seeking an offer of political sovereignty, or at the very least, cautionary towns for France. Winwood and Carew were inclined to discount these stories, but they were widespread and plausible enough to create doubts in London.[75]

As for the French, they felt that England was more afraid of domination of the United Provinces by the French than by the Archduke, and they were worried about the impact on English politicians of Spanish pension money, about which they had been carefully informed by the Spaniards themselves.[76] In Paris's view what Eng-

[73] See, e.g., May 2/12, 1606, Henry Wotton to Cecil, P.R.O., S.P. 99/3, ff. 76–77; Sept. 2, Carew to Cecil, P.R.O., S.P. 78/53, ff. 154–56. Wotton was passing on an intercepted letter which explained Henri's coddling of the Jesuits in terms of assuring the Dauphin's succession.

[74] Wotton reported that a Venetian senator had compared Henri's behavior in this matter to Dante's *Inferno*: no one understands it. P.R.O., S.P. 99/3, ff. 90–91. Carew remarked that Villeroy was responsible because he wanted a red hat. P.R.O., S.P. 78/53, f. 134.

[75] Nov. 9, 1606, Jan. 3/13, Jan. 18, 1607, Browne to Lisle; Feb. 8, 1607, Carew to Cecil, *De L'Isle* III, 323–27, 340–43, 344–45, 345–46. Mar. 23, 1607, Winwood to Cecil, P.R.O., S.P. 84/66, ff. 4–5.

[76] Oct. 6, 1604, Parry to Cecil, P.R.O., S.P. 78/51, ff. 277–79. Cecil disingenuously replied to Parry that he would like to see the list of those allegedly pensioned by Spain, "although I think all will prove smoke." *Ibid.*, ff. 290–93. Cecil himself was one of the recipients. The English reputation in this connection was very bad; the Venetian ambassador wrote in 1604, "Bribery is so general in this country that it is useless to hope for anything unless this method be adopted." *C.S.P. Venetian 1603–1607*, pp. 182–83. For a discussion of the whole question of Spanish bribery in England see C. H. Carter, *The*

land wanted was to push France back into war with Spain and then sit back and enjoy the spectacle, reaping a golden harvest the while. This, it was thought, was partly Machiavellianism, partly genuine pacifism, and partly cowardice—England, said Sully to Carew, flinched at the enemy. Carew replied that England had no enemy, and that, after all, France had made peace with Spain first.[77] The Venetian ambassador believed in the genuineness of the pacifism: the new French ambassador, Antoine le Fèvre de la Boderie, urged England to back the Dutch, "but, although here they understand their own interests quite well, they wish to live in peace with everyone."[78] James's laziness also came in for unfavorable comment. His neglect of business, wrote Boderie, led to delays, as the Council disliked acting without his approval. Boderie also rather gleefully reported that the king had received an anonymous letter urging him to stop hunting and get to work, or all his dogs would be poisoned.[79]

Immediately after the signing of the Anglo-Spanish peace the French had feared that James might move closer to Spain and abandon the Dutch, or even turn against them. This fear was now dispelled, but Henri was occasionally disturbed by the recurrent rumors that James would attempt to mediate a peace between the Dutch and Spain and that there might be an Anglo-Spanish marriage alliance with the Low Countries as dowry.[80] The Dutch made it

Secret Diplomacy of the Habsburgs 1598–1625 (New York, 1964), pp. 123–27, and A. J. Loomie, "Sir Robert Cecil and the Spanish Embassy," *Bulletin of the Institute of Historical Research* XLII (1969), 31–56, esp. pp. 54–56.

[77] Mar. 25, 1606, Carew to Cecil, P.R.O., S.P. 78/53, ff. 59–61.

[78] July 2/12, 1606, Giustinian to the Doge and Senate, *C.S.P. Venetian 1603–1607*, pp. 373–74.

[79] Aug. 18/28, Aug. 22/Sept. 1, 1606, Boderie to Villeroy, *Boderie* I, 300–309, 309–14.

[80] Oct. 17, Nov. 9, 1604, Parry to Cecil, P.R.O., S.P. 78/51, ff. 288–89, 303–306; Oct. 20, Cecil to Parry, *ibid.*, ff. 290–93. In the summer of 1604 the French ambassador in Spain allegedly feared an Anglo-Spanish move against Guienne. P.R.O., S.P. 94/10, ff. 82–84. See also Jan. 3/13, 1605, Molin to the Doge and Senate, *C.S.P. Venetian 1603–1607*, pp. 208–209, and Apr. 23, 1606, Edmondes to Cecil, P.R.O., S.P. 77/8, f. 93.

clear from the beginning, however, that they would make peace only if their independence were acknowledged,[81] and in 1604 neither Spain nor the Archduke was prepared to do that. James's virtual repudiation of Sully's treaty[82] Henri regarded with contempt, and, as the English knew he would, he made as much political capital as he could out of the fact that, in 1605, he continued to give aid to the Dutch while English aid stopped.[83] He also made a good deal of his disgust that James permitted the Archduke to recruit in England. He very skillfully gave to all concerned, especially the Dutch, the impression of a man champing at the bit and holding back only because of the pusillanimity of his alleged ally.[84]

By the end of 1605, having made his point, Henri began to change his tune. Aerssens, the Dutch agent in Paris, wrote to Winwood that in spite of the hostility engendered by the plot against Marseilles, France would not take any action against Spain: she could not fight without an alliance with England. Henri was now complaining more loudly than ever that he was bearing the burden of the Dutch war, and that others were profiting from it.[85] He was perhaps trying, in the wake of the Gunpowder Plot, to galvanize James into action— at least James had instructed Edmondes to notify the English officers serving the Archduke that he would look with disfavor on those who did not throw up their commissions.[86] Henri made an anti-Spanish

[81] Dec. 19/29, 1604, Molin to the Doge and Senate, *C.S.P. Venetian 1603–1607*, pp. 200–202.

[82] Carew's instructions make it clear that England no longer considered herself bound by this treaty. P.R.O., S.P. 78/52, ff. 314–22.

[83] By the same token Cornwallis occasionally tried to make political capital with Spain out of this state of affairs. See his memorandum of Nov., 1605, *Winwood* II, 160–63.

[84] See, e.g., Feb. 24, 1605, Browne to Sidney, *De L'Isle* III, 149–50. Henri left the same impression with the Archduke, who was annoyed at French propaganda to the effect that the Low Countries ought to seek French protection. May 3, July 10, Edmondes to Cecil, *Salisbury* XVII, 173–74, P.R.O., S.P. 77/7, ff. 198–201.

[85] *Winwood* II, 181–82.

[86] Dec. 12/22, 1605, Molin to the Doge and Senate, *C.S.P. Venetian 1603–1607*, pp. 304–306.

speech to Carew in January, 1606, and raised the question of an alliance; Carew was noncommittal and turned the conversation to a discussion of a general alliance against the Turks.[87] It was clear enough that England would not fight—at least not yet.

So Henri resumed his cautious policy. At the beginning of 1606 he set out to discipline the fractious duke of Bouillon. His language to Carew, and the number of men he was raising for this purpose, led the ambassador to suspect that the king's intentions were far more aggressive, that this was to be the pretext for an attack on the Archduke. Some people in England hoped so; there were corresponding fears in Spain. If this was Henri's original plan, he abandoned it, and in March, 1606, made a settlement with Bouillon which, in Carew's opinion, he could have got without stirring from Paris.[88]

The Bouillon episode had one important result. At the beginning of 1606, Carew told the Venetian ambassador in London that the Dutch were hoping for substantial French aid this year; they had elaborate plans for naval harassment of the Spanish coast.[89] The cost of the army which was raised to deal with Bouillon jeopardized the subsidy, and made the Dutch reflect on the precariousness of their situation and the difficulty of military planning which was contingent on money which, at the last minute, might not be available.[90] The immediate consequence was a considerable increase in the amount of peace talk at The Hague, and in the number and vehemence of the Dutch pleas for financial aid.[91]

The French king's instructions to his new ambassador in London reflected his growing concern with the problem of the Dutch. Boderie was to tell James that Spain was boasting that James, acting

[87] P.R.O., S.P. 78/53, ff. 5–6.

[88] *Pays-Bas* VI, 110–11. Jan. 21, Feb. 16, Mar. 7, Mar. 25, Apr. 22, 1606, Carew to Cecil, P.R.O., S.P. 78/53, ff. 7–8, 26–27, 40–42, 59–61, 84–85. Apr. 10/20, Giustinian to the Doge and Senate, *C.S.P. Venetian 1603–1607*, pp. 338–39.

[89] *C.S.P. Venetian 1603–1607*, pp. 320–21.

[90] See Carew's letter of Feb. 16, 1606, P.R.O., S.P. 78/53, ff. 26–27.

[91] Mar. 5, 1606, Winwood to Cecil; June 6, Cecil to Winwood, P.R.O., S.P. 84/65, ff. 164–65, 212–15.

as mediator, was going to arrange a peace on terms favorable to them; Henri said he was sure James would not do that. There was some justification for French concern on this score. Spain had made such suggestions to England, but the English Privy Council was not receptive: the Dutch wanted no such interference, and if James persisted, he would simply drive them into the arms of France.[92] Boderie was also to tell James that it was the French view that it was necessary to support the Dutch to prevent their being driven to an unfavorable peace; France and England should consult on the whole problem. Henri told Boderie to cooperate with Caron, even though the Dutch agent was more friendly to England than to France. Villeroy followed up the official instructions with a more detailed set of inquiries. Boderie was to discover how angry the English were over the Gunpowder Plot, whether the pro-Spanish faction was strong enough to make its views felt, whether Spain had made an offer attractive enough, in terms of a marriage alliance, with the Low Countries as dowry, to win James over. Boderie was not to believe all he heard on this last score, Villeroy said; the English were quite capable of lying about this to induce the French to make counterproposals "tant nous avons mauvaise opinion de leur disposition et vertu." If English statesmen favored a Dutch-Spanish peace, Boderie was not openly to oppose it, but simply to point out all the objections.[93]

Boderie approached the problem cautiously. In his first interview with the king he avoided the question of help to the Dutch and tried to keep alive James's hostility to Spain over the refusal to de-

[92] Mar. 17, 1606, the Privy Council to Cornwallis, *Winwood* II, 199–201. See also Mar. 5, Winwood to Cecil, P.R.O., S.P. 84/65, ff. 164–65; May 7, Carew to Cecil, P.R.O., S.P. 78/53, ff. 90–92.

[93] Boderie's instructions are dated Apr. 5/15, 1606; *Boderie* I, 1–29. May 6/16, 1606, Villeroy to Boderie, *ibid.*, pp. 30–38. James liked Caron, in spite of his "native German prolixity," which occasionally prevented the equally prolix king from talking as much as he liked: "had I not interrupted him it had been tomorrow morning before I had begun to speak." James to Cecil, *Salisbury* XVIII, 374–75. This letter is undated, but the content suggests that it was written in the latter part of 1605.

liver Owen and Baldwin. James showed his annoyance with Spain, and at the same time his anxiety for peace; he was pleased over the settlement with Bouillon since the army the French raised had frightened the Archduke. Boderie summed up the king as "timide et irresolu."[94] In late May Boderie raised the Dutch question, and made clear the French opposition to a peace. The Dutch should be encouraged, he said; allowing English troops to serve with the Archduke did not encourage them. James replied that he could not withdraw them without violating the Anglo-Spanish treaty, although he would like to do so. He could not help the Dutch with money.[95] He told Boderie to consult with Cecil as to ways and means of helping them.

Boderie's impression was that the king favored peace between Spain and the Dutch, but not so single-mindedly that he could not be shaken into a change of view.[96] Shortly thereafter the ambassador had his interview with Cecil, an interview which was really decisive. In reply to Cecil's observation that England did not want to strengthen Spain, Boderie said that a Spanish-Dutch peace would do just that. Cecil's rejoinder was that England simply could not afford to support the Dutch with money. To Boderie's suggestion that an Anglo-French fleet sent to the West Indies would dissipate Spanish energies and thus be helpful, Cecil replied that such an action would be a breach of faith. Boderie concluded that England would do nothing to endanger her peace with Spain; she would go on allowing France to support the Dutch and making her profit from that support.[97] At about the same time Winwood was making it clear to Oldenbarnevelt that there would be no financial help from England, that there would not even be remission of any part of the Dutch debt unless the Dutch made some substantial payments.[98]

[94] May 12/22, 1606, Boderie to Villeroy, *Boderie* I, 38–49.
[95] Cecil had already told Beaumont that such aid would be a breach of the Anglo-Spanish treaty. *Salisbury* XVIII, 69–71.
[96] May 28/June 7, 1606, Boderie to Villeroy, *Boderie* I, 79–96.
[97] June 8/18, 1606, Boderie to Villeroy, *ibid.*, pp. 111–23.
[98] June 28, 1606, Winwood to Cecil, P.R.O., S.P. 84/65, ff. 222–24.

For a time French policy wavered uncertainly. King Henri returned occasionally to what Carew called the *veteram cantilenam*, that England and France should join forces against Spain, and frequently to the need to aid the Dutch financially. Sully tried the idea of a joint campaign to set up an independent prince in the Low Countries; he slid over the awkward question of dynastic right by saying that "the title of la bienséance et la repos de la chrestianité supported with force would always be good enough"—an argument unlikely to appeal to James.[99] Boderie's report that England had abandoned the idea of promoting negotiations between Spain and the Dutch was encouraging, however. Boderie, who was thoroughly anti-Spanish, had hopes that the Pope might denounce James publicly; such action might lead to a break between England and Spain and shake James out of his neutrality.[100]

The French ambassador did his best to keep James's suspicions alive, laying heavy stress on Spanish bad faith—proverbial, like that of the Carthaginians, he said—and Spanish propensity for conspiracy and assassination plots.[101] He was pleased that Cecil, whose fundamental suspicion of Spain he came quickly enough to appreciate, encouraged merchants to complain to James about Spanish misbehavior, in order to keep the king's anti-Spanish sentiments alive.[102] But by September Boderie had concluded that James would not break with Spain, in spite of Spanish provocations, in spite of a bellicose public opinion, which was very anti-Spanish and jealous of the rewards which Dutch belligerency brought them in the East Indies. The English government believed that it was unnecessary for

[99] June 2, June 30, 1606, Carew to Cecil, P.R.O., S.P. 78/53, ff. 106–108, 125–28.
[100] June 26/July 6, 1606, Boderie to Villeroy, *Boderie* I, 174–86. For Boderie's reputation see Apr. 12, Edmondes to Cecil, P.R.O., S.P. 77/8, ff. 80–81. Henri, on the other hand, wanted no open breach between James and the Pope. See G. Ascoli, *La Grande-Bretagne devant l'opinion francaise au XVIIe siècle* (Paris, 1930) I, 9.
[101] See, e.g., his letter of July 10/20, 1606, to Henri, *Boderie* I, 195–202.
[102] Aug. 2/12, 1606, Boderie to Henri, Aug. 18/28, Boderie to Villeroy, *ibid.*, pp. 249–61, 300–309.

them to support the Dutch, since the French had to do so; their whole policy, Boderie concluded, was based on the permanence of Franco-Spanish antagonism. The only hope Boderie could see was in a session of Parliament, provided it met while the merchants' grievances were still unsettled. Then the pressure for a rupture would be great, especially from "the third chamber, which is entirely made up of merchants, mostly Puritan."[103] In Paris things went no better from the French point of view. Carew, whom Villeroy regarded as anti-Dutch and much too prone to talk in terms of equity and justice rather than reason of state, proposed to the French king in October that England and France should join together to mediate a peace, lest Spain and the Dutch should eventually agree on a settlement which would be unfavorable to them.[104]

French exasperation at the negative and imprecise character of English policy was rising. The commercial agreement had apparently brought about no change in England's aloof and suspicious political stance toward France. At the end of August Villeroy was of the opinion that, since the English did not value French goodwill, the only thing to do was to try to coerce them into following France's lead.[105] At the end of November the French tested this theory: they threatened to hold up the Dutch subsidy for the following year.[106] Sir William Browne, the English commander at Flushing, reported that his Dutch informants were sure that Henri would fight if James would, and blamed the latter for their dangerous situation. Browne was convinced that Henri's threat was designed to smoke James out.[107]

If this was the king's purpose, it did not work, and it may well

[103] Oct. 12/22, 1606, Boderie to Villeroy, *ibid.*, pp. 392–98. See also his letters of Sept. 3/13 to Henri and of Nov. 11/21 to Pierre Brulart, vicomte de Puisieux, another of the French secretaries of state, *ibid.*, pp. 331–35, 419–26.

[104] Aug. 10/20, 1606, Villeroy to Boderie, *ibid.*, pp. 283–88. Oct. 4, Carew to Cecil, P.R.O., S.P. 78/53, ff. 176–79.

[105] Aug. 30/Sept. 9, 1606, Villeroy to Boderie, *Boderie* I, 322–31.

[106] Nov. 28, 1606, Winwood to Cecil, P.R.O., S.P. 84/65, ff. 275–77.

[107] See Browne's letters of December, 1606, in *De L'Isle* III, 335ff, especially that of Dec. 28, 1606/Jan. 7, 1607, pp. 337–38.

have helped to produce the result which, above all others, Henri wished to avoid. James picked this time, December, 1606, to reopen formally the matter of the French debt to England, an action which his government had been threatening to take ever since the signing of the commercial treaty.[108] The Dutch were alarmed by the direction of English and French policy, and by the constant bickering of the two countries over the matter of support for the United Provinces. It was no longer possible, in their view, to drift on this way, depending for support on the goodwill of such uncertain allies. There was more to be hoped for from France than from England; Oldenbarnevelt believed—or so he told Paul Chouart, seigneur de Buzenval, the French agent at The Hague—that English unhelpfulness was deliberate, and was inspired by her fear of Dutch commercial and maritime rivalry.[109] In late October and November the Dutch had talked of sending an embassy, which would include Oldenbarnevelt himself, to Paris to put their case to King Henri and ask for aid. They had even put out feelers to Henri as to the possibility of his assuming sovereignty in the Netherlands, and therefore responsibility for the war, with the clear implication that the alternative for them was to open negotiations for peace.[110] Buzenval was cool to this suggestion: England would be angry, and, he felt, the Dutch might very well stop fighting and let France carry the entire burden. At the same time Sully was suggesting to the nuncio that the only real solution was to make the Low Countries independent of England, France, and Spain alike.[111] Then came Henri's statement that he could no longer support the Dutch all by himself and the English decision to reopen the question of the French debt. The Dutch dropped the plan for the embassy, and the astonishing news leaked out that, without consulting their allies, they had begun negotiations

---

[108] Mar. 5, 1606, Cecil to Beaumont, *Salisbury* XVIII, 69–71.
[109] Feb. 17/27, 1606, Buzenval to Villeroy, *Beaumont* I, 288.
[110] *Prinsterer*, pp. 369–74.
[111] *Ibid.*, pp. 369–74. Nov. 28, 1606, Carew to Cecil, P.R.O., S.P. 78/53, ff. 191–93.

for a truce with the Archduke.[112] The wheels had been set in motion which were to bring the long war to a temporary end.

English policy must bear a greater share of the responsibility than that of France for this result, so distasteful to both parties. King James's well-known pacifism, his financial difficulties, his unwillingness to take a diplomatic initiative or, indeed, to act at all until he was compelled to do so, all led the Dutch to despair of his ever being willing to aid them to any substantial degree. Caron simply did not believe James's vague promises to follow the French lead if Henri declared openly for the Dutch. Winwood reported that the Dutch were in serious financial difficulties, but Cecil made it clear that England simply could not help them.[113] King James was clearly prepared to let the French bear the burden alone, but even here his financial necessity, which led him to raise the question of the debt, threw obstacles in France's way. The French, however, bore their share of responsibility too. Henri was not yet prepared to contemplate seriously a renewal of open war with Spain, and the English knew it. If the French were scornful of English feebleness and irresolution, and doubtful of her power and good faith, French maneuvering often appeared to London to be slippery and dishonest. They were trying to lure England back into the war so that they could profit from neutrality or from a bilateral bargain with Spain. French naval preparations were sufficiently disquieting to cause Cecil to decide that France was not to be allowed to buy ships in England.[114]

Because of this mutual suspicion and mistrust it was impossible for the two countries to work out a common policy of support for the Dutch, or even to discuss seriously the possibility of working out such a policy. Neither government was pro-Spanish; neither was

[112] Edmondes reported this rumor to Cecil on Dec. 10, 1606, P.R.O., S.P. 77/8, ff. 193–94. The Archduke notified Lerma the next day; *Pays-Bas* VI, 125.

[113] Nov. 20/30 1606, Giustinian to the Doge and Senate, *C.S.P. Venetian 1603–1607*, p. 437. Nov. 28, Winwood to Cecil, P.R.O., S.P. 84/65, ff. 275–77. Dec. 8/18, Dec. 13/23, Boderie to Brulart, *Boderie* I, 448–60, 466–77.

[114] P.R.O., S.P. 78/53, ff. 176–79.

actively seeking alliance with Spain; but each feared that the other would use any overt action on its part to make such an alliance—a somewhat inconsistent attitude for the English to take, given their belief in the permanence of Franco-Spanish hostility. The incompatible personalities of the two monarchs created further difficulties. Henri let his contempt for James show: James was unwilling to take any risks that might interfere with his hunting. He would talk but not act, especially if action meant clashing with Spain.[115] On the other hand the royal theologian was afraid of a Jesuited king who occasionally intervened on behalf of English Catholics. So paralysis set in, and the Dutch, reading the signs aright—their agents in London and Paris were very astute men—decided to explore the avenue which the Archduke had opened to them.

[115] See, e.g., Sept. 20/30, 1606, Piero Priuli (Venetian ambassador in France) to the Doge and Senate, *C.S.P. Venetian 1603–1607*, p. 405.

CHAPTER IV

❋ ❋

Spain and the Dutch: Peace or War?

FROM THE BEGINNING of 1607 until the conclusion of the Truce of Antwerp in March, 1609, the prospect of the settlement of the long conflict between Spain and her rebels, a conflict which had begun even before King James was born, dominated the western European diplomatic scene. Neither the English nor the French government had changed its view that the continuation of the war would be very desirable, and English opinion, especially in the merchant community, was occasionally positively bellicose. Both countries feared that, given a breathing spell, Spain's former power might revive. Both were aware of the commercial strength of the Dutch, which peace would vastly enhance.[1] Nor did everyone within the two rival camps want peace. The government of Philip III found the concessions the Dutch demanded most unpalatable, and gave way very slowly and grudgingly. In the United Provinces Prince Maurice and his friends were, on the whole, hostile to peace. The unity of the provinces, precarious enough in wartime, might very well dissolve altogether once the military threat was removed, and a revived Spain might, at some future date, absorb them piecemeal at her leisure. Furthermore, the great position of the House of Orange would decay; it was a position created by war, and in peace the mercantile

[1] See, for instance, July 6, 1607, Robert Savage to Cecil, *Salisbury* XIX, 175. Savage was a London merchant in the Spanish trade.

oligarchy would gradually erode it. The groups most eager for peace were that oligarchy, headed by Oldenbarnevelt, and the war-weary and impoverished government of the Archduke in Brussels,[2] and in the end they had their way.

They had their way largely because of the unwillingness of England and France to make the necessary sacrifices to keep the war going. The two governments were not precisely working at cross purposes during the negotiations, and the two sets of commissioners sent to "advise" the Dutch, headed by Winwood and the veteran French diplomatist Pierre Jeannin, got on reasonably well together. But the mutual suspicions persisted. Because each was afraid that the other would, somehow, commit it to open military support of the Dutch and withdraw to a profitable neutrality, peace appeared, in the end, to be the least of evils.

The key to any settlement was Spanish acknowledgement of Dutch sovereignty. Caron had said as much to Cecil as early as the beginning of 1605;[3] the Archduke's willingness to discuss this concession had touched off the negotiations for a truce at the end of 1606. It took the Archduke three months to make the distasteful statement; once he did so, Oldenbarnevelt overrode the opposition of Maurice and arranged a truce to run for eight months from April 10, 1607, which Spain was to ratify within three months. The truce was originally confined to operations on land; the Archduke wanted it extended to the sea as well, and in due course it was.

The months before the Archduke's concession represented the best opportunity to block the negotiations; during this time English and French policy floundered. Part of the difficulty, certainly, stemmed from England's reopening of the question of the French debt. The French believed that the timing of this move meant that

---

[2] The letters of the commander in the Netherlands, Ambrogio Spinola, to Philip III bear eloquent testimony to this; see, e.g., that of Feb. 5/15, 1607, *Pays-Bas* I, 244–45.
[3] *Salisbury* XVII, 2–3.

England's protestations that she wanted the war to continue were insincere, and that the move was designed to convince the Dutch that England was too poor to help them. Carew had stressed that England really needed the money, but Cecil, according to Boderie, had virtually admitted to Caron that he did not expect the maneuver to produce any real fiscal results. So the French reverted to the ancient red herring of Sully's treaty. If James would acknowledge their interpretation of that treaty and concede that one-third of all the payments they had made to the Dutch since 1603 could be deducted from the debt, they would admit to the balance, and, furthermore, they would make the Dutch repay that third, which, in effect, provided the Dutch could be compelled to accept it, would transfer the burden to their shoulders. Carew reported the suggestion on January 8; its great advantage, in his view, was that it would mean the repayment of the money which England conceded to have been legitimately deducted from the debt in 1603 and 1604 in accordance with Sully's treaty.[4]

Sully was very touchy about the validity of his treaty, which, the French insisted, was a binding contract. Carew gave the standard English response: it was only a preliminary draft of articles for a future contract, made obsolete by the Anglo-Spanish peace. Carew expressed the opinion in March that Sully had painted the treaty's fiscal advantages too glowingly to Henri, who had not received the English demands well: Sully was afraid of what the consequences to himself of the hardening English attitude would be. As Carew saw it, there were three matters to be considered: the total amount of the debt, how much was validly deducted by payments to the Dutch, and the conditions of repayment. It was hard enough to get anyone in the French government to talk about the debt at all; Carew was constantly being referred from one high official to another. When he could persuade someone to talk, he discovered that

[4] P.R.O., S.P. 78/53, ff. 220–23. See also Jan. 1/11, 1607, Brulart to Boderie; Jan. 19/29, Boderie to Brulart, *Boderie* II, 17–24, 39–45.

they wanted to talk about the total, which would clearly take a long time to calculate; to Carew the key question was the matter of the deductions.[5]

It was against this background of bickering about the debt and about the implementation of various clauses of the recently signed commercial treaty that the two governments attempted to assess each other's attitude to the prospect of the Spanish-Dutch negotiations. The air was full of trial balloons. Carew tried one: he suggested to Aerssens—or so Aerssens said—that, if Prince Henry married Henri's eldest daughter, James would arrange that Philip would acknowledge them as sovereigns of Holland and Zealand.[6] This was utterly fantastic; somewhat less so was Winwood's report that Aerssens—a busy talebearer—told him that Henri was ready to fight, in alliance with England and the German Protestants, in order, as Aerssens rather grandiloquently put it, to confine Spain behind the Pyrenees. Winwood was chilly to this proposal; the negotiation of the various alliances involved would take a lot of time, and time was what the Dutch did not now have. This was hardly a new suggestion, in any event; the French, said Winwood, had made such proposals before, and had disavowed them. A week later Winwood reported that the Dutch themselves were not enthusiastic about this.[7] The war-weariness of the Dutch, which became more and more obvious with the first real prospect of peace, was to be a crucial factor in the diplomats' calculations.

One matter which helped to increase English suspicions of the sincerity of France's professed eagerness to fight for the Dutch was what the English regarded as her equivocal policy in Italy, in the quarrel between the Pope and the government of Venice. There was a connection between events in Italy and the negotiations in the

[5] Mar. 20/30, 1607, Brulart to Boderie, *ibid.*, pp. 123–30. Mar. 21, Carew to Cecil, P.R.O., S.P. 78/53, ff. 250–53.

[6] Jan. 1/11, 1607, Brulart to Boderie; Jan. 19/29, Boderie to Brulart, *Boderie* II, 17–24, 39–45.

[7] Jan. 14, Jan. 21, 1607, Winwood to Cecil, *Salisbury* XIX, 7–8, 17–18. Cecil on Feb. 21 praised Winwood for his caution. *Winwood* II, 297–98.

north; as Spinola pointed out to Philip III, Spanish difficulties in Italy would lead the Dutch to adopt a stiffer and more bellicose attitude.[8] It would therefore seem logical for France to do all that she could to keep Italy in turmoil, to keep Spain busy there, in order to encourage the Dutch to fight on. Instead, France's Italian policy was just the opposite: she was actively trying to prevent a serious eruption in the peninsula. James complained to the Venetian ambassador, Georgio Giustinian, that France was double-dealing, and pointed out that Spanish behavior in Italy was such as to give Henri an admirable excuse for a breach with Spain without offending the Pope.

There was a good deal of discussion of a league to support Venice, raised first by Henry Wotton, who hoped to involve the French. James told Giustinian that he favored a league in principle, and would join one when France had committed herself so far that she could not back out. The French reaction was very cool; when the Venetian ambassador in Paris raised the question of a league, he was told not to rely on English promises. Henri, he reported, was not averse to a league after a settlement was arranged, but it should be a league which included the Pope rather than England. Giustinian commented that the policy of the two governments in Italy had the same general anti-Spanish cast, but that England wanted to give any league an anti-Papal edge, and France did not.[9] Wotton, whose view of French policy coincided with Giustinian's, did what he could to keep the pot boiling, but his French colleague in Venice was utterly unhelpful and pointed out to Wotton that English policy was inconsistent: how could England simultaneously urge France to involve herself in Italy and demand repayment of the French debt?[10]

---

[8] *Pays-Bas* I, 243. See also Jan. 29/Feb. 8, 1607, Giustinian to the Doge and Senate, *C.S.P. Venetian 1603–1607*, pp. 464–65.

[9] Feb. 12/22, Mar. 18/28, 1607, Piero Priuli to the Doge and Senate; Feb. 12/22, Feb. 17/27, Giustinian to the Doge and Senate, *C.S.P. Venetian 1603–1607*, pp. 467–68, 469–71, 471–74, 484. Jan. 22/Feb. 1, Villeroy to Boderie, *Boderie* II, 46–49.

[10] Feb. 27/Mar. 9, 1607, Wotton to James, L. P. Smith, *The Life and Letters of Henry Wotton* (Oxford, 1907), I, 382–83. Feb. 20/Mar. 1, 1608, Wotton to Cecil, P.R.O., S.P. 99/5, ff. 46–49. Boderie also made this point in connection

By April, 1607, the Italian crisis was over, thanks in large part to the mediation of Cardinal Joyeuse, the archbishop of Rouen, whom the French government frequently employed to deal with the Papacy, and the possibility of seriously distracting Spain had vanished. Cecil, who had always felt that the quarrel between Venice and the Pope would be peacefully settled, complained to Boderie of the uncooperativeness of the French ambassador in Venice, and raked up various grievances going back as far as the Treaty of Vervins. His assurances that England would join in a war with Spain if France took the lead were hardly convincing; Boderie and his superiors had heard that song many times before, and besides, England was unprepared for war.[11] The French were convinced that England would never fight in Italy; all such discussions were "pour amuser le tapis."[12] In fact they were convinced that England would not fight at all, in spite of the generally bad relations between England and Spain—the old commercial difficulties were again acute. "To remain in the terms we do," wrote Cornwallis on March 31, "the inconveniences are great, neither is there in my weak conceit a greater difference of disease and unrest to Christendom by a peace of this nature and an open war."[13] The words on both sides were brave,

---

with French help to the Dutch in discussing the debt with Cecil. Jan. 31/Feb. 10, 1607, Boderie to Brulart, *Boderie* II, 50–65.

[11] Jan. 31/Feb. 10, 1607, Boderie to Brulart; Feb. 21/Mar. 3, Brulart to Boderie, *Boderie* II, 50–65, 93–100. For Cecil's attitude see Feb. 18/28, Giustinian to the Doge and Senate, *C.S.P. Venetian 1603–1607*, pp. 474–75. The Venetian ambassador added that Cecil had not emphasized his opinions in talking to James, who did not feel that a settlement in Italy was likely and who disliked hearing views which ran counter to his own.

[12] *Lettres de Henri IV, Roi de France, et de Messieurs de Villeroy, et de Puisieux, à M. Antoine Le Fèvre de la Boderie, Ambassadeur de France en Angleterre Depuis 1606 jusqu'en 1611* (Amsterdam, 1733), pp. 136–42.

[13] P.R.O., S.P. 94/13, ff. 207–208. See also Jan. 8/18, 1607, Boderie to Brulart, *Boderie* II, 25–32. When the Spanish ambassador in England complained that people threw stones and mud at him in the street, Cecil replied that the throwers were friends and relatives of the merchants who were victims of Spanish injustice. Jan. 31/Feb. 10, Boderie to Brulart, *ibid.*, pp. 50–65.

wrote Boderie, and the resolutions were feeble—and he was right to the extent that Cecil certainly wanted no rupture with Spain on this issue. The English preferred that Spain sap their strength bit by bit, wrote Boderie contemptuously, adding that James resembled Henri III, and that his reign might be as disastrous as was that of the last of the Valois.[14]

The professional diplomatists had been skeptical that anything would ever come of the conversations between the Dutch and the Archduke's government; the news of the eight-months' truce therefore came as a surprise and something of a shock, and put an entirely different complexion on Anglo-French relations. The Dutch made the agreement without prior consultation with their allies, and the news was most unwelcome to both kings.[15] Edmondes reported that it was the opinion in Brussels that the Dutch had acted because France had asked for too much in return for continued financial support.[16] English opinion, reported Boderie, was troubled; they wondered whether the reopening of the question of the debt, which inhibited further French aid to the Dutch, might have driven the latter to make the truce. Cecil wrote to Cornwallis that he found it hard to believe that the Archduke had made the concession respecting Dutch independence, or that Spain would accept it. The English suspected that France might have had a hand in the negotiations; for reassurance's sake they would now welcome French initiative in the matter of an Anglo-French league. Suspicions on this score were mutual; Henri instructed his ambassador to discover what part James had had in the making of the truce and what his attitude now was; Aerssens had said that Winwood had favored the truce. Villeroy noted the inconsistency between Winwood's alleged attitude

[14] Jan. 11/21, 1607, Brulart to Boderie; Feb. 11/21, Boderie to Brulart, *Boderie* II, 32–39, 76–81.

[15] Mar. 29, 1607, Carew to Edmondes, B.M. Stowe Mss. 169, ff. 1–2. Apr. 10, Cecil to Edmondes, P. R. O., S.P. 77/8, ff. 272–73.

[16] Feb. 15, 1607, Edmondes to Cornwallis, *Downshire* II, 452–54. Apr. 8, Edmondes to Cecil, P.R.O., S.P. 77/8, ff. 270–71.

(which Aerssens had mistakenly reported) and that of London as reported by Boderie, and instructed the ambassador to see whether the English government could be persuaded to initiate discussions for a league; if France spoke first, England would simply revert to her maddening policy of balance.[17]

Boderie's report of the English attitude was quickly proved correct. Caron, who told the Venetian representative in London frankly that Anglo-French irresolution had prompted his government's action,[18] had to exert himself to mollify James, which he did with considerable success. He explained that the Archduke had given them so little time to make up their minds that they had had to decide without asking James's advice, and promised that the Dutch would certainly not make any final settlement without full consultation. This appeared to satisfy the king. The immediate English reaction was that there must be close cooperation from now on with France. Cecil said as much to Boderie, adding that he hoped that Spain would not ratify the truce, and that she would not if there were an accommodation in Italy—a belated acknowledgement that perhaps Henri's policy there had not been so foolish after all, given the apparent ascendancy of the peace party at The Hague.[19]

A few days after this interview with Cecil, Boderie saw the king. James asked if the French were as surprised as he at the truce. Boderie said yes, and went on to ask James if he felt that the two governments should support or oppose the peace; his master, he said, would follow the English lead. James replied that he did not favor peace; the problem was how to prevent it. France and England must not oppose it directly, he said, lest the Dutch sign anyway; such a line would antagonize both the United Provinces and Spain—James

---

[17] Mar. 28/Apr. 7, 1607, Boderie to Brulart; Apr. 4/14, Henri to Boderie; Apr. 4/14, Villeroy to Boderie, *Boderie* II, 141–49, 149–56, 156–62. Apr. 20, Cecil to Cornwallis, Cott. Mss. Vesp. CX, ff. 81–82. For Winwood's attitude see Feb. 24, Winwood to Cecil, *Salisbury* XIX, 53–55.

[18] Apr. 15/25, 1607, Giustinian to the Doge and Senate, *C.S.P. Venetian 1603–1607*, p. 492.

[19] Apr. 6/16, 1607, Boderie to Brulart, *Boderie* II, 174–87.

evidently believed, as did political circles in Brussels, that Spain wanted peace, though probably from the worst of motives.[20] The proper line was to point out to the Dutch how untrustworthy Spain was, and how disadvantageous peace would be; if that failed, then the negotiations themselves would provide some opening for disruption. Peace must be prevented at all costs. This line of reasoning must have provoked a few wry smiles in Paris; it was precisely the tack which the French had so unsuccessfully attempted with James in 1603 and 1604.

Boderie was convinced that the English king meant what he said. There was, said the ambassador, no devious Anglo-Spanish plot. But whether James would commit himself to war in order to prevent the distasteful peace from taking place—that was another question. Cecil, Boderie reported, was rather more bellicose. He also wanted no peace, and talked of an Anglo-French alliance. He brought up the current causes of English irritation with France: her policy in Italy, the rumored marriage negotiations with Spain—there were always such rumors in connection with both parties and Spain, and they had, in some measure, impeded serious discussions of the possibility of an alliance in recent months[21]—French shuffling over the debt, and her telling the Dutch that the English demand for repayment meant that France could no longer subsidize them. Cecil's purpose in all this was not to score points, but rather to work out an accommodation. The tone of Boderie's report indicated that real cooperation might at last be possible.[22]

The next French move temporarily revived all the English doubts, however. In mid-April Henri dispatched a special embassy, headed by Pierre Jeannin, to the Low Countries to ascertain the true state of Dutch opinion. In his instructions the king stressed that his goodwill

[20] Cornwallis had been saying so since January. See, e.g., B.M. Cott. Mss. Vesp. C IX, ff. 646–57. Apr. 15, 1607, Edmondes to Cecil, P.R.O., S.P. 77/8, ff. 274–75.

[21] On this point see Feb. 19/Mar. 1, 1607, Boderie to Brulart, *Boderie* II, 82–92.

[22] Apr. 10/20, 1607, Boderie to Henri, *ibid.*, pp. 174–87.

to the Dutch had not diminished, that he would support them whether they opted for peace or war, and that he had no notion of compelling them to make him an offer of sovereignty by cutting off his support. The ambassadors were to urge the Dutch not to relax their military posture, and to point out that, given Spanish untrustworthiness, peace would not mean disarmament for them. Henri wanted to know the Dutch conditions for peace; he was particularly interested that they should insist on the removal of Spanish troops from the Archduke's dominions. He was also hopeful that toleration for Catholics in the United Provinces could be successfully forwarded, but Jeannin was instructed not to raise this question if it would be badly received. If there was a division of opinion among the Dutch as to peace or war, France would back the stronger party, so as to prevent the disruption of Dutch unity.

The king's instructions indicated that he was highly suspicious of the English. He still believed James might have had a hand in the truce; Boderie's report of James's annoyance he discounted on the ground that James was irritated only because he had not been able to fill his favorite role of mediator.[23] Nevertheless, Jeannin was instructed to cooperate with King James's representatives, if they asked for cooperation, on the understanding that the principal aim was the welfare of the Dutch.[24] Villeroy, in informing Boderie of this embassy, told him to stress French willingness to cooperate, and excused France's failure to consult England before sending Jeannin by emphasizing that speed was essential, to prevent peace fever from getting too tight a grip on the Dutch. If the Dutch were to be persuaded to fight on, an offer of assistance must be made at the right moment—not, he added, as tardily as Elizabeth had made hers at the time of the Franco-Spanish peace talks in 1598.[25] To Carew King

---

[23] There was some justification for this view. See June 7, 1607, Cornwallis to Cecil, B.M. Cott. Mss. Vesp. C X, ff. 98–102.

[24] The instructions, dated Apr. 12/22, 1607, are in *Jeannin* XI, 466–95.

[25] Apr. 18/28, 1607, Villeroy to Boderie, *Boderie* II, 187–92. See also May 8, Cecil to Winwood, P.R.O., S.P. 84/66, ff. 21–22.

Henri stressed that Jeannin and his colleagues were sent chiefly as observers in the first instance.

The French explanations and the request for joint action relieved the English, whose first reaction was that Jeannin's purpose was to get the Dutch to rely exclusively on French advice. Boderie felt that it was necessary to assure the English that there was no substance to their belief that the Pope was promoting a Franco-Spanish reconciliation.[26] James, for his part, was willing to accept the French explanations, and also the principle of cooperation; but he insisted that, before England did anything, the Dutch must send a delegation to England to explain their recent behavior, so that he could determine the best policy to follow. Cecil's letter to Winwood on May 17 reflected James's uncertainty: the king, wrote Cecil, had no desire to oppose peace, or to further it if it were unsafe.[27] This sort of irresolution prompted Villeroy to write in exasperation that France, no matter what she did, would be criticized in England. If she talked of peace, the English would say that she wanted Dutch gratitude, if of war, that she wanted political control of the United Provinces.[28]

James agreed, with Boderie, that the Spanish purpose was ultimately to weaken and reabsorb the Dutch; he gave the ambassador a vehement account of Spanish wrongdoing. Cecil, when Boderie approached him, was rather more reserved and mentioned such awkward matters as the rumored Franco-Spanish marriage negotiations and France's mediation in Italy. Cecil was genuinely anxious for cooperation with France at this stage, however; in June he scolded his aggressive and quarrelsome agents in the Ottoman Empire for getting into an unnecessary row with their French opposite number there.[29] It was Boderie's view that, partly because of her

[26] Apr. 28/May 8, 1607, Boderie to Brulart; May 5/15, Boderie to Villeroy, *Boderie* II, 203–209, 209–12.

[27] *Winwood* II, 310–11.

[28] *Jeannin* XII, 122–27.

[29] P.R.O., S.P. 95/7, ff. 166–68. See also May 18/28, 1607, Ottavio Bon (Venetian representative in Turkey) to the Doge and Senate, *C.S.P. Venetian 1603–1607*, p. 485

financial difficulties, England hoped to find a satisfactory solution
without undertaking any new obligations; above all, without fighting.[30]

It was July before the Dutch delegation arrived in London and
August before Winwood (who returned briefly to London in July
to advise his government) and Sir Richard Spencer were commissioned as King James's special envoys. For a time it was not at all
certain that they would have anything to do; before negotiations
could take place, Spain had to ratify the Archduke's concessions.
That ratification was a long time in coming; when it finally did
come, its form was such that, as Cornwallis reported, Spanish officials believed that its concessions respecting sovereignty could
easily be explained away.[31] It seems likely that Spain gave in because
of her own financial troubles, her belief that France and England
were hostile to the peace,[32] and unremitting pressure from the Archduke and Spinola. In their correspondence with Madrid the latter
laid heavy stress on the exhaustion of the loyal provinces and the
cost of continuing the war—it would take 200,000 écus (£50,000)
a month, said Spinola, merely to keep his army from mutiny, and
300,000 to run the war properly. Archduke Albert pointed to the
adverse reaction of Spain's ill-wishers as a telling argument in favor
of peace, and his wife suggested that the opponents of peace were
those, like the constable of Castile, whose friends and relatives profited from the war. They were all distressed at Philip's decision to
send the fire-eating Don Diego de Ibarra to Brussels; Ibarra was
very coldly received. He found that the war party, though noisy,
had little influence, and he could make no dent on the unanimity of
the Archduke and his officials as to the necessity of peace. His swift

[30] Apr. 20, 1607, Cecil to Winwood, *Winwood* II, 305–306. May 5/15,
Boderie to Brulart, *Boderie* II, 212–28.

[31] Aug. 24, 1607, Cornwallis to Cecil, P.R.O., S.P. 94/14, f. 127. See also his
letters of May 24 and June 14, *ibid.*, ff. 25–26, 51–53. Spencer, who played no
independent role in the negotiations, was the brother of Lord Treasurer
Dorset's daughter-in-law.

[32] On this point see June 7, 1607, Cornwallis to Cecil, B.M. Cott. Mss. Vesp.
C X, ff. 98–102.

ANGLO-SPANISH PEACE CONFERENCE, 1604

Louis Verryken, Jean Richardot, Count of Aremberg, Alessandro Rovida, Count of Villa Mediana, Constable of Castille, Lord Buckhurst, Earl of Nottingham, Lord Mountjoy (Devonshire), Henry Howard (Earl of Northampton), and Robert Cecil

Marc Gheeraedts the Younger, National Portrait Gallery, London

JAMES I

Van Somer, Hatfield House, Hertfordshire
Courtesy of the Marquess of Salisbury, K.G.

HENRI IV

Pourbus, Louvre, Paris
Reproduction from the Musées Nationaux

ARCHDUKE ALBERT

Rubens, Musées Royaux des Beaux-Arts, Brussels

SIR RALPH WINWOOD

Mierevelt, Palace House, Beaulieu, Brockenhurst
Courtesy of Lord Montagu

JOHAN VAN OLDENBARNEVELT

Mierevelt, Rijksmuseum, Amsterdam

NICOLAS DE NEUFVILLE, SEIGNEUR DE VILLEROY

Larcher, Reproduction from the Musées Nationaux

PIERRE JEANNIN

École fr. XVIIeme, Reproduction from the Musées Nationaux

recall, early in July, coupled with the recent disbanding of the army collected by the Spanish viceroy of Milan, the disposition of which was being carefully watched as an earnest of Spanish intentions, was taken as an indication that Spain was ready to negotiate.

The Dutch evidently believed so. They would not accept the Spanish ratification in its present form, because of the inadequacy of the language, and the fact that King Philip had signed it *Jo el Rey* instead of with his name, which implied that he was addressing his subjects rather than a free people. Nevertheless they did ratify the extension of the land truce to the sea, to the great annoyance of Henri, agreed to an exchange of prisoners, and accepted the assurances of the Archduke's agent Louis Verreyken that a second Spanish ratification, in more satisfactory form, would be forthcoming in a month.[33] It was still quite possible, however, that the war party in Madrid, encouraged by the Spanish clergy, would get the upper hand. Father Jean Neyen, the most active of the Archduke's go-betweens in the negotiations, reportedly said that his Spanish brothers in Christ had done their best to discredit him, even to the point of saying that his parents were Lutherans.[34]

There was more division of opinion in the United Provinces than in the Archduke's territories; it was very apparent to the English and French envoys, each of whom occasionally tried to play upon it to gain some advantage over the other.[35] The Dutch also had some suspicion of the intentions of their protectors, who, they knew, had their own selfish reasons for wanting the war to continue. Toward the end of May Jeannin sent back to his government an analysis of

[33] For the Archduke's policy see the correspondence in *Pays-Bas* I, 245–67, VI, 131–34. See also Edmondes's letters in P.R.O., S.P. 78/8, ff. 281ff., esp. ff. 293–94, 309–10, 312–13, 320, 328. July 17, 1607, Ogle to Cecil, P.R.O., S.P. 84/66, f. 35. B.M. Stowe Mss. 169, f. 126. Aug. 14, Carew to Cecil, P.R.O., S.P. 78/53, ff. 317–19. According to Edmondes, the Archduke had not wanted the Spanish forces in Italy sent to Flanders.

[34] P.R.O., S.P. 94/14, ff. 114–15.

[35] Jeannin, for instance, reported that Winwood had told the bellicose Maurice that James and the English people favored war, but that France favored peace. May 30/June 9, 1607, Jeannin et al. to Henri, *Jeannin* XII, 80–90.

Dutch opinion, the gist of which was that the lesser people, and some towns which profited from the war, wanted it to go on, but that the merchant oligarchy favored peace.[36]

Peace soon appeared to Jeannin to be the lesser of evils. He started out by being rather suspicious of Winwood, but quickly changed his mind and in his reports back to Paris began to praise Winwood's openness and honesty. Partly this was because the two ambassadors analyzed the problem in the same way. There were three solutions: an Anglo-Franco-Dutch league and open war, the best result, but the least likely; peace; or a continuation of the existing situation, with England and France helping the Dutch more than before. This last seemed the most likely to Jeannin at first, since he did not believe that Spain was sincere about peace;[37] but gradually his views came to alter. His superiors in Paris kept assuring him that England was secretly treacherous and hostile to France. The king continued to accuse James and his advisers of malice, feebleness and nonchalance, and Villeroy was bitterly anti-English. King James, he said, was irresolute and anti-Dutch; he wanted to see them subjected to the Archduke, and Cecil was malicious and prevaricating: "Les Anglais sont et seront à jamais ennemis jurés de la France."[38] Henri and Villeroy also distrusted Oldenbarnevelt, whom they regarded as the leader of the peace party, and as pro-English. Oldenbarnevelt's behavior disgusted Villeroy; he would, wrote the Frenchman, always behave "secrètement et infidèlement, suivant le style du comte de Salisbury." Nevertheless Oldenbarnevelt was so important that every effort should be made to wean him from his pro-English proclivities and make him sympathetic to France.[39] Villeroy was not the

[36] May 23/June 2, 1607, Jeannin et al. to Henri, *ibid.*, pp. 56–71.

[37] May 19/29, 1607, Jeannin et al. to Henri, May 25/June 4, Jeannin to Boderie, *ibid.*, pp. 24–43, 74–78.

[38] Aug. 14/24, 1607, Villeroy to Jeannin, *ibid.*, pp. 316–23. See also July 8/18, Jeannin et al. to Henri, *ibid.*, pp. 212–19, and Aug. 5/15, Giustinian to the Doge and Senate, *C.S.P. Venetian 1607–1610*, pp. 22–23.

[39] July 26/Aug. 5, 1607, Villeroy to Jeannin, *Jeannin* XII, 267–71. See also his letter of June 7/17, *ibid.*, pp. 122–27.

only French minister who felt suspicious of England; in June Brulart wrote to Boderie that Winwood and his associates had spoken so convincingly of England's desire to join with France in furthering whatever might be to the Dutch advantage that the French might almost believe them, if they did not know better, and Boderie himself remarked that the best way to get England to favor a war policy was to indicate that France favored peace.[40] It was clear to Jeannin that genuine Anglo-French cooperation, as well as a good deal more financial support, was essential if the Dutch were to be persuaded to go on fighting; given the existing atmosphere in Paris, such cooperation was impossible.

The fault was not all on one side, of course. Cecil was not disposed to trust the French, whose continued evasiveness over the debt he and Carew found most exasperating. Also exasperating was France's spreading the story, which had some impact on Dutch opinion, that Carew had told Henri that the French debt to England was not to be used to aid the Dutch; this was a cheap way of lowering England in Dutch eyes.[41] Cecil also still believed—or so he told Caron—that Henri still had designs on the sovereignty of the Low Countries.[42] The slowness of the English government in making up its mind what to do also contributed to the atmosphere of indecision, and therefore to the likelihood of an end to the fighting. James's insistence that the Dutch send a delegation to him before he sent commissioners to them, a decision which Caron vainly tried to persuade him to change, his emphasis on his offended dignity in this connection, was a pretext, in the French view: he was waiting to see how Jeannin fared in the United Provinces before he committed

[40] *Lettres de Henri IV*, pp. 188–91. July 10/20, 1607, Boderie to Jeannin, *Jeannin* XII, 228–32.

[41] See, for instance, Carew's letters of July 1 and 17, and Oct. 19, 1607, P.R.O., S.P. 78/53, ff. 292–95, 298–301, 345–49. Aug. 7/17, Jeannin to Villeroy, *Jeannin* XII, 301–308.

[42] June 5/15, 1607, Boderie to Brulart, *Boderie* II, 273–82. Winwood shared this suspicion. May 16, Winwood to Edmondes, B.M. Stowe Mss. 169, ff. 38–39.

himself to anything.[43] By early June Villeroy had concluded that, in view of the state of Dutch opinion and the unreliability of the English—"ils sont tous trompeurs"—France had better work for peace.[44]

There was, besides war and a final peace settlement, a third alternative: a long truce. By the end of May Jeannin was convinced that this was a very likely solution. Spain was apt to grant no more than this, since it would permit her to reopen the question of sovereignty at some future date. For this reason Henri thought it very dangerous, but Jeannin was able to persuade him that a truce was no more fragile than a peace, and that a truce would actually serve French interests better, since it would keep alive Dutch suspicion of Spain and, therefore, her friendliness to France. Jeannin also pointed out that England preferred a truce to war, an argument in its favor from the ambassador's point of view, since he was genuinely eager to collaborate with the English.[45] But of course the idea of a long truce could not be put forward at this stage of the negotiations. The Dutch wanted peace; only if they could not get it would the idea of a truce become practical politics.

In July the Dutch deputation finally arrived in London and asked the king to appoint commissioners to advise with them. James granted the request at once, which indicates that his offended dignity was more than just a pretext, although there was some delay in making the nominations, owing to the difficulty of finding people willing to go.[46] Another cause of delay involved the nature of the commissioners' instructions; they could not be precise, Winwood observed, until the nature of the Spanish ratification became known, if, indeed, there ever was to be such a ratification. Many people in

---

[43] June 6, 1607, Cecil to Winwood, *Winwood* II, 313–15. June 20/30, Brulart to Boderie, *Boderie* II, 303–307.

[44] June 5/15, 1607, Villeroy to Jeannin, *Jeannin* XII, 113–17.

[45] The relevant correspondence is in *ibid.*, pp. 71–74, 92–105, 146–61, 168–76, 179–90.

[46] On this point see July 9, 1607, Winwood to Edmondes, B.M. Stowe Mss. 169, ff. 82–83.

England doubted that Spain ever would ratify; when she did, Dudley Carleton commented to Chamberlain that "the news you write will get our statesmen and some of their principals new to school, who grounded their counsels upon an infallible supposition that this thing called an agreation would never be assented unto by Spain."[47]

Approximately a month passed between the official English decision to send commissioners and the drawing-up of their instructions; James's government now had to decide what its policy would be. The Dutch deputation made it clear that there were only two possibilities: peace, or open war on Spain by England and France. A mere continuation of aid would not do. They pressed Cecil and the king to say plainly what they would do in the event of war; what they got was evasion. James told them that, if the Dutch decided for peace, he would do all he could to further it; if for war, he would "take such a resolution as will content them, or, rather, as his affairs will permit." He repeated this cryptic remark to Boderie, and asked him to transmit it to his master. The Dutch deputies had the firm impression that James, and even Cecil, both wanted peace.[48] So, too, had the Venetian ambassador Giustinian, who reported that James was angry at certain preachers who spoke against the peace. London opinion, on the other hand, was noisily anti-Spanish. Edmondes reported the Marquis Bentivoglio as saying that "the rudeness of the people of London is such as no man can pass the streets in Spanish attire but that he is publicly reviled and assaulted with stones."[49]

Giustinian reported that on the whole the Dutch deputies were pleased with the result of their mission, since their real purpose was not to get aid to continue the war, but rather to get an eventual Anglo-French guarantee of the peace terms. It was the general view in England, he added, that there would be peace, since the Dutch wanted it and the English and French were too suspicious of each

[47] P.R.O., S.P. 14/28, no. 23.

[48] July 10/20, 1607, Boderie to Jeannin; July 15/25, July 23/Aug. 2, Boderie to Brulart, *Boderie* II, 328–34, 340–43, 343–52.

[49] P.R.O., S.P. 77/8, ff. 330–31. Bentivoglio was the nephew of the nuncio in Brussels. See also May 20/30, 1607, Boderie to Brulart, *Boderie* II, 242–49.

other to cooperate successfully. A week later he wrote that if peace could be made on the basis of Dutch independence, England would favor it, since her purpose was to prevent the United Provinces from falling into the hands of either Spain or France.[50] Boderie suggested that England had decided to send the deputies mainly in order to avoid leaving the whole business in the hands of France.[51]

On August 10 Winwood and Spencer received their instructions, which were rather general. They were to collaborate with Jeannin, to be sure Dutch unity was preserved, and to commit England to nothing without approval from London. They were not to give any indication that they were opposed to peace, since England was at peace with Spain; rather they were to give such advice as would be best for the States—a Delphic utterance—and to point out the dangers of peace, including the probable end of the East Indian trade and the likelihood that Spain would try to regain control after a peace by means of corruption or a coup at a time of civil dissension. In the actual peace negotiations Winwood and Spencer were to encourage the Dutch to press for the exclusion of foreign soldiery from Flanders and the introduction of liberty of conscience there; the Dutch, however, were to maintain their own foreign soldiery, including the English and Scottish companies. The envoys were to find out what the Dutch really wanted: if they inclined to war, they were to be encouraged to go on fighting, but England would not be drawn in. There was also the question of an alliance, which the Dutch were likely to raise. The envoys could give a generally favorable response to a league to guarantee a peace, but they were to refer the details back to London. If the Dutch asked for money, the envoys were to say that England had none to spare, having spent so much on them already.[52]

These instructions were designed to gain still more time for

[50] June 10/20, July 22/Aug. 1, July 29/Aug. 8, 1607, Giustinian to the Doge and Senate, *C.S.P. Venetian 1607–1610*, pp. 6, 18–19, 21–22.
[51] Aug. 6/16, 1607, Boderie to Brulart, *Boderie* II, 362–69.
[52] P.R.O., S.P. 84/66, ff. 50–65.

England to make up her mind; as Cecil explained in a letter to the earl of Dunbar, the Scottish lord treasurer, it was James's view that he could not advise the Dutch as to either peace or war until he had more information and had consulted with France. Cecil did not think there was any particular need for hurry, since Spain was "resolved to proceed in all things by degrees, taking that to be greatness."[53] When Winwood and Spencer arrived they began diligently to take soundings. They got into a slightly acrimonious discussion with Jeannin over the matter of the French debt, and rejected out of hand his suggestion of a three-year Anglo-French treaty to subsidize the Dutch. They also declined his suggestion that they press the Dutch to make no treaty without the consent of England and France; the Dutch would not do this in any event, and would resent the pressure. The Dutch at once raised the question of what assistance they could expect if the war went on; Winwood and Spencer requested instructions on this as soon as possible.[54]

Jeannin, in reporting his initial conversations with Winwood and Spencer, made it perfectly clear why such instructions were needed. If England was unwilling to commit herself as to what she would do if the war went on, she was in effect supporting a peace policy, and Jeannin told Winwood so. All Winwood could reply was that they did indeed believe that the continuation of the war would be preferable, but that the Dutch wanted peace. Jeannin agreed that the way in which the Dutch had put their request for aid to continue the war, without specifying what aid they wanted, was designed to court a refusal and strengthen the hand of the peace party. The French ambassador concluded that if worst came to worst, the English would help the Dutch rather than abandon them, but that they would do all they could for peace first.[55]

It was still not at all clear whether there would be any peace ne-

[53] *Salisbury* XIX, 237–38.
[54] P.R.O., S.P. 105/92, pp. 23–29, 31–34, 37–38.
[55] Sept. 14/24, 1607, Jeannin et al. to Henri; Sept. 26/Oct. 6, Jeannin to Villeroy, *Jeannin* XII, 375–402, 415–22.

gotiations, however, since the Dutch would not talk until a satisfactory ratification came from Spain. King Henri was convinced that England would push for peace whether it came or not, but Winwood and Spencer told Jeannin that they had orders to withdraw if the ratification was unsatisfactory, or if negotiations began before it arrived. Jeannin was skeptical, and urged Oldenbarnevelt to resume war preparations in order to smoke the English out, but the Dutch feared that if they did this all chance for peace would vanish.[56] When the new *agréation* finally did arrive, in mid-October, the Dutch asked the opinion of their associates. Winwood and Spencer told the Dutch that they felt that it was suitable, even though its form was faulty and it was signed *Jo el Rey*, because it contained the necessary concession respecting independence.[57] Jeannin's view was that the ratification would do, except for one clause which nullified the concession of a free status to the Dutch if the parties failed to reach agreement on all their claims, religious and other. This seemed to mean that Spain would insist on toleration for Catholics in the United Provinces, and this the Dutch simply would not accept. The prospect worried Jeannin as well as the Dutch. If Spain were stubborn on this point, the negotiations would be wrecked, and in the worst possible way for France, since this was the one issue on which France could not support the Dutch. The French envoys nevertheless joined Winwood in urging the Dutch to accept the ratification, since, they said, the Spaniards did not make the religious issue a *sine qua non* and, Jeannin added, toleration was something they might well grant.[58]

---

[56] Sept. 28/Oct. 8, 1607, Henri to Jeannin et al.; Oct. 6/16, Jeannin et al. to Henri, *Jeannin* XII, 423–29, 434–39.

[57] Oct. 17, 1607, Winwood and Spencer to the Privy Council, P.R.O., S.P. 105/92, pp. 46–50.

[58] Oct. 17/27, 1607, Jeannin et al. to Henri, *Jeannin* XII, 465–72. Oct. 20/30, Jeannin to Boderie, *Boderie* II, 417–22. Spinola also opposed introducing the question of toleration at this stage; see his letter of Aug. 29/Sept. 8 to Philip, *Pays-Bas* I, 268–69.

At first the English government supported the position Winwood had taken, possibly because of a dispatch from Edmondes reporting a conversation with Richardot. The Archduke's principal diplomatic adviser explained that the language King Philip employed amounted to an acknowledgement of the freedom of the United Provinces, provided that peace or a long truce was made.[59] Then, in mid-November, James and Cecil began to have second thoughts. Winwood and Spencer reported the Dutch qualms,[60] and the qualms spread to London. James wanted to avoid any implication that he was encouraging the Dutch to negotiate, lest he be blamed if the peace turned out to be unsatisfactory.[61] He had a conversation with Boderie in which he announced his intention of scolding his agents for urging the Dutch to accept so defective a document. Boderie rejoined that unless James was prepared to fight, the Dutch must have peace.[62]

King James's flare-up over the question of the ratification, which implied a momentary turning from the policy of peace, may well have been prompted by the flight of the earl of Tyrone, who took refuge with the Archduke in the autumn of 1607. Tyrone, the leader of the great Irish revolt of the last decade of Elizabeth's reign, had been restored by King James. He speedily became disenchanted with the new government's policy in Ulster, and his behavior gave rise to the suspicion that he was about to renew the rebellion; his flight was precipitated by an order to come to London. Edmondes demanded that the Archduke send Tyrone back to England; the Archduke refused, though he did hustle the fugitive out of his territories as promptly as possible. King James was naturally incensed;

[59] Oct. 21, 1607, Edmondes to Cecil, P.R.O., S.P. 77/8, ff. 358–59. Nov. 8, the Privy Council to Winwood and Spencer, P.R.O., S.P. 105/92, pp. 74–80.
[60] Oct. 27, 1607, Winwood and Spencer to Cecil, P.R.O., S.P. 105/92, pp. 56–57.
[61] So Cecil explained to Edmondes on Nov. 17, 1607, P.R.O., S.P. 77/8, ff. 382–87.
[62] Nov. 12/22, 1607, Boderie to Brulart, *Boderie* II, 441–56.

he was reminded of the Archduke's behavior at the time of the Gunpowder Plot. A distinct if temporary chilliness between the two
governments was the natural result.

The Tyrone affair had repercussions on Anglo-French relations
as well. Henri heard of the earl's flight before Carew, and relying
on an erroneous report that Tyrone had gone straight to Spanish
territory, made a righteous speech to Carew sympathizing with
James and declaring that he would be very offended if any neighbor
of his received his fugitives. He was greatly embarrassed when
Tyrone turned up in France on his way to Flanders. Carew reminded
the king of his fine words and asked that Tyrone be detained. The
French were evasive. Tyrone, they said, had not been convicted of
anything; his "crimes" were religious, not political; he was probably gone already. It soon developed that Henri had given permission for Tyrone to move on to Flanders.[63] As Cecil put it in a letter
to the earl of Shrewsbury, "When the French king heard he
[Tyrone] was in Spain, he spoke much of the discourtesy the K. of
Spain should offer if he should give them any favor, but now being
wished to stay them till the King might be advertised, he changed his
style, and said that France was free."[64] The Venetian ambassador in
France suggested that Henri behaved as he did deliberately to annoy James.[65] Villeroy predicted that England would make a fuss
with the Archduke, be rebuffed as she had been at the time of the
Gunpowder Plot, and swallow the insult through cowardice rather
than try to avoid the inevitable rejection by being prudent.[66] Apart
from the imputation of cowardice, this turned out to be an accurate
prediction.

After Tyrone's friendly reception in Flanders Henri again tried

[63] Oct. 1, Oct. 2, Oct. 19, 1607, Carew to Cecil, P.R.O., S.P. 78/53, ff. 337–
41, 342–43, 345–49.

[64] Edmund Lodge, *Illustrations of British History, Biography, and Manners
in the Reigns of Henry VIII, Edward VI, Mary, Elizabeth, and James I* (London, 1838) III, 328.

[65] *C.S.P. Venetian 1607–1610*, pp. 50–51.

[66] Oct. 12/22, 1607, Villeroy to Jeannin, *Jeannin* XII, 444–49.

to make capital of the affair, by pointing to the difference in treatment: Tyrone had not received even "a cup of cold water" in France. Carew's reply was that England expected more of France than of Spain, and that—as Edmondes had reported—Henri's behavior had supplied the Archduke with a precedent and an excuse.[67] Not, indeed, that Tyrone fared so well in Flanders; Edmondes wrote late in December that he and his friends "liberally drink sack instead of husquabagh for the digesting of their melancholy."[68] James was obviously aggrieved at Henri's attitude, but Boderie advised his government not to worry. England had no means of damaging France. She was short of money, usable warships, pilots, and seamen, and besides "je crois certes que qui plus leur fera du mal sera d'avantage respecté d'eux."[69] In any case James was far more annoyed at the Archduke—Edmondes reported that the Brussels regime was startled by James's vehemence—and eventually the king accepted Boderie's explanation that Henri believed Tyrone had fled for religion's sake, and that he gave the earl passage only when he was sure Tyrone would not stay.[70] And in fact Tyrone did become another source of friction between England and Spain. During the next few years there was apprehension in London that Spain might use Tyrone (who settled in Rome) along with other Irish refugees, who lived in the Spanish peninsula or in Flanders, to create trouble in Ireland, a fear which France tried occasionally to exploit.[71] Henri's misstep cost him nothing in the end.

Winwood and Spencer, in defending to their government their decision to advise the Dutch to accept the Spanish ratification, took

[67] Nov. 28, 1607, Carew to Cecil, P.R.O., S.P. 78/53, ff. 360–62. Dec. 3, Carew to Edmondes, B.M. Stowe Mss. 169, f. 223. See also Oct. 14, Edmondes to Cecil, P.R.O., S.P. 77/8, ff. 356–57.

[68] P.R.O., S.P. 77/8, ff. 409–10.

[69] Oct. 20/30, 1607, Boderie to Brulart, *Boderie* II, 411–17.

[70] Nov. 18/28, 1607, Giustinian to the Doge and Senate, *C.S.P. Venetian 1607–1610*, pp. 65–66. Dec. 2, Edmondes to Cecil, P.R.O., S.P. 77/8, ff. 398–99.

[71] For instance, in June, 1608, Henri told Carew that he had heard that Spain was planning to send seven warships to Ireland. P.R.O., S.P. 78/54, ff. 102–107.

much the same line as had Boderie in his conversation with King James: open intervention was the only alternative to peace. It would be much safer for the Dutch to go on fighting, they said, and stressed "how convenient this war would be for the good of his majesty's realms if it might be maintained without his charge." The implication was that since it could not—Winwood was under no illusions on that score— there was nothing for it but to negotiate.[72]

Faced with this situation, the English government in December came to a decision which in effect determined its policy for the next eighteen months, a policy typical of James, namely, to take no initiative and let the French take the lead, since any initiative might turn out badly. On December 5 Sir Thomas Lake reported the king's decision to Cecil respecting the ratification: Winwood's and Spencer's actions were approved, but they were not to meddle in it any further. If England were to advise clarification of the document and the negotiations fell through, the Dutch would hold them responsible for the failure of the peace. If England advised acceptance and it turned out that Spain was playing false, the English would look like conspirators. So the Dutch were to be told to rely on the advice of those who urged them to negotiate in the first place.[73] Eleven days later the new policy was carefully spelled out in a long dispatch to Winwood and Spencer, the gist of which was "that you be not leaders but followers." With respect to the principal issue, that of war or peace, the envoys were to do nothing in particular to encourage peace, but were not to leave themselves open to the accusation that they broke up the negotiations. If the Dutch asked their advice as to whether or not to press for a new *agréation*, they were to point out the inconveniences of the present one but make no positive statement.[74] The French position in support of acceptance

---

[72] Nov. 22, 1607, Winwood and Spencer to Cecil, P.R.O., S.P. 105/92, pp. 85–87. See also their letter of the same date to the Privy Council, *ibid.*, pp. 81–85.

[73] *Salisbury* XIX, 358–60.

[74] P.R.O., S.P. 105/92, pp. 103–12. See also P.R.O., S.P. 84/66, ff. 85–87.

did not waver, and in mid-December the Dutch decided to accept the ratification and begin negotiations.[75]

England's decision to follow in the French wake in the forth-coming negotiations was not owing to any confidence in the honesty and good intentions of France. King James was about as critical as he could be of his good brother in Paris in describing him to Cecil as a man "who only cares to provide for the felicity of his present life without any respect of his life to come."[76] Nor was it, as Boderie suggested when he wrote of James as "plunged" in repose,[77] a policy stemming from mere laziness. The real roots of English policy were caution, uncertainty, financial problems which made England most unwilling to adopt any line which involved additional expense, and unwillingness to offend anyone—it was, indeed, in James's words, a "perplex and thankless" situation.[78] There were obvious arguments in favor of the war policy. As long as the war went on, England's chief enemy would have her hands full and the danger of Dutch commercial competition would be minimized. But not all the arguments cut the same way. Peace, by reopening the Archduke's ports, would benefit English trade. The Dutch and French might actually pay their debts. There would be less likelihood of renewed involvement in war; the diplomatic game of balancing between France and Spain would become much less dangerous. It might also be more successful, since Spain, once relieved of the incubus of the Dutch war, would be a greater danger to France than to England. Once the Dutch were free and secure, a major cause of Anglo-Spanish friction would be gone, and England really would have the choice of allies. Yet a revived Spain would menace England, her ideological

[75] *Jeannin* XIII, 111–12. See also Nov. 13/23, 1607, Henri to Jeannin et al., *ibid.* XII, 515–28.

[76] *Salisbury* XIX, 351–53.

[77] Dec. 19/29, 1607, Boderie to Jeannin, *Boderie* II, 492–97.

[78] Oct. 19, 1607, James to Cecil, *Salisbury* XIX, 285–86. R. S. Ashton, in *The Crown and the Money Market 1603–1640* (Oxford, 1960), p. 37, points out that the four or five years after 1606 represented a "great period of debt reduction."

foe, as well as France. It was an agonizingly difficult decision to make, and so, in the end, England refused to decide.

The French were scornful of James's timidity, and at the same time unwilling to credit it. The English government, they felt, was deliberately coddling the Archduke, whose desire for peace was obvious. By creating the impression that only France wanted the war to continue, they were hopeful of reviving the old Anglo-Burgundian alliance.[79] That this suspicion was baseless should have been obvious to the French after the Tyrone episode, but they periodically reverted to it, especially as they believed that a large number of important English officials were in Spanish pay.[80]

By abandoning the diplomatic initiative to France the English government hoped to avoid any major errors in the negotiations between Spain and the Dutch. Her caution earned her no good-will, and inspired no confidence in many of her own officials. Dudley Carleton, for instance, a man with some diplomatic experience who was to have a distinguished career, commented to Edmondes, "Here we stand still like lookers on . . . as if it concerned us but little which way the game went."[81] This was an overstatement: England may have eschewed the initiative, but she was hardly an impartial spectator. She was still committed to the Dutch, as the next six months were to show.

[79] See, for instance, among other examples, Nov. 13/23, 1607, Henri to Jeannin et al.; Dec. 12/22, Villeroy to Jeannin, *Jeannin* XII, 515–28, XIII, 107–11.
[80] May 16/26, 1608, Brulart to Boderie, *Boderie* III, 290–96.
[81] B.M. Stowe Mss. 169, ff. 247–48.

CHAPTER V

✤ ✤

Spain and the Dutch: The Treaties of Guarantee

ALMOST FROM the beginning of the discussion of a possible Spanish-Dutch peace the question of guarantees had been in the back of the diplomatists' minds. The Dutch quite naturally expected France and England to guarantee the peace, since it was being made with their advice and since they had supported the war effort for so long. The question was never whether there would be such guarantees, but rather, what form they would take. The rather half-hearted Spanish effort in the autumn of 1607 to distract the English by reviving the idea of a marriage between an Infanta and an English prince, with the Netherlands as dowry, though it caused some worry in Paris, was never taken seriously in London. Even Cornwallis, who had shown some enthusiasm for this plan in the past, was aware that at this time it was mere mischief-making, designed to embroil England with France.[1] The serious Spanish effort to disrupt the incipient coalition by a marriage offer was made later, and was focused on France.

Almost as soon as Jeannin and his associates arrived in the United Provinces the Dutch raised the question of a league. Jeannin, in reporting this, expressed his belief that it should be a triple league, in-

[1] Oct. 20, 1607, Cornwallis to Cecil, P.R.O., S.P. 94/14, ff. 185–86. Jeannin fed these rumors to Maurice, to make him less hostile to peace. Dec. 15/25, Jeannin to Villeroy, *Jeannin* XIII, 116–24.

97

cluding England. Henri instructed Jeannin to find out what terms the Dutch had in mind. England could join if she wanted to, said the king, but James was unlikely to do so, since he was poor and lazy and attached to "cette espèce de neutralité" he had adopted. So, Henri felt, two leagues might be necessary: a defensive one, guaranteeing the settlement, which England would probably sign, and a secret offensive one.[2]

The Dutch quickly made it clear that what they wanted was a triple league, defensive in nature, which would guarantee the peace, but which was not conditional on the peace. As to the timing, they were flexible: they would negotiate with France alone or with both countries, now or after the peace was signed. They did not want an offensive league, which would involve renewal of the fighting; furthermore, a secret league would violate the terms of their treaty of 1585 with England. Henri and Villeroy were disgusted with Oldenbarnevelt's cautious attitude. The French king regarded speed as a matter of some urgency; the league must come before the peace was signed, or—given the treacherous nature of the English—France might find herself diplomatically isolated. Nevertheless, since it was necessary to settle for a defensive league, it would be wise to await the English deputies before beginning negotiations, now that the French had made clear their desire for such a league.[3]

Winwood and Spencer, when they arrived, expressed approval in principle of the idea of a defensive alliance, and of negotiating it before peace was made. But they were not prepared to negotiate until it became clear that there would be a peace. Jeannin felt that this meant that France should not negotiate either, not alone with the Dutch and not yet, lest she get trapped into being the sole support of the Dutch in a renewed war. The king did not agree. Immediate negotiation would give the French a diplomatic advantage at The Hague, and make England jealous. It was true that France must not

[2] June 17/27, 1607, Jeannin to Villeroy; June 28/July 8, Henri to Jeannin et al., *Jeannin* XII, 168–76, 179–87.
[3] *Ibid.*, pp. 234–54, 267–71, 288–301, 316–23, 323–29, 331–40.

be left holding the bag if the war resumed, but the fact of negotiation might very well incline Spain and the Archduke more toward peace.[4] Winwood and Spencer, for their part, were anxious to negotiate, and pressed London repeatedly for detailed instructions.[5] Until such instructions came, all they could do was to stall, say that there was no hurry, and discuss various theoretical alternatives, such as a perpetual triple league with a guarantee of mutual assistance against rebels.[6] These delaying tactics annoyed Henri, especially as Carew was pressing him again on the French debt. He was prepared to negotiate separately with the Dutch but left the tactical decision in Jeannin's hands.[7]

At the end of October the Dutch presented the English and French envoys with a draft of a triple alliance which was defensive in nature but which included a clause which bound France and England to continue subsidizing the Dutch armed forces even if peace was made. Oldenbarnevelt could hardly have expected to get anything like this, and in fact Winwood told him that in the event of peace the money should flow the other way: the Dutch should pay off their debt.[8] In mid-November the Dutch produced a second draft which contained a set of more modest generalities respecting financial aid, and did their best to get the French and English envoys to make some precise proposals themselves.[9] The indefiniteness of the Dutch on the matter of the amount of money they would need to continue the war bothered Cecil; he repeated that England could

[4] Sept. 14/24, 1607, Jeannin et al. to Henri; Sept. 28/Oct. 8, Henri to Jeannin et al., *ibid.*, pp. 375–402, 423–29.

[5] See, e.g., their letters of Oct. 17 and 27, 1607, P.R.O., S.P. 105/92, pp. 51–52, 53–55.

[6] Oct. 27/Nov. 6, 1607, Jeannin et al. to Henri, *Jeannin* XII, 485–500. Henri was prepared to consider such a plan, for the sake of his children. *Ibid.*, pp. 515–28.

[7] Oct. 24/Nov. 3, 1607, Henri to Jeannin et al., Villeroy to Jeannin, *ibid.*, pp. 477–80, 481–85.

[8] Nov. 7, 1607, Winwood and Spencer to Cecil, P.R.O., S.P. 105/92, pp. 62–66.

[9] Nov. 14/24, 1607, Jeannin et al. to Henri, *Jeannin* XII, 537–51.

not afford a large subsidy, and a small one would simply embroil her with Spain without benefiting the Dutch.[10] Boderie thought that England was too weak to fight, and that she would try to dispense whatever aid she gave the Dutch in the event of a renewal of the war as secretly as possible, to avoid antagonizing Spain.[11] England's precarious financial position was a potent argument for peace.

The matter of debts, both Dutch and French, was a decisive factor in causing James and Cecil to reject the idea of a triple alliance in favor of a series of bilateral pacts, a policy which they believed would have the added advantage of not antagonizing Spain. On November 8, 1607, the Council at last sent Winwood and Spencer their instructions, and rather limited instructions at that. They were authorized to discuss the league, but not until they learned whether the Dutch were really disposed to peace, and what the Dutch would do about the debt and the payment of the garrisons of the cautionary towns. Above all, they were to remember that James had no intention of breaking the peace with Spain. With respect to the precise amount of aid to be provided, this was, if possible, not to be particularized; but if it had to be, Winwood and Spencer could promise 6,000 men, 20 ships, and 300,000 crowns (£90,000) a year, at the charges of the party requiring it. The Dutch were to pay the garrisons of the cautionary towns, and at least £60,000 a year on their debt in peacetime. If it was necessary to have a triple league—which Winwood and Spencer were carefully not authorized to conclude, but only to discuss informally—the French were to be asked to make the same contribution in manpower, half as many ships and twice as much money, and pay off their debt to the tune of £50,000 a year.[12] In informing Cornwallis and Edmondes of the English decision,

[10] Oct. 22, 1607, Cecil to Winwood and Spencer, P.R.O., S.P. 105/92, pp. 58–59. In November Winwood and Spencer reported that Maurice had informed Henri that he could fight for one and one half million crowns (£450,000) a year. *Ibid.*, pp. 72–74.

[11] Nov. 7/17, 1607, Boderie to Jeannin, *Boderie* II, 436–40.

[12] Nov. 8, 1607, the Privy Council to Winwood and Spencer, P.R.O., S.P. 105/92, pp. 74–80. See also Cecil's memorandum, *Salisbury* XIX, 483–84.

Cecil stressed that any such treaty would become operative only if there was a peace, that the French had already accepted the idea, that this was the only way James would ever get any money from the Dutch, and that Spain's and Flanders' interests would not be damaged. To Carew, Cecil stressed the special considerations—the debt and the cautionary towns—which made a bilateral agreement desirable.[13] The English government was keeping its fences mended as carefully as it could.

Winwood and Spencer were not entirely pleased with some aspects of their instructions. They rather favored the triple league, since, they argued, the failure to make a treaty with France would not make Spain any more friendly, and would simply antagonize the French and Dutch. They did not like the idea of tying the question of the French debt to the negotiations, since this, they believed, would wreck the treaty. In the event of a triple league, the matter of the Dutch debt and the cautionary towns could be simultaneously settled in a separate agreement. With respect to the cautionary towns, they urged their superiors to consider the possibility of getting out altogether, if peace were made, in return for a public bond for the money that was owed; remaining there would be politically risky. The Dutch would argue, and with some justice, that they could not pay both the garrisons and the debt, and they would probably not be able to pay at the rate of £60,000 a year anyway, not for a while at least.[14]

These arguments failed to move the London government. On December 16 the Council informed the English envoys that England still preferred separate bilateral pacts; only if the Dutch and French insisted would they authorize a triple league, and then it was to be limited strictly to the matter of defense of the Dutch, and involve

[13] Nov. 9, 1607, Cecil to Carew, P.R.O., S.P. 78/53, ff. 351–56. Nov. 17, Cecil to Edmondes, P.R.O., S.P. 77/8, ff. 382–87. Nov. 18, Cecil to Cornwallis, P.R.O., S.P. 94/14, ff. 214–18.

[14] Nov. 22, 1607, Winwood and Spencer to Cecil, and to the Privy Council, P.R.O., S.P. 105/92, pp. 81–85, 85–87. Dec. 9, Dec. 17, Winwood and Spencer to Cecil, *ibid.*, pp. 94–96, 98–99.

no Anglo-French obligations to each other. If the French raised the question of an Anglo-French league, they were to stall until they saw how the peace negotiations turned out, and to tell the French that such a league did not hinge on the peace negotiations. The Council did accept Winwood's logic on payment of the garrisons, but the £60,000 a year on the debt was a *sine qua non*. The November instructions were altered in a few other particulars as well. There were 400 horse added to the 6,000 foot and 20 ships, and if necessary the envoys could go as high as 600 horse, 8,000 foot, and 26 ships. The aid clause was to be optional in the sense that the party in need could ask for money instead of ships and men, since England was more apt to need the former than the latter. If possible, a satisfactory commercial settlement should also be reached.[15]

These instructions meant that the treaty could not be negotiated quickly; the question of the debt, all by itself, would take considerable time to resolve. Furthermore, by insisting on bilateral treaties the English government gave the French an opportunity to score a diplomatic success of which they proceeded to take advantage, by promptly negotiating their own bilateral agreement with the Dutch. By late November Henri and Villeroy resolved to go ahead, whether or not the English were willing to join them in the negotiations.[16]

One factor in the French decision may well have been Carew's renewed pressure respecting the French debt. He got nowhere; the French, he said, promised everything but payment. In fact, at one point, in December 1608, the ingenious Sully produced a set of figures which showed that England owed France money. Carew, Brulart remarked, was "un peu etonné" at this; Sully apparently thought it funny. Carew was not amused, and huffily told Aerssens that this sort of joke was not calculated to produce cooperation in

---

[15] Dec. 16, 1607, the Privy Council to Winwood and Spencer, *ibid.*, pp. 103–12. See also Dec. 1, James to Cecil, *Salisbury* XIX, 351–53. In February, 1608, the Council authorized Winwood and Spencer to drop the commercial question, which meant mainly the regulation of the position of the Merchant Adventurers, if it proved too difficult to settle. P.R.O., S.P. 105/92, pp. 134–43.

[16] Nov. 28/Dec. 8, 1607, Henri to Jeannin et al., *Jeannin* XIII, 39–50.

the matter of the league. Henri's reply, when Carew again pressed for payment, was that, since England had not renewed the Elizabethan treaty with France and had denied the validity of Sully's treaty, the whole status of Anglo-French relations had to be reviewed. This was an obvious stalling tactic, though Carew admitted to Cecil that the idea as such had some merit. Cecil was dubious; the French move looked to him like an attempt to force England to negotiate a general league with France, a matter Jeannin had raised with Winwood and Spencer, and which James did not wish to undertake at this stage. Henri, meanwhile, informed Boderie that he did not mind paying what he owed, but the figures had to be clarified before he would pay anything.[17] Relations between the two governments became chillier still when Boderie got involved in a losing dispute over precedence with the Spanish ambassador at one of Queen Anne's masques.[18] Under these circumstances the French decision to go ahead alone with the Dutch is hardly surprising.

On December 12/22 Henri and Villeroy wrote parallel letters to Jeannin and his colleagues, expressing even more suspicion and contempt for England than usual—"trompeurs, vrais ennemis de la France," wrote Villeroy, "et qui préfèrent aussi imprudemment que malignement leur haine à leur propre bien"—and instructing Jeannin to go ahead and conclude with the Dutch, after making a final effort to include England in the pact.[19] It was safe to do this now that it was fairly certain that peace negotiations would take place, so that France would not be left as the sole support of the Dutch in a renewed war.[20] Jeannin did so, after one last series of general discus-

---

[17] Nov. 28, Dec. 14, 1607, Carew to Cecil, P.R.O., S.P. 78/53, ff. 360–62, 364. Dec. 19/29, Brulart to Boderie, *Boderie* II, 497–503. Jan. 5, 1608, Carew to Cecil, P.R.O., S.P. 78/54, ff. 11–15. Jan. 10/20, Henri to Boderie, *Boderie* III, 31–33. Jan. 17, Cecil to Winwood and Spencer, P.R.O., S.P. 105/92, pp. 124–29.

[18] Cecil wrote a lengthy memorandum to Carew about this on Jan. 3, 1608, P.R.O., S.P. 78/54, ff. 1–10.

[19] *Jeannin* XIII, 102–107, 107–11.

[20] Dec. 19/29, 1607, Henri to Jeannin et al., Villeroy to Jeannin, *ibid.*, pp. 128–33, 135–38.

sions with the English envoys. Jeannin's final effort to get a triple league was a suggestion that the three states make a general pledge of mutual assistance, with the specific details to be worked out after the peace was signed. Winwood and Spencer accepted this, but then, hobbled as they were by their instructions, they said that the general pact could not take effect until after the particular treaties were made, which was, in effect, to nullify everything.

Jeannin therefore went ahead with the Dutch, after expressing to Winwood his regret at having to do so. The principal clauses of the pact, which was to take effect with the peace, were that in case of need France would supply 10,000 men—more, if the Dutch paid for more—and the Dutch 5,000 men, or warships, at the French choice. France further agreed to pay its troops in Dutch service, some 4,000 men, for two years after the peace. Jeannin and his superiors in Paris were delighted. They had won a considerable propaganda advantage over England. The Dutch peace party, now clearly in the ascendant, regarded the treaty as evidence that France really wanted peace, and they could hardly be sure what England wanted. Furthermore, Jeannin felt, the treaty would help keep England out of a league with Spain, though he was not above suggesting to Maurice that England's unwillingness to make a league with France was precisely because she was negotiating with Spain. Despite these slippery tactics Jeannin had no desire to antagonize England, and suggested to Boderie that he should emphasize the fact that France had acted at Dutch insistence. English susceptibilities should be carefully cultivated; she could do the Dutch immense damage if she should ever decide to sell the cautionary towns to Spain.[21]

In mid-December, 1607, about a month before the signing of the defensive league with France, the Dutch government formally

[21] The text of the treaty, dated Jan. 13/23, 1608, is in *ibid.*, pp. 148–57. Jan. 18/28, Jeannin et al. to Henri; Jan. 26/Feb. 5, Jeannin to Boderie, *ibid.*, pp. 157–75, 186–90. Jan. 23, Winwood and Spencer to Cecil, P.R.O., S.P. 105/92, pp. 122–24. For the French reaction see Feb. 2, Carew to Cecil, P.R.O., S.P. 78/54, ff. 24–25, Feb. 14, Carew to Edmondes, B.M., Stowe Mss. 169, f. 291.

agreed to negotiate with the Archduke's representatives. There had already been a good deal of speculation on all sides as to the issues which would prove difficult. The Dutch had made it clear to everyone that recognition of their independence was the *sine qua non*; the Venetian ambassador reported that they had told Cecil that even if Spain met all their other demands there would be no peace without independence.[22] The French government feared that the Dutch would give way on everything else if they got their sovereignty, and that England would encourage them to do so.[23] There was general agreement that the most awkward problems would be the Spanish demand that Catholics be tolerated in the United Provinces and the Dutch demands that the Spanish army be removed from the Archduke's territories and that they be allowed to participate in the East Indian trade.[24] One the first point there might well be a rupture between England and France; both countries were eager for the second and not at all eager for the third.

These speculations proved correct. The Archduke's instructions to his negotiators stressed the religious question and were uncompromising on the matters of foreign troops and colonial trade.[25] The Archduke, according to Edmondes, was pleased by the Dutch decision to negotiate, and to prolong the cease-fire for another four to six weeks; at the end of December he formally requested the English and French governments to aid in the negotiations.[26] Cecil's reaction was to summon the Archduke's ambassador, scold him for his master's reception of Tyrone, and ask him what the Archduke wanted James to do to further peace. The ambassador's reply was vague on most of the concrete issues, but he did give renewed as-

[22] July 22/Aug. 1, 1607, Giustinian to the Doge and Senate, *C.S.P. Venetian 1607–1610*, pp. 18–19.

[23] See Henri's and Villeroy's letters of July 25/Aug. 4, 1607, *Jeannin* XII, 256–64, 264–67.

[24] See, e.g., Nov. 18/28, 1607, Giustinian to the Doge and Senate, *C.S.P. Venetian 1607–1610*, pp. 65–66.

[25] The instructions are in *Jeannin* XI, 510–19.

[26] Dec. 23, Dec. 30, 1607, Edmondes to Cecil, P.R.O., S.P. 77/8, ff. 409–10, 413.

surances on the matter of sovereignty. Boderie, in reporting this episode, suggested that Cecil's angry speeches respecting Tyrone were partly for France's benefit, to dispel the suspicion that the English government was pro-Spanish.[27]

Sovereignty would be the first issue discussed, and both Winwood and Jeannin had forebodings: *prima coitio est acerrima*, wrote Winwood. Jeannin was afraid that the Archduke's envoys would press for a *quid pro quo* for their concessions on this question, and spin out the negotiations if they failed to get it.[28] The English Council approached the question very circumspectly. If the Dutch asked the English envoys' advice, they were to say that what Spain had granted in the ratification was a good beginning, but that an absolute renunciation would be desirable in the final treaty. Caution was again urged on Winwood and Spencer: James must not be liable to any criticism for promoting a rupture.[29] As it turned out, the English need not have worried. Spinola, who in Winwood's view was the principal member of the Archduke's delegation, was smooth as butter to the Dutch representatives, and the Archduke's commissioners, to the surprise of Winwood, who had predicted considerable delay, and of Villeroy, gave way very promptly on the issue of sovereignty, provided that a peace treaty actually resulted. King James, wrote Boderie, was disappointed; he had hoped that the issue would serve to break up the negotiations.[30]

The most difficult issue in the negotiations turned out to be trade. The Dutch demanded that they be allowed to do business in the Spanish colonial world as a matter of right, a demand which Spain

[27] Jan. 14, 1608, Cecil to Edmondes, B.M. Stowe Mss. 169, ff. 251–55. Jan. 19/29, Boderie to Brulart, *Boderie* III, 42–51

[28] Jan. 23, 1608, Winwood and Spencer to the Privy Council, P.R.O., S.P. 105/92, pp. 119–22. Jan. 26/Feb. 5, Jeannin to Boderie, *Boderie* III, 84–89.

[29] P.R.O., S.P. 105/92, pp. 134–43.

[30] Dec. 17, 1607, Feb. 4, 1608, Winwood and Spencer to the Privy Council, *ibid.*, pp. 96–97, 129–31. Nov. 29, 1607, Feb. 25, 1608, Winwood to Edmondes, B.M. Stowe Mss. 169, ff. 216–17, 293–94. Feb. 17/27, Boderie to Brulart; Feb. 18/28, Villeroy to Boderie, *Boderie* III, 121–33, 133–42. For Spinola's behavior see Feb. 2, Browne to Lisle, *De L'Isle* IV, 5–6.

was not disposed to grant. She had made no such concessions to England and France in her peace treaties with them, and this was one demand which neither London nor Paris would support too strongly, in part because they hoped to persuade Dutch businessmen to emigrate if they found business conditions too awkward after a peace. In February Villeroy wrote to Jeannin that he had discussed these problems with Aerssens, who had given it as his opinion that the Dutch merchants, if they had to move, would prefer England to France because there was less red tape and better justice in England; Villeroy tried to persuade him otherwise.[31] At one time in March it was believed in England that the trade question might be settled and a peace signed, "dont on ne se réjouit ici nullement," wrote Boderie, not only because of the adverse economic consequences for England of heightened Dutch commercial rivalry, but also because they feared, in the wake of Tyrone's flight, that Spain, once her hands were free, would meddle in Ireland.[32] The trade issue had another aspect which could make it useful for Spain; it was potentially divisive, not only of the Dutch and their allies, but also of the United Provinces themselves. It was the mercantile provinces, Holland and Zealand, which pushed this demand; the other five had much less interest in it. It was the one major issue in the negotiations on which there was a serious division of opinion inside the United Provinces, apart, of course, from the fundamental question of whether there ought to be any negotiations at all.

The discussions on trade very quickly reached an impasse. Winwood suggested a compromise: that the Dutch be allowed to trade in the Indies for fourteen years. This pleased nobody, and so Winwood proposed to the Dutch that they drop this question for a while and take up other matters.[33] This was done, but the awkward question kept cropping up. Winwood and Spencer believed that the

[31] *Jeannin* XIII, 228–32.
[32] *Boderie* III, 185–92.
[33] Feb. 19, 1608, Winwood and Spencer to the Privy Council, P.R.O., S.P. 105/92, pp. 143–47.

Archduke's commissioners were deliberately aiming at a rupture within the United Provinces on this issue, and that if they failed to achieve it they would turn to the religious question.[34] The English envoys underestimated the Archduke's eagerness for peace; he was willing to compromise on this and everything else if only a settlement could be reached. His commissioners were willing to discuss the possibility that the Dutch be allowed to trade in the Indies for nine years, at least to the point of sending Father Neyen to Spain to discuss the problem with the Spanish government. Jeannin thought that the Archduke was willing to be accommodating on this matter because he believed that the Dutch would find the East Indian trade unprofitable in the long run and voluntarily relinquish it, as long as they could deal in Spain.[35]

Although it was clear that there could be no final settlement until the question of trade in the Indies was cleared up, there were a good many other awkward problems to discuss—the frontier, for example, and the reopening of Antwerp to trade, which Holland and Zealand fiercely opposed. All sides were anxious to avoid the religious question; Spinola was sure that the Dutch would never yield on it, and the Dutch and everyone else knew that this was the one issue on which they could get no French backing.[36] The war party in Spain was anxious to stress this issue, and its noisiness made Cornwallis rather pessimistic about the chance of peace. If it came, he wrote, "I shall think it like the peace of God, which passeth all understanding."[37] Yet he himself reported the chief inducement to Spain to make peace: her desperate financial condition. The Dutch, he heard, were demanding a huge indemnity from Spain to pay off

[34] Mar. 12, 1608, Winwood and Spencer to Cecil, *ibid.*, pp. 162–63.

[35] Mar. 29, May 28, 1608, Winwood to Edmondes, B.M. Stowe Mss. 170, ff. 3, 47–48. Mar. 19/29, Jeannin to Villeroy, *Jeannin* XIII, 322–31. See also Mar. 20/30, Spinola to Philip, *Pays-Bas* I, 280–81.

[36] Feb. 2, 1608, Carew to Cecil, P.R.O., S.P. 78/54, ff. 24–25. June 6/16, Spinola to Philip, *Pays-Bas* I, 283.

[37] Apr. 19, 1608, Cornwallis to the Privy Council, B.M. Cott. Mss. Vesp. C XII, ff. 6–12. See also his letter of Apr. 2 to Cecil, *Winwood* II, 385.

their debts. "This soil," he wrote, "as our present estate standeth, is hardly able to afford them so many cucumbers."[38] The rumor concerning the indemnity turned out to be false, but Spain's poverty was real enough. In May Cornwallis wrote that King Philip's servants were unpaid; he had not met his obligations to his Genoese bankers, and had even asked the Pope to allow the alienation of some Church property to relieve his financial difficulties.[39]

Opinion in England and France fluctuated, but most people believed that peace was more likely than not—Maurice, who was becoming more and more alarmed, talked rather wildly to Jeannin of forcing a renewal of war[40]—and their views were confirmed when, in May, the Dutch, against the advice of England and France, renewed the truce with Spain and the Archduke until the end of the year. The Anglo-French objection was not to the principle of renewal, but to its length: it would simply encourage the Spaniards to stall. Oldenbarnevelt rejoined that a statement that there must be a settlement within two months of the resumption of negotiations after Father Neyen's return would obviate this difficulty.[41] England and France decided in the end not to make an issue of Dutch disregard of their advice, in order to retain their influence with Oldenbarnevelt and the peace party.[42]

The completion of the Franco-Dutch league and the opening of the peace talks at The Hague forced James and Cecil to take stock of their position. They realized that an agreement with the Dutch was now a necessity, unless they were prepared to see French in-

[38] Mar. 6, 1608, Cornwallis to Edmondes, B.M. Stowe Mss. 169, f. 310.

[39] May 12, 1608, Cornwallis to the Privy Council, P.R.O., S.P. 94/15, ff. 60–62.

[40] May 4/14, 1608, Jeannin to Villeroy, *Jeannin* XIII, 455–60.

[41] May 11/21, 1608, Spinola to Philip, *Pays-Bas* I, 282. June 15/25, Giustinian to the Doge and Senate, *C.S.P. Venetian 1607–1610*, pp. 142–43. May 14/24, Jeannin et al. to Henri, *Jeannin* XIV, 6–18. May 18, Edmondes to William Trumbull, *Downshire* II, 58–59. Trumbull was Edmondes's secretary.

[42] So Henri put it to Carew; June 20, 1608, Carew to Cecil, P.R.O., S.P. 78/54, ff. 102–107.

fluence predominant in the United Provinces; much more open to question was the matter of a new agreement with France. On the surface relations were friendly enough. The collaboration between Winwood and Jeannin continued, in spite of occasional tremors of suspicion on both sides. King Henri decided to overlook Queen Anne's alleged snub to Boderie at her masque, and invited her to stand godmother to his new son. James sent his good brother a present of deer; Henri reciprocated with a gift of twenty-six ostriches. Carew inspected them: "Being kept in a boat divers days that was covered with canvas, their smell was not of the best."[43] James's reaction to this gift—one wonders if anyone thought it symbolic—is not recorded.

There were still several causes of friction between England and France. The implementation of the commercial treaty of 1606 was not satisfactory to the English. The French were slow about appointing conservators. Some *parlements* had not registered the treaty; others kept jurisdiction over cases the conservators could not decide, instead of referring them to Paris for speedy judgment. Some towns, notably Rouen, Caen, and Bordeaux, still imposed local levies. Above all, faulty English cloth was still being confiscated instead of being returned; this was the issue which had brought about the negotiation of the treaty in the first place.[44] The French did agree to appoint conservators in Rouen, but on other matters they were disposed to dally, in spite of Henri's assurances and Cecil's prodding of Boderie; "I am at my wits' end about it," wrote Carew in May.[45] The ambassador had come to believe what Villeroy believed of the English: that the only way to get anywhere with the French was to be stern with them; politeness simply increased their insolence.[46] The English decision in June to increase their own customs

[43] Apr. 28, 1608, Carew to Cecil, *ibid.*, ff. 65–70.
[44] Feb. 26, 1608, Cecil to Carew, P.R.O., S.P. 78/54, ff. 30–36.
[45] *Ibid.*, ff. 88–90. See also Apr. 1/11, 1608, Boderie to Villeroy; Apr. 15/25, Brulart to Boderie, *Boderie* III, 206–10, 231–35.
[46] Feb. 16, 1608, Carew to Cecil, P.R.O., S.P. 78/54, f. 28.

duties to what Cecil described as a true 5 percent naturally displeased French merchants and was not calculated to galvanize Paris into action respecting the English complaints.[47]

More serious was the perennial question of the debt. At the beginning of 1608 there was a lull in this seemingly endless controversy, as Cecil waited for the French to make a constructive gesture of some sort. When none was forthcoming, Cecil finally decided to send the original accounts to France, accompanied by an expert named George Bingley and a set of figures showing that the French owed a total of £355,125/10s/2d. Before sending the books off, Cecil showed them to Boderie (who could make nothing of them, since they were kept in English) and explained to the ambassador what he was doing. In his instructions to Carew he authorized the latter to defalk any specific item in the accounts to which the French objected. Cecil, who was soon to be lord treasurer, wanted a settlement.[48] He was not to get one—not yet. Sully did consent to a preliminary survey, but he complained—and Carew was embarrassed to discover—that the accounts Cecil sent over had not been countersigned by any French official, and in June Villeroy flatly informed Boderie that France would not pay. He repeated Sully's canard that England really owed France money, and anyhow paying England off would not assure France of her friendship.[49]

In adopting this attitude the French government was going counter to the advice of both Boderie and Jeannin. The two ambassadors firmly believed that France should give England some satisfaction, and offer England support if she had trouble in Ire-

[47] June 23, 1608, Cecil to Carew, *ibid.*, ff. 110–12. June 10/20, Boderie to Brulart, *Boderie* III, 314–26. Boderie did not believe that complaint about the customs duties would succeed; English financial necessity was too pressing. On May 31/June 10 Henri authorized the appointment of conservators in London. *Ibid.*, pp. 308–10.

[48] Apr. 16, 1608, Cecil to Carew, P.R.O., S.P. 78/54, ff. 59–61. See also *ibid.*, ff. 57–58. Apr. 16/26, Boderie to Brulart, *Boderie* III, 235–37. Cecil became lord treasurer in April, after the death of the earl of Dorset.

[49] May 9, June 20, 1608, Carew to Cecil, P.R.O., S.P. 78/54, ff. 80, 102–107. June 18/28, Villeroy to Boderie, *Boderie* III, 329–35.

land, because both believed that an English alliance was a necessity
to France. Otherwise Spain might buy England up, as Boderie put
it, and solidify her position by promising not to fish in Irish waters.[50]
England must be cultivated, untrustworthy though she was, because, given the hostility between France and Spain, it was King
James who had the choice of allies. Villeroy, in spite of his violent
hostility to England, believed this too. France wanted an alliance, he
told Boderie.[51] The problem was what sort of alliance it should be,
and when and where it should be made. In February Boderie reported that there was talk once again in England of a general anti-
Habsburg coalition, and in the United Provinces there was some
general discussion amongst the commissioners of the possibility of a
comprehensive review of the treaties between England and France.[52]

In March the French took a chance remark of Winwood's as a
feeler. Winwood was apparently speculating on the possibilities of
an Anglo-French marriage alliance. The Dutch, who were very
eager to cement the bonds between their two potential protectors,
eagerly seized on this, and Caron even mentioned it to Cecil, who
snubbed him: it was no concern of the United Provinces.[53] It was
made clear that Winwood's remarks were unauthorized, but there
was a brief flurry of discussion. Jeannin in particular urged the advantages to France of a marriage alliance with England rather than
with Spain. King James, he said, had no sinister designs on France.
Villeroy was unconvinced; such an alliance with England could not
benefit France, and would keep her from making advantageous mar-
riages elsewhere.[54] But in fact, as both governments well knew, all

[50] May 28/June 7, 1608, Boderie to Jeannin, *Boderie* III, 303–308. See also
May 4/14, Jeannin to Boderie; May 26/June 5, Boderie to Brulart, *ibid.*,
pp. 274–80, 297–303, June 4/14, Jeannin to Villeroy, *Jeannin* XIV, 60–68.
[51] June 29/July 9, 1608, Villeroy to Boderie, *Boderie* III, 347–53.
[52] *Ibid.*, pp. 119–21, 170–73.
[53] Mar. 20, 1608, Cecil to Winwood and Spencer, *Winwood* II, 378–79.
Apr. 4/14, Jeannin to Boderie, *Jeannin* XIII, 372–77. Apr. 23/May 3, Boderie
to Jeannin, *Boderie* III, 237–41.
[54] Mar. 31/Apr. 10, 1608, Brulart to Boderie; Apr. 23/May 3, Boderie to
Jeannin, *Boderie* III, 200–205, 237–41. Apr. 30/May 10, May 26/June 5,

talk of an alliance was premature. There was no real possibility of serious Anglo-French discussions in the early part of 1608, because neither side knew what to discuss. Until some sort of settlement between Spain and her erstwhile rebels was reached—or the war resumed—there was no way to negotiate an Anglo-French treaty intelligently. In late March Cecil stated that his government wanted an agreement with France, but not until the outcome of the peace negotiations was known, and the French accepted this without demur.[55]

The Anglo-Dutch league was a different matter, however. As the French had predicted, the signing of the agreement between France and the Dutch forced the English hand.[56] The news of this agreement was received in England with astonishment and displeasure, wrote Boderie; it also increased English uncertainty, since they saw that France could do without them.[57] By April, after considerable preliminary fencing, they had settled down to serious negotiations with Caron. Their first thought had been to limit the league to one year, subject to renewals, as a way of avoiding too great a commitment; the Dutch disliked this, and eventually James agreed that the league could last as long as the Franco-Dutch treaty. He also consented to the Dutch request that they put off any payment on their debt until two years after the peace was signed.[58]

There were no major difficulties in the actual negotiations. England flatly rejected the Dutch suggestion that she subsidize the Dutch after the peace. The Dutch acknowledged a debt of £818,408, to be paid in installments of £60,000 a year beginning two years after the peace. They ratified their "placart" of 1599 in favor of English merchants; the question of the privileges of Dutch

---

Jeannin to Villeroy, *Jeannin* XIII, 420–28, XIV, 39–43. May 13/23, Villeroy to Jeannin, *ibid.*, XIV, 1–5.

[55] Mar. 29/Apr. 8, 1608, Boderie to Brulart; Apr. 15/25, Brulart to Boderie, *Boderie* III, 192–99, 231–35.

[56] Dec. 22, 1607/Jan. 1, 1608, Boderie to Brulart, *ibid.*, pp. 1–8.

[57] Feb. 17/27, 1608, Boderie to Jeannin, *Jeannin* XIII, 214–18.

[58] Mar. 29/Apr. 8, 1608, Boderie to Brulart, *Boderie* III, 192–99.

merchants in England was to be the subject of a future conference. The Dutch were reluctant to make this concession, and at one stage in the negotiations Winwood asked Jeannin to help convince the Dutch of the necessity of confirming the English merchants' privileges.[59] In one of his reports the Venetian ambassador pointed to a matter which would certainly be discussed at such a conference and which was to cause considerable controversy: the activity of Dutch fishermen in English (and Scottish) waters.[60] There was some discussion of the proportion of Dutch aid to English. The Dutch wanted to promise only half the English commitment; England insisted on, and got, two-thirds.[61] In the treaty England promised 6,000 foot, 400 horse, and 20 ships if the Dutch were attacked; the Dutch promised the same number of ships, and either 4,000 foot and 300 horse or the equivalent in money, at England's choice. The assisted party agreed to repay the cost of the aid. The language of the treaty also made it clear that James could call on Dutch aid if an outside power aided an uprising in Ireland. The treaty was to run for James's lifetime and that of his successor, provided it was confirmed within a year of the latter's accession. These were for the most part the provisions England had wanted from the beginning. The only thing they failed to get— and they had discounted this earlier—was Dutch agreement to pay the garrisons of the cautionary towns.[62]

In the latter stages of the negotiations the English government was careful to keep Spain and the Archduke informed, and to make it very clear that the league was purely defensive, would become

---

[59] June 6/16, 1608, Jeannin et al. to Henri, *Jeannin* XIV, 68–75. The problem, according to Jeannin, was that the Amsterdam business community wanted to get a part of the English cloth trade, now concentrated at Middleburg, in Zealand.

[60] Feb. 25/Mar. 6, 1608, Gustinian to the Doge and Senate, *C.S.P. Venetian 1607–1610*, pp. 101–102.

[61] Apr. 13/23, 1608, Jeannin et al. to Henri, *Jeannin* XIII, 386–95.

[62] The treaty, dated June 26, 1608, is printed in T. Rymer, *Foedera* XVI, 667–70. The separate financial and commercial agreement, with the same date, is in *ibid.*, pp. 673–76. See also May 1, Cecil to Winwood and Spencer, *Winwood* II, 392–94.

operative only with the conclusion of the peace, involved no agreement with France, and was made in part in order to prevent French
predominance at The Hague. England believed that such a league
would be conducive to peace; King James, said Cecil, favored peace
even though it might create new problems for England. Furthermore, such a league was the only way to persuade the Dutch to repay their debt.[63] Cecil brushed aside the objection that this agreement
violated the Anglo-Spanish peace treaty. It was, he said, in accord
with the peace treaty, in which James had promised to try to end the
war on suitable conditions; without the league the Dutch would be
afraid to negotiate at all. Cecil also suggested to the Spanish and
Archducal representatives in London that England might be willing
to make a similar league with them, once this was finished. England,
said Cecil, had deliberately spun out the negotiations, so that the
Dutch would not become too stiff in their demands at the peace table,
but now she was pushing ahead, since Spain and the Archduke had
not complained about the Franco-Dutch league.[64]

Cecil's dealings with the Habsburg representatives constituted a
skillful piece of fence-mending, and were undoubtedly in some part
sincere. Cecil shared in some measure at least his father's conviction
that if the difficulties in the Low Countries could be settled, Anglo-
Spanish relations should greatly improve, "except it be set down
there [Spain] for a principle, that the king must needs be enemy to
Spain because he is not a vassal to the Pope." Cornwallis also harped
on this string. England and Spain, he said, were friends by nature
and enemies by accident; just the reverse was true with France.[65]

The Anglo-Dutch league was signed late in June of 1608, in
the hope and expectation, on England's part, that it would never
be necessary for the Dutch to call upon her to fulfill the obligations

[63] Nov. 17, 1607, Apr. 13, 1608, Cecil to Edmondes, P.R.O., S.P. 77/8, ff.
382–87, B.M. Stowe Mss. 170, ff. 15–18.
[64] May 31, 1608, Cecil to Edmondes, B.M. Stowe Mss. 170, ff. 45–51. See
also May 19, June 30, Cecil to Cornwallis, *Winwood* II, 400–403, 413–16.
[65] Feb. 6, 1608, Cecil to Cornwallis, B.M. Cott. Mss. Vesp. C X, ff. 317–19.
Oct. 16, Cornwallis to the Privy Council, P.R.O., S.P. 94/15, ff. 149–52.

she had assumed. The fact that it was necessary for England to make such a treaty was an indication of the unreality of the policy of balance which James and Cecil had been pursuing since the Anglo-Spanish peace. Despite the appearances which the antagonism between the governments of Henri IV and Philip III created, England did not have the choice of allies, because for both ideological and political reasons she could not abandon the Dutch. For the time being, however, the agreement was useful to England. It enabled her to recover some, but not all, of the ground she had lost in Dutch opinion by her previous shuffling. Like the Franco-Dutch league, it marked a commitment to peace. Both governments were now convinced that peace was the only alternative to far greater military and financial support of the Dutch than either would give alone, and their mutual distrust still precluded any attempt at negotiating the sort of agreement which would have been the essential preliminary to support of, or participation in, the Dutch war effort. The independent policy of the Dutch, who were determined not to be anyone's client, their failure to consult England and France before making the initial truce, increased the mutual uneasiness. Each power suspected that the Dutch initiatives had resulted from secret consultation with, and encouragement from, the other. It seems likely, in view of the policy France was to adopt in the Cleves-Julich crisis, that Henri's suggestions that France would fight if England would were sincerely meant, but England had no intention of fighting, and James's occasional flashes of bellicosity were rightly discounted in Paris.

The real gainers from this situation were the supporters of peace in the United Provinces and on the Habsburg side. It was not at all clear yet, however, whether they would be able to come to an agreement—whether King Philip and his advisers could be persuaded or browbeaten into making the necessary concessions, whether Oldenbarnevelt and his allies could keep the upper hand of Maurice and the war party and preserve the fragile unity of the seven disparate United Provinces. Almost every week opinion in government circles in London and Paris seemed to shift—peace was assured, peace was most unlikely. The leagues strengthened Oldenbarnevelt's hand. What the Dutch wanted was known, and they now had their desired guarantees of a future settlement. The decision now rested in Madrid.

CHAPTER VI

❖ ❖ ❖ ❖ ❖

Spain and the Dutch:
The Truce of Antwerp

WITH THE SIGNING of the two treaties of guarantee in the first half of 1608 the major remaining question was what sort of settlement, if any, they would be guaranteeing. The negotiations between the Dutch and the Archduke's commissioners were incredibly lengthy and repetitious; by late summer they reached a crisis. In July King Philip III finally made up his mind: there would be no peace, no recognition of Dutch sovereignty, unless the Dutch agreed to grant religious freedom to Catholics and accept exclusion from the Indies trade. This did not necessarily mean resumption of the war, however. Dutch freedom was unpalatable enough to Spain, but even acknowledging freedom was preferable to the incorporation of the seven provinces into either England or (more probably) France, and this, Spain believed, was a distinct possibility if the war went on. Philip was prepared, therefore, to accept a truce of some length— five or six years. During the truce the Dutch themselves would grant toleration, and the benefits of peaceful trade would lead them to give up their demand to trade in the Indies, so that peace on Spanish terms would eventually result—or so Philip professed to believe.[1]

This decision, when it became known, almost caused the collapse of the negotiations. The Dutch would not make peace on

---

[1] July 5/15, 1608, Philip to the Archduke, *Pays-Bas* I, 284–86.

Spain's terms, while a truce meant the reopening of the question of sovereignty. Philip had made his original concession on this matter only in the event of a peace treaty; nothing had been said about a truce. Spain might not acknowledge Dutch freedom at all, or she might agree to acknowledge it only for the duration of the truce. Jeannin, who had just returned from a brief visit to France, and Winwood urged the Dutch to accept the idea of a truce, provided, of course, that there was no going back on the Archduke's statement respecting Dutch sovereignty. Their plan was that religion not be mentioned at all, and that a formula be found on the problem of trade which would be empty and vague enough to satisfy both sides —which, in other words, they and the Dutch could interpret as a Spanish concession for the duration of the truce. They also wanted a much longer truce, one which would run for not less than twelve years.[2]

The Dutch were disgruntled and uneasy, and the English and French commissioners were gloomy, since Richardot and Spinola were being very difficult on the sovereignty question.[3] The war party in the United Provinces revived; Jeannin expressed the opinion that only the steady pressure exercised by himself and Winwood kept Oldenbarnevelt and his friends in control.[4] The Archduke himself finally broke the deadlock. In violation of instructions from Spain he conceded the principle of sovereignty for a short truce, seven years or possibly ten, and at the same time raised the possibility of a much longer truce, of as much as twenty years, without mention of sovereignty.[5] The formulation of the sovereignty clause remained to be worked out, but with the concession of the principle negotiations could resume.

[2] Aug. 14/24, 1608, Jeannin et al. to Henri, *Jeannin* XIV, 84–98. Aug. 27, Winwood to Edmondes, B.M. Stowe Mss. 170, ff. 144–45. See also *Jeannin* XIV, 105–108.

[3] See, e.g., Aug. 19/29, 1608, Jeannin to Villeroy, *Jeannin* XIV, 114–28.

[4] Sept. 21/Oct. 1, 1608, Jeannin to Villeroy, *ibid.*, pp. 219–24.

[5] Oct. 1/11, 1608, Jeannin et al. to Henri, Oct. 6/16, Richardot to the English and French commissioners, *ibid.*, pp. 251–55, 281–83.

In making known their decision against peace the Spanish government laid heavy stress on the religious question in the hope of causing friction between France and her Protestant associates. The Spanish ambassador in Paris, for instance, remarked to Carew that Spain preferred peace if the Dutch would only grant toleration; on commerce "it would not stick."[6] At the same time Spain tried to drive a further wedge into the coalition by dispatching Don Pedro de Toledo on a special mission to France. By May, 1608, the rumors were flying that he was to offer a marriage alliance to France, possibly with the stipulation that the pair might inherit the Low Countries after the death of the Archdukes, who were childless.[7] The French believed that Spain's chief purpose was to make the Dutch mistrustful of them, and possibly to try to divert France from giving the Dutch any further aid.[8] There was also the chance that the Dutch would accept less favorable terms from Spain if they thought that France might desert them.

There was alarm in England over Don Pedro's mission too, especially since it coincided with Jeannin's departure for Paris. They suspected that the Pope was behind it. If France abandoned the Dutch and the war went on, they would have to act, or see the Dutch beaten.[9] Winwood's London man of business, John More, wrote that England could extricate herself by a close alliance with the Dutch, and by reentering the war; the two powers would have naval superiority and could successfully strike at "both his [Philip's] Indies. . . . But all this discourse is but wind," More went on. "His Majesty is a lover of peace, and having conceived I know not what opinion of the States, is miserably poor."[10] Winwood's circle con-

[6] Aug. 24, 1608, Carew to Cecil, P.R.O., S.P. 78/54, ff. 141–45.
[7] This possibility was mooted as early as December 1607. Dec. 31, 1607/Jan. 10, 1608, Villeroy to Jeannin, *Jeannin* XIII, 142–48.
[8] On this point see F. T. Perrens, *Les Mariages Espagnols sous le Règne de Henri IV et la Régence de Marie de Médicis* (Paris, n.d.), p. 111.
[9] So Boderie reported on June 22/July 2, 1608, *Boderie* III, 340–47.
[10] June 25, 1608, More to Winwood, *Winwood* II, 412–13.

tinued to be distressed at the timidity of English policy. "We are afraid of every shadow," wrote Sir Henry Neville, the Puritan-minded former ambassador to France, on June 21, "lest it should give a pretense unto Spain to foment the rebellion we expect in Ireland; as if when he resolves and finds himself ready to do it, he will forbear for want of a pretext."[11]

The French were prepared to listen to Don Pedro. A marriage alliance with Spain would assure a quiet succession for the Dauphin, as Cornwallis pointed out.[12] A serious offer would allow France to conduct a sort of diplomatic auction between Spain and England, and give her the choice of allies on the most favorable possible terms. Early in July Carew was reporting that some people in France believed not only that Henri welcomed the possibility of marriage discussions with Spain, but also that he had made the first move.[13] Cecil refused to get excited. He doubted very much that France would jettison the Dutch for a "cradle contract," though he did take the precaution of talking to Boderie once again in general terms about an Anglo-French league.[14] As it turned out, Cecil was right. Don Pedro was indeed authorized to discuss a marriage alliance, but he began his mission in the most tactless possible way, by a violent protest against French aid to the Dutch.[15] He went on to ask that France urge the Dutch to accept Spanish terms respecting sovereignty, toleration, and the Indies, with the implication that the marriage negotiations were contingent upon France's giving Spain satisfaction on these matters.[16] The French were not disposed to trade immediate advantage for the remote possibilities of gain in-

[11] *Ibid.*, pp. 411–12.

[12] June 18, 1608, Cornwallis to Cecil, B.M. Cott. Mss. Vesp. C XI, ff. 43–47.

[13] July 9, 1608, Carew to Edmondes, B.M. Stowe Mss. 170, f. 87.

[14] July 14/24, 1608, Boderie to Villeroy, *Boderie* III, 366–81. July 22, Cecil to Wotton, P.R.O., S.P. 99/5, ff. 153–55.

[15] July 20, 1608, Carew to Cecil, P.R.O., S.P. 78/54, ff. 124–27.

[16] July 16/26, 1608, Villeroy to Boderie, *Boderie* III, 384–86. July 26, Cecil to Winwood and Spencer, Aug. 7, the Privy Council to Winwood and Spencer, *Winwood* II, 421–23, 427–29.

volved in what Cornwallis called "discourse of swaddling clothes";[17] and so, when Don Pedro raised the marriage question, his proposals were politely turned aside.[18]

Even if Spain had not so crudely and obviously tied the marriage proposal to her negotiations with the Dutch, there were good reasons for Henri to reject it at this time. The reaction abroad might well be a powerful Protestant coalition headed by England to which the Huguenots would look with sympathy for leadership and moral support. If France tried to get control of the Low Countries by means of such a marriage, wrote Carew, she would run into the same difficulties as the duke of Anjou had in 1581.[19] So the Spanish effort to deflect King Henri from his chosen course was a failure. Don Pedro lingered on for several months in France, where his presence caused occasional flashes of uneasiness in London and The Hague. By February, 1609, he was gone, and with him the most promising Spanish chance of dividing the coalition.

Cecil's reopening of the question of an Anglo-French league with Boderie was a tactical maneuver; he was determined not to enter into any auction to buy French friendship from Spain,[20] and he had no desire to make an agreement with France until the situation in the Low Countries was resolved. This became apparent when the two parties got down to particulars. It was the English position that the treaty should not mention the Dutch, a view which gravely disturbed many of the English in the United Provinces.[21] If a settlement between the Dutch and Spain was made, the newly made treaties of guarantee were ample—both England and France had declared that the guarantees held good for a truce as well as for a peace. If no settlement was reached, an Anglo-French treaty promising

[17] Sept. 7, 1608, Cornwallis to the Privy Council, *Winwood* II, 431–33.
[18] Aug. 20/30, 1608, Villeroy to Boderie, *Boderie* III, 428–32.
[19] Oct. 8, 1608, Carew to Cecil, P.R.O., S.P. 78/54, ff. 177–80. See also Aug. 18/28, Villeroy to Jeannin, *Jeannin* XIV, 108–12.
[20] Aug. 6, 1608, Cecil to Levinus Munck, P.R.O., S.P. 78/54, ff. 130–31. Munck was Cecil's secretary.
[21] See, e.g., Aug. 6, 1608, Browne to Cecil, P.R.O., S.P. 84/66, f. 114.

aid to the Dutch might lead to war. Cecil felt that French insistence on dragging the Dutch into the treaty was simply a device to force England into a breach with Spain; Boderie's argument that such a treaty would persuade Spain to offer better terms to the Dutch did not move him.[22] Villeroy, for his part, did not believe in the English professions of desire for an alliance; in any event, given England's poverty, such a connection would not be of much use to France. But, to keep England from an agreement with Spain, it was necessary to talk.[23] Jeannin, who seems to have been the most ardent advocate of the league, was distressed. France, he felt, should make the league even on England's terms. England would try to block the truce otherwise, for fear that a Franco-Spanish bargain would follow it, or else she would herself bargain with Spain. Furthermore, such a league would lead to a marriage alliance, which would be the most useful such alliance France could make.[24]

There was, indeed, some desultory talk of an Anglo-French marriage alliance in the summer of 1608, but it was not very seriously meant. Villeroy believed, and with justice, that Don Pedro's mission had prompted the English feelers, and the idea of a double marriage, which the English said they wanted, was thoroughly unfeasible, in view of the disparity in the ages of the Dauphin and Princess Elizabeth, who were, respectively, seven and twelve. He was willing to talk about a marriage alliance, but only in the most general terms and with no idea of a commitment for a long time to come.[25] Jeannin, while he was in Paris, advocated the English league to the king; Henri said that he was willing, but he was convinced that the English hated France and wanted only to disrupt France's discussions with Don Pedro.[26] And, indeed, as soon as it became apparent in London

[22] Aug. 8/18, 1608, Boderie to Villeroy, *Boderie* III, 408–19. Aug. 14, Sept. 2, Cecil to Carew, P.R.O., S.P. 78/54, ff. 139–40, 149–54.

[23] July 25/Aug. 4, 1608, Villeroy to Boderie, *Boderie* III, 393–405.

[24] Aug. 31/Sept. 10, Oct. 16/26, 1608, Jeannin to Villeroy; Sept. 3/13, Jeannin to Boderie, *Jeannin* XIV, 137–45, 148–49, 341–46.

[25] July 25/Aug. 4, Aug. 20/30, 1608, Villeroy to Boderie, *Boderie* III, 393–405, 428–32. Aug. 18/28, Villeroy to Jeannin, *Jeannin* XIV, 108–12.

[26] Aug. 20/30, 1608, Jeannin to Boderie, *Jeannin* XIV, 131–33.

that Don Pedro's mission was not going to produce a revolution in French policy, Cecil and his master lost what little enthusiasm they had had for an immediate alliance.[27] Both sides agreed to postpone negotiations—which they still professed to want—until after the agreement between the Dutch and Spain.

One reason for France's reluctance to negotiate seriously with England at this stage was the matter of the debt; they knew England would insist on satisfaction of her claims as part of a settlement.[28] Sully tried to turn the connection between the league and the debt to France's advantage, or alternatively to frighten England into dropping the connection, by suggesting that France's willingness to pay depended on England's signing a league on French terms. Carew waxed indignant at this attempt to make payment of past obligations contingent on future behavior;[29] indeed, he found Sully very exasperating. France was building 20 new warships, which alarmed Carew. He asked Sully if they were for use in the Indies; Sully, instead of answering directly, urged on Carew an Anglo-French alliance to drive Spain out of the Indies and set up free trade there. Carew replied that payment of the French debt might be an inducement to such an adventure.[30] In March, 1609, when he felt there was some prospect of Sully's fall, he wrote that this would be a good thing for England. Not only was Sully opposed to paying the debt, but also his naval policy was dangerous, and the other Protestant states of Europe would look to England for leadership once Henri's principal Huguenot adviser was gone. Furthermore, France's finances would become disordered, which Carew evidently believed would be to England's advantage, though how this would help England recover her money Carew did not say.[31]

Carew told Sully that the debt amounted to more than one million crowns—well over £300,000. Sully scoffed and said that England

[27] Sept. 21/Oct. 1, 1608, Boderie to Jeannin, *ibid.*, pp. 216–19.
[28] Sept. 8/18, 1608, Villeroy to Jeannin, *ibid.*, pp. 181–84.
[29] July 20, 1608, Carew to Cecil, P.R.O., S.P. 78/54, ff. 124–27.
[30] Nov. 1, Nov. 18, 1608, Carew to Cecil, *ibid.*, ff. 196–201, 207–14.
[31] Mar. 14, 1609, Carew to Cecil, P.R.O., S.P. 78/55, ff. 55–57.

would be glad to get half that amount.[32] The king was a bit more polite; he disavowed the idea that payment depended upon England's future political attitude. But he echoed what now came to be Sully's line: that France would do nothing about the debt until the situation in the Low Countries was clarified. If the war there went on, and France continued to support the Dutch, clearly she could not pay her debt to England. If there were peace, she would indeed pay something, but nothing like as much as England was demanding.[33] To their ambassadors, who were anxious for an accommodation on the debt, the French government explained that, owing to England's chronic ingratitude, there was no political advantage in paying the debt.[34] At first Cecil was unwilling to accept the French response and told Carew to insist on an answer—though not money —now; but by the end of the year he instructed Carew to press the demand no further for the time being.[35] Carew extracted what moral advantage he could from Cecil's decision, telling the king that James would ask for no more "by way of suit," but would wait to see what Henri's sense of honor and justice would lead him to do. Henri smoothly replied that he would pay what he ought—though he did not say when—and that he always stood ready to help England in case of need.[36]

One reason for England's acquiescence, however reluctant, in Sully's stalling on the debt was that, by early December, it looked as though a settlement between Spain and the Dutch was not far off. For the most part Jeannin and Winwood continued to work harmoniously together in urging the truce on both parties, though each side occasionally suspected the other of supporting the truce only on

[32] July 20, 1608, Carew to Cecil, P.R.O., S.P. 78/54, ff. 124–27.

[33] Aug. 24, Sept. 15, 1608, Carew to Cecil, *ibid.*, ff. 141–45, 160–65.

[34] Oct. 1/11, Oct. 23/Nov. 2, 1608, Brulart to Boderie, *Boderie* IV, 27–34, 57–62. Boderie believed that France should test England's alleged ingratitude. If the first payment produced no tangible results, no more would be made. Nov. 2/12, Boderie to Brulart, *ibid.*, pp. 67–74.

[35] Oct. 9, Dec. 23, 1608, Cecil to Carew, P.R.O., S.P. 78/54, ff. 187–91, 233–36.

[36] Jan. 23, 1609, Carew to Cecil, P.R.O., S.P. 78/55, ff. 19–23.

the surface, and of surreptitiously working against it.[37] This was a far cry from the situation at the beginning of the negotiations, when each suspected the other of only pretending to want the war to go on, and of secretly working for peace. Jeannin was also a bit bothered that Winwood constantly let him take the lead in pressing for the truce, since Prince Maurice was likely, in consequence, to look more favorably upon England than France.[38] Winwood, however, went further than Jeannin, once the Archduke had made the necessary concession on sovereignty, by threatening the Dutch with withdrawal of English aid if they failed to accept the truce,[39] a line which Jeannin soon found it necessary to follow. In November he and Winwood addressed the States-General, discoursing on the virtues of unity and promising support to the Dutch only if Spain, and not they, caused a rupture in the negotiations.[40] By the middle of that month Maurice had given in to the pressure; he ceased openly to oppose the truce and reconciled himself to Oldenbarnevelt, possibly because Oldenbarnevelt "had almost lost his credit by juggling in this treaty but recovered it again by standing so resolutely for religion."[41] It was clear enough to everybody that the superficial unity within the United Provinces might crack; given Dutch war-weariness, this was more apt to happen if the fighting resumed. But it might happen anyway, in which case a truce was a good deal safer than war.[42]

[37] See, e.g., Aug. 24, 1608, Edmondes to Cecil, P.R.O., S.P. 77/9, ff. 108–10, Aug. 19/29, Jeannin to Villeroy, *Jeannin* XIV, 114–28.

[38] Sept. 21/Oct. 1, 1608, Jeannin to Villeroy; Oct. 1/11, Villeroy to Jeannin, *Jeannin* XIV, 219–24, 243–49. In October Carew reported that Maurice angered Henri by a threat to join with England if France continued to follow her present pacific policy, which, Maurice said, was disruptive of Dutch unity. P.R.O., S.P. 78/54, ff. 177–80.

[39] Oct 11/21, 1608, Jeannin et al. to Henri, *Jeannin* XIV, 300–306.

[40] *Ibid.*, pp. 394–402.

[41] Nov. 10/20, 1608, Jeannin to Sully, *ibid.*, pp. 414–17. The quotation is from John Chamberlain's letter of Oct. 21 to Dudley Carleton. N. E. McClure, ed., *The Letters of John Chamberlain* (Philadelphia, 1939) I, 265.

[42] So Villeroy believed. See his letter of Oct. 23/Nov. 2, 1608, to Boderie, *Boderie* IV, 55–56.

Then, in December, Richardot, whether intentionally or not it is impossible to say, wrote a letter which almost produced a rupture in the coalition. During the recent discussions of the sovereignty question the idea had been put forward that, instead of a short truce with a renewed guarantee of Dutch freedom, there might be a much longer truce, of twenty or twenty-five years, without such a guarantee. Virtually everybody connected with the negotiations save the Dutch had suggested this at one time or another; virtually everybody was sure that he—and by extension his government—had not been the first to make the suggestion, since it was generally felt that the Dutch would not accept it, not even the peace-loving Oldenbarnevelt.[43] In late November, on orders from Madrid, the Archduke sent a special envoy, Don Fernando Giron, to London to thank King James for his good offices, possibly because the English attitude on the truce had altered rather abruptly. At first England had been very cautious about it; Cecil had told Boderie that, unlike a permanent peace, a truce would benefit only Spain.[44] Then the English seemingly became its leading advocates, so eager, in fact, that Jeannin felt it necessary to try to restrain them.[45] The French were suspicious of Giron's mission; their agent in Brussels wrote Jeannin that Giron's real objective was to persuade James to abandon the Dutch unless the latter became less intransigent.[46] Then, on November 29, came Richardot's letter, to the effect that King James himself had suggested the plan of a long truce with no declaration on sovereignty, which, said Richardot, reopened the whole question.[47]

This letter produced an explosion, particularly in Paris. Henri was very angry at what he regarded as another piece of English duplicity, and a pointless one at that, since there was no chance that the Dutch would accept this, even if England threatened to turn over the cautionary towns to Spain. In Villeroy's view the English ma-

[43] See, e.g., Dec. 3/13, 1608, Jeannin to Villeroy, *Jeannin* XIV, 464–73.
[44] Sept. 3/13, 1608, Boderie to Villeroy, *Boderie* III, 444–50.
[45] Oct. 12/22, 1608, Jeannin to Villeroy, *Jeannin* XIV, 314–23.
[46] *Ibid.*, pp. 454–55.
[47] The letter is in *ibid.*, pp. 462–64.

neuver might well wreck the whole negotiation.[48] Winwood and
Spencer, who had feared the revival of the idea of a long truce without sovereignty, and hardly expected it to come about in this way,
were embarrassed and denied to Jeannin that their government had
ever made such a proposal. On December 11 they joined Jeannin in
a formal reply to Richardot, declaring that they had put no such
suggestion to the Dutch because they knew that the Dutch would
never accept it, and ten days later wrote a separate letter to Richardot to the same effect. Jeannin inclined to believe Winwood. If the
English ever had made such a proposal, he thought, it was done when
they were trying to break up the negotiations, which they were not
doing now. In Jeannin's view Richardot's maneuver was essentially
a face-saving device; if England and France stood firm, Spain would
authorize the Archduke to negotiate.[49]

In November Winwood and Jeannin, weary of the long delay in
getting a firm commitment from Spain on the question of sovereignty, had sent Charles de l'Aubespine, abbé de Préaux, one of
Jeannin's subordinates, to Brussels to ask the Archduke point-blank
what King Philip would do. The Archduke replied that Philip had
been willing to ratify his action but had changed his mind because he
had heard, especially from Don Pedro de Toledo, that he might get
a long truce without making the distasteful concession, a proposal
which de Préaux had been instructed specifically to reject. A week
later the explanation was different: now the Archduke said that
Cornwallis had assured the Spanish government that King James
could obtain such a truce.[50] Cecil, who was very angry at the slur

[48] Dec. 6/16, 1608, Villeroy to Jeannin, *Jeannin* XV, 1–7. Dec. 9/19, Villeroy to Boderie, *Boderie* IV, 113–17.

[49] *Jeannin* XV, 26–27. Dec. 6/16, 1608, Jeannin to Villeroy; Dec. 22/Jan. 1,
1609, Jeannin et al. to Henri, *ibid.*, pp. 7–10, 59–63. Nov. 27, 1608, Winwood to
Edmondes, B.M. Stowe Mss. 170, ff. 256–57. Dec. 21, Winwood and Spencer
to Richardot, P.R.O., S.P. 84/66, f. 149.

[50] Nov. 30, Dec. 7, 1608, Edmondes to Cecil, P.R.O., S.P. 77/9, ff. 194–95,
197–98. De Préaux's instructions, dated Nov. 20/30, are in *Jeannin* XI, 501–
506.

on his master (and himself), and who naturally preferred to attribute the story to Don Pedro, rejected this at once; Cornwallis, he said, had had less than anyone else to do with the negotiations. He told Boderie that he was upset that the French so readily believed the story, and he tried to track it to its source. The ambassadors of both Spain and the Archduke in London denied having reported anything which might have given rise to it.[51]

Cecil's protests were a trifle overvehement. At one point, in September, in order to steer Spain away from striking a bargain with France, he had told Edmondes to hint to Richardot that if Spain or the Archduke approached James, "it may be, peradventure, some such midway may be thought of, for reconciling their opposite respects about the sovereignty."[52] Cornwallis, however, was not involved. Cecil notified his ambassador of the allegations of the Archduke's government and told him to deny them formally, but without protesting overmuch. The most logical explanation, Cecil felt, was that the lie had to be invented somewhere, in Madrid or Brussels, in order to justify Spain's failure to support the Archduke on the sovereignty question.[53]

The English protests continued loud and indignant, and James took advantage of Giron's leave-taking to deny publicly and elaborately that he had ever suggested that there should be a truce without an acknowledgement of Dutch sovereignty. It was, said the king, a strange and impertinent request, to ask the Dutch now to accept less than the Archduke had already conceded.[54] The English denials were accepted, especially after Giron's departure emptyhanded from England, though Henri characteristically made use of the episode to try to prejudice the Venetian ambassador in Paris against

[51] Dec. 23, Dec. 31, 1608, Cecil to Winwood and Spencer, *Winwood* II, 466–67, 469–71. Dec. 31, Cecil to Edmondes, B.M. Stowe Mss. 170, ff. 280–82. Dec. 31,1608,/Jan. 10, 1609, Boderie to Jeannin, *Boderie* IV, 172–75.
[52] Sept. 14, 1608, Cecil to Edmondes, B.M. Stowe Mss. 170, ff. 159–61.
[53] Dec. 31, 1608, Cecil to Cornwallis, P.R.O., S.P. 94/15, ff. 189–94.
[54] Feb. 2, 1609, Cecil to Carew, P.R.O., S.P. 78/55, ff. 25–26. Feb. 4, Cecil to Winwood and Spencer, B.M. Stowe Mss. 170, ff. 318–19.

James who, he said, had been a fraudulent trickster from birth.[55] The king believed that James, to curry favor with Spain, would have urged the Dutch to accept such a truce if he had believed there was a chance of success,[56] but it was tacitly agreed on all sides that there was nothing to be gained by identifying any culprit. It was all an honest misunderstanding, probably, so Cecil came to believe, on the part of the Spanish ambassador in London—which in point of fact it may well have been.[57]

This contretemps seemingly disturbed the Dutch less than it did anyone else. In December, while it was at its height, they granted a further short extension of the cease-fire, with, apparently, every expectation of a successful conclusion to the negotiations. They were not deceived. At this stage, since the Dutch refused absolutely to discuss religion, and the Archduke did not press the point, there were only two major issues, the wording of the sovereignty clause and the matter of the Indies trade. There was also the problem of duration: the Archduke had offered ten years, the Dutch wanted fifteen and ultimately settled for twelve.[58] The sovereignty clause was still the key to the settlement. The Archduke sent his confessor Inigo Brizuela to Spain to make Philip and Lerma see reason on this. Brizuela carefully pointed out the financial consequences of a renewal of the fighting, while Spinola emphasized to the king that there was no break in the solid front of the coalition; they were firmly behind the Dutch demand, and Jeannin was even talking of a rupture with Spain if she persisted in her stubbornness.[59]

[55] Jan. 18/28, 1609, Antonio Foscarini (Venetian representative in France) to the Doge and Senate, *C.S.P. Venetian 1607–1610*, p. 224.

[56] Jan. 20/30, 1609, Henri to Jeannin et al., *Jeannin* XV, 156–61.

[57] Feb. 12, 1609, Cecil to Cornwallis, *Winwood* II, 478–80. See also P.R.O., S.P. 94/16, ff. 41–43. In April Richardot, in apologizing for his error, suggested that the Spanish ambassador in London might have acted out of malice, since he did not get on well with the Archduke's envoy there, who happened to be Richardot's son-in-law. Apr. 6, 1609, Winwood and Spencer to Cecil, P.R.O., S.P. 84/66, ff. 183–84.

[58] Nov. 20/30, 1608, Jeannin et al. to Henri, *Jeannin* XIV, 426–33.

[59] Dec. 19/29, 1608, Spinola to Philip III, *Pays-Bas* I, 314–15.

At long last the Archduke had his way. On January 19 King Philip agreed to accept the Archduke's formula on sovereignty, provided Giron was unable to change the English position.[60] So, in the final treaty, both Spain and the Archduke announced their willingness to deal with the United Provinces "in the capacity of, and as taking them for free lands, provinces, and estates, over which they claim nothing."[61] There was a small loophole here, in the use of the word "as." The recognition of independence was not absolute; as Carew put it, the States were recognized as free but not sovereign.[62] This was perfectly satisfactory to England and France, since it would keep Dutch suspicion of Spain alive—not that it was likely to die down. The Dutch would have liked more, but since they had already accepted this formula as satisfactory for a peace treaty, they could hardly argue that it would not do for a truce. They had gotten the main point for which they had been contending: there was no suggestion that the recognition was for the duration of the truce only. They did ask the French and English commissioners to give them a guarantee that they recognized Dutch sovereignty as perpetual, but this was rejected on the ground that it could serve no useful purpose. To the Dutch objection that Spain might not ratify, the reply was that Spain was committed by the powers she had given to the Archduke, and Winwood and Spencer added that Spanish refusal to ratify could be taken as an infraction of the truce, in which case the treaties of guarantee would become operative. With that the Dutch had to rest content.[63]

The question of the Indies trade proved more difficult. Richardot at first was adamant that there should be no mention of this in the treaty at all, which meant in effect that Spain would continue

---

[60] *Ibid.*, pp. 320–22. This document is in the form of a reply to a memorandum by Brizuela, which is in *ibid.*, pp. 304–13.

[61] The text of the treaty, with its attached declarations, is in *Jeannin* XV, 365–83.

[62] Dec. 30, 1608, Carew to Cecil, P.R.O., S.P. 78/54, ff. 237–40.

[63] Mar. 11/21, 1609, Jeannin et al. to Henri, *Jeannin* XV, 305–10. Spain ratified the truce in June.

her absolute prohibition of all trade there other than her own. Since no concessions had been made to France or England in their respective peace treaties with Spain, Richardot calculated, and correctly, that the two governments would not be anxious to obtain a legal advantage for a commercial rival. Winwood and Jeannin felt, however, that it was necessary to get something for the Dutch. The commercial oligarchy was the backbone of the peace party in the United Provinces; if they received no satisfaction on this point, Maurice and his friends might yet carry the day and the war be resumed. At this moment, furthermore, the English government was not pleased with Maurice, who had recently made some insulting remarks about James, for which he had to apologize.[64] So a certain amount of pressure was applied to Richardot, and once again a face-saving compromise emerged. Clause IV of the truce declared that the Dutch could trade with the Spanish possessions in Europe and in other areas where other powers had the right to trade. In other Spanish possessions the Dutch were not to trade without King Philip's permission, but Spain would make no effort to impede their dealing with other "princes, potentates, and peoples"—which, presumably, meant in those areas not occupied by Spain. Jeannin, by telling Richardot that he had heard from The Hague that there might be a rupture otherwise—the final negotiations were being held at Antwerp—obtained one more concession: that the truce was not to go into effect "outside these limits" for a year, or until the parties there could be notified. "Outside these limits" meant the Indies, to Jeannin, which was an indirect way of making the concession Spain would not make directly.[65]

The clause as drawn was certainly vague enough to admit of several interpretations, and the Dutch understandably pressed for more. The French and English commissioners were willing to sign a statement to the effect that, if the Dutch could trade in Spanish possessions in the Indies only with Spanish permission, the same held true

[64] Jan. 22/Feb. 1, 1609, Jeannin to Villeroy, *ibid.*, pp. 174–79.
[65] Mar. 2/12, 1609, Jeannin to Villeroy, *ibid.*, pp. 281–83.

for Spain in those areas which the Dutch held—in other words, that their guarantee extended to the Indies if Spain made any effort to drive the Dutch out of those places they had occupied. Here again the phraseology was imprecise: such an attack by Spain was not precisely a breach of the truce, but simply an act which demanded reparation.[66] The Archduke's deputies, in addition, were prepared to give an explicit oral promise that their government would make no effort to shut off the Dutch trade, but no such promise could be got from Madrid. The Dutch wanted more: they wanted to be apprised of those places from which Spain proposed to exclude them. This demand was not satisfied, nor were various other demands which even the sympathetic Winwood regarded as exorbitant. He and Spencer complained that the Dutch were aggrieved if every proposal of theirs did not receive automatic Anglo-French support.[67] It is a truism that coalitions tend to dissolve once their goals have been achieved, and already the fissures in this one were beginning to show.

The Truce of Antwerp was signed on March 29, 1609. It has been appraised at its true value both at the time and since. Winwood regarded it as very advantageous to the Dutch; Pieter Geyl, the greatest of recent historians of the Netherlands, called it "an astonishing victory" for the United Provinces.[68] Their freedom, for which they had struggled so long and so heroically, was recognized. They had not committed themselves to exclusion from the Indies. They had given up no territory in return for the truce, which was signed on the basis of *uti possedetis*. They had made no concessions respecting religion, save in the small segments of Brabant which they held.

[66] *Ibid.*, pp. 381–82. See also Mar. 16, 1609, Winwood and Spencer to the Privy Council; Mar. 29, Winwood and Spencer to Cecil, *Winwood* II, 488–90, III, 1–2.

[67] Mar. 2, 1609, Winwood to Edmondes, B.M. Stowe Mss. 170, ff. 360–61. Apr. 6, Winwood and Spencer to the Privy Council, P.R.O., S.P. 84/66, ff. 185–86. See also Feb. 28/Mar. 10, Foscarini to the Doge and Senate, *C.S.P. Venetian 1607–1610*, pp. 238–39.

[68] P. Geyl, *The Revolt of the Netherlands* (London, 1958), p. 254. Apr. 5, 1609, Winwood to Chamberlain, P.R.O., S.P. 77/9, ff. 243–44.

Jeannin's final effort, before his departure, on behalf of his coreligionists in the seven provinces was politely turned aside.[69] They had made no promises or commitments respecting the reopening of the Antwerp trade; in subsequent discussions with the Archduke's government they held to their position, the blockade continued, and so did the decay of the great port. They had their guarantees for the duration of the truce from their two powerful protectors, guarantees specifically renewed in June, with the explicit addition that the guarantees applied if their trade to the Indies was disrupted by Spain or the Archduke, in return for their own promise to make no treaty with Spain or the Archduke during the truce without the consent of France and England.[70] They had, in fact, just about everything they could expect, excepting permanency; in twelve years the whole question could be reopened.

For the two guarantors the truce was anything but an astonishing victory. It was something they could not prevent, short of full-scale intervention on behalf of the Dutch, which England would not contemplate at all and France would not undertake alone. Given the high level of suspicion and mistrust, the two sets of commissioners worked well together, and Jeannin, in particular, was lavish in his praise of his English counterparts, possibly because he wished to counterbalance the hypercritical attitude of his superiors in Paris. Henri indicated no public dissatisfaction with the results of the negotiation. He professed to be contemptuous of the present regime in Spain; he called Philip III stupid and Lerma corrupt, and said that he would never have advised the truce if Philip II had still been king. He also told Carew, with great assurance, that the truce was not dangerous, since Spain would not recover in spite of the breathing-space the cessation of hostilities would provide.[71] His actions in the

[69] His address to the States-General on the subject is in *Jeannin* XV, 474–84. See also P.R.O., S.P. 84/66, f. 231.

[70] P.R.O., S.P. 103/36, ff. 123–24. See also *ibid.*, ff. 117–18.

[71] See Carew's letters to Cecil on Aug. 10, Sept. 27, and Nov. 18, 1608, P.R.O., S.P. 78/54, ff. 132–36, 169–73, 207–14.

following year showed how little he believed in this confident statement.

For France, Spain was still the enemy, and anything which benefited her, as the truce surely would, was bound to be detrimental to French interests. Henri had not achieved one of his major goals; there were still Spanish soldiers in the Low Countries, and Spain was now in a better position to meddle elsewhere—perhaps in Italy, where France had been encouraging the duke of Savoy in his occasional attempts to shake himself free of Spanish domination. True, the amount of money France spent annually to support the Dutch would be reduced, but it was not eliminated—in June, 1609, France again promised to continue to support two regiments of foot-soldiers and some light horse for two years.[72]

Thanks to the skill of Henri and his subordinates, France had gone a long way toward recovery from the horrors and devastation of the civil wars. The country was prosperous and the government shared in the prosperity owing to the heavy taxation. France herself had nothing to fear from Spain in the immediate future. Her diplomatic position, however, had not been improved by the truce. The Dutch might be thankful for French help in the past, but gratitude is a notoriously frail reed upon which to lean in international relations, and the ultra-Protestants and the war party in the United Provinces (which groups overlapped a good deal) were disappointed. Prince Maurice remarked that Jeannin was a false man and that Henri was becoming more Catholic every day.[73] For the future there were only two choices before France: she could adopt a passive foreign policy, or, if she wished to be aggressively anti-Habsburg, she must seek most of her allies among the Protestant states. The Scandinavian kingdoms, Denmark and Sweden, were relatively strong, but they were preoccupied with their own detestation of each other, and Spain represented no threat to them. The United Provinces were

[72] *Jeannin* XV, 494–96.
[73] Mar. 18, 1609, Browne to Cecil, P.R.O., S.P. 84/66, f. 173.

weary from their long struggle, and King James's government was profoundly pacifist. France's diplomatic prospects looked rather unpromising in the spring of 1609.

On the surface the English position looked considerably better, for all of James's and Cecil's unadventurousness during the long negotiations. For it was England who had apparently emerged with the choice of allies, provided she could make her alliance seem worth having. Philip might be stupid and Lerma corrupt, as Henri said, but they were not complete fools and they knew who their enemy was. Only England, among all the major states of Europe, was a potentially useful friend. King Philip's Austrian cousins were more of a liability than an asset at this point, with old Emperor Rudolf slipping further and further into his peculiar form of mental decay. The English ambassador, Sir Stephen Lesieur, remarked that he "ought to be walled up in a cloister with a necromancer, an alchemist, a painter, and a whore."[74]

Cecil was fully aware of what he believed to be the advantages of England's position. He instructed Cornwallis to make it very clear to the Spanish government that England had done more than France to further the truce, especially in the final stages, by threatening to abandon the Dutch if they proved unreasonable. The Spanish may not have believed this, but they said that they did, and Cornwallis was even able to report that there had been a few decisions favorable to English merchants handed down by Spanish courts.[75] Furthermore, there was a group of high officials in England, including Cecil himself, who were in receipt of Spanish pensions. This did not mean, of course, that they danced to Spanish piping—far from it. A recent authority has put it this way. "It [Cecil's pension] did not buy friendship: a point had simply been reached where refusal to grant it would create more than normal hostility. Spain, far from being

---

[74] Nov. 17, 1610, Lesieur to Cecil, P.R.O., S.P. 80/2, ff. 105–106.

[75] Feb. 5, Apr. 13, 1609, Cornwallis to the Privy Council; Apr. 7, Cornwallis to James, P.R.O., S.P. 94/16, ff. 29–30, 61–62, 67–69. Feb. 12, Cecil to Cornwallis, B.M. Cott. Mss. Vesp. C XI, ff. 280–86.

in control of its hireling, was rather in the position of a hapless diner who must 'bribe' a surly waiter with tips to avoid getting soup spilled on him.'"[76] This is substantially accurate, but it does neglect one factor: the diner's hope that the tips, under the proper circumstances, might make the waiter more accommodating. There was the possibility that that time had come, a fact which was recognized in Paris. A month or so after the signing of the truce Sully remarked to Carew, during another of their seemingly endless discussions of the debt, that now that peace had come to the Low Countries there was nothing to keep France and England friendly.[77] This comment was one of those profound and misleading half-truths to which politicians, and even statesmen, are prone. It was certainly true that the greatest and most obvious common interest of France and England since the accession of King James, and even before, was the support of the Dutch in their struggle for their independence, and that was now achieved. Unless and until that war resumed, the bond was dissolved, and the dissolution had been underscored by England's steady refusal to make a triple treaty of guarantee.

England was seemingly in a far better position to strike a bargain with Spain than was France. In actuality the English advantage was entirely imaginary, and Spain's unwillingness to make a permanent settlement with the Dutch should have opened the eyes of James and his minister to the falsity and contradictory nature of their assumptions. Any genuine alliance with Spain would have to be at the expense of the Dutch, to whom England was committed by treaty. Furthermore, in an age in which ideology counted for so much, one cannot simultaneously play both ideological partisan and *tertius gaudens*. There was no real possibility of genuine friendship between the two powers which regarded themselves as the champions of their respective faiths. At this very time, in the spring of 1609, King James was once again in the throes of controversial composition—an

[76] C. H. Carter, *The Secret Diplomacy of the Habsburgs 1598–1625*, pp. 126–27.
[77] May 9, 1609, Carew to Cecil, P.R.O., S.P. 78/55, ff. 84–86.

activity which all the diplomatists of France and England deplored but could not prevent. Angered by Cardinal Bellarmine's attack upon his anonymously published book, *Triplici nodo, triplex cuneus*, defending the oath of allegiance imposed on English Catholics after the Gunpowder Plot, the king reissued the book, under his own name this time, with a long preface entitled *A Premonition to all Most Mightie Monarches, Kings, Free Princes, and States of Christendome*. James was proud of his theological skills, and wanted to present a copy of his tract to all the governments with which England had diplomatic relations, including Catholic powers, because, he said, the book was not an attack on Catholic dogma, but on the unjustified claims of the Pope to temporal authority.

Henri was in an awkward dilemma. Boderie had reported that the book was pernicious and called the Pope Antichrist. Henri could hardly be expected to approve such a sentiment. But if he refused the book altogether, James would be insulted. An unsatisfactory compromise was all that was possible—Henri accepted the book from Carew but declined to read it.[78] James's activity created problems for his diplomatists; his severe attack on his self-exiled Catholic subjects led Philip and the Archduke to value them the more highly, for their obvious nuisance value if for nothing else, and made it far less likely that the efforts of Cornwallis and Edmondes to have them expelled, or their activities restrained, would be successful.[79] The lives of French diplomatists were made more complicated too; the French government had to exert itself to prevent a violent Papal reaction to James's insults by pointing out that the first result of such a reaction would be the further persecution of English Catholics.[80] Small wonder that Henri told Carew that he wished the book had not been written.[81]

[78] Boderie's letters in the spring of 1609 are full of this matter. See especially that of May 17/27, *Boderie* IV, 328–34.

[79] See, e.g., Mar. 30, 1609, Carleton to Edmondes, B.M., Stowe Mss. 171, ff. 5–6.

[80] June 9/19, 1609, Brulart to Boderie, *Boderie* IV, 360–63.

[81] June 15, 1609, Carew to Cecil, P.R.O., S.P. 78/55, ff. 105–108.

It was certainly not necessary for James to engage in controversy with Cardinal Bellarmine and his fellow pamphleteers, or to put pressure on the Dutch government to cancel the appointment to the chair of divinity at Leyden of a man whose theological views James found distasteful.[82] But even if James had been as much of a *politique* as his predecessor, the religious gulf would still have been there, and, as is well known, religious enthusiasm in England was rising, especially among just those elements who were most hostile to any sort of bargain with Papists, and especially with Spain.

James's policy of peace and balance, then, had a good many weaknesses, of some of which the king and Cecil were not fully aware. The rising Puritan tide made it much more difficult for the king to win support for such a policy at home, even if he had thought it necessary to bid for such support by explaining his policy to Parliament, which he did not. Furthermore, such a policy, if it is to be effective, requires military preparedness, and England was notoriously unprepared. The difficult financial position of the government was no secret, and Cecil's policy of retrenchment after he became lord treasurer underscored England's unwillingness to fight to maintain the balance. James was under no illusions as to the attitude of Spain. She had accepted the truce because she had no choice; she was an unfriendly power, and would remain so. Cornwallis's letters from Madrid sounded the alarm repeatedly—Spain was fitting out a fleet for use in Ireland, or possibly in Virginia. James had not yet come under the spell of Gondomar, who did not arrive in England till 1613; he did not yet believe in the kind of coexistence which Gondomar was to advocate, the kind which involved genuine cooperation between the leading Catholic and the leading Protestant power, a policy which, in the end, Gondomar could not persuade his own government to adopt.

James's whole policy, then, continued to hinge upon a factor over which he had no control—the continuing hostility between

[82] For this matter see M. Lee, Jr., "The Jacobean Diplomatic Service," *American Historical Review* LXXII (1966–67), 1269–72.

France and Spain. The truce might well have the effect of diminishing that hostility. If, as Sully said, the war between Spain and the Dutch formed a bond between England and France, it also was a major bone of contention between France and Spain. Franco-Spanish antagonism in large measure hinged upon the life of Henri IV. Not only must Henri remain both steadfast and above ground; he also had to live long enough to train his successor to continue in his footsteps. Historians have made much of the Spanish faction at James's court. There was also a Spanish faction in Paris—or, at least, a strongly Catholic, anti-English faction, many of them former Leaguers, the most prominent of whom was Villeroy. If the king should die prematurely, leaving behind a minor heir, this faction might well achieve a reorientation of French policy in the interest of keeping peace during that minority. If both England and France turned pacifist, what was then to prevent Spain from renewing her aggressive ways, especially since she no longer had the Dutch war to distract her and eat up her resources?

George Carew, when he was recalled from his ambassadorial post in the fall of 1609, wrote an account of the state of France in imitation of the Venetians, a practice which he urged be made a rule for all English ambassadors. He was full of praise of Henri IV, of the administrative efficiency of the French government, and of its wealth. But there were weaknesses in the French state. Taxation was heavy, said Carew, the nobility had a great deal of power in local affairs—the kingdom was "cantonized"—and there was no uniformity of religion. Above all, Carew stressed the questionable legitimacy of Henri's heir and the dangers of a minority.[83] The English government did not lack for information as to the perils of the policy it pursued. But in James's regime there was lack of application and, above all, lack of thought. "Ses chasses et ses lévriers le possèdent

[83] Carew's account, a long one, is printed in T. Birch, *An Historical View of the Negotiations between the Courts of England, France, and Brussels from the year 1592 to 1617* (London, 1749), pp. 415–528. See especially pp. 513–25.

entièrement" wrote Brulart scornfully of James in March, 1609.[84] In the course of the negotiations between Spain and the Dutch, English policy had drifted to the view that the cessation of hostilities between the two would be the least of evils; after the truce it continued to drift, as it had, really, ever since the signing of the peace with Spain in 1604. There was no attempt to think through the consequences of the policy of peace and balance, or to plan out its implementation. James and his officials simply continued to react to the initiative of others. In the following year, the last year of the life of the king upon whom English policy depended, this passivity was to lead England to the brink of war.

[84] *Boderie* IV, 275–79.

CHAPTER VII

✻ ✻

The Cleves-Julich Succession

PEACE OF A SORT had come to western Europe with the signing of the Truce of Antwerp. For the first time in more than forty years none of the major powers was engaged in hostilities against another or against rebellious subjects. It was a highly precarious peace; there were repeated predictions that it would end very soon—because of the chronic aggressiveness and malice of the other side, of course. In April, 1609, Henry Wotton wrote to Edmondes that Venetian opinion was unhappy about the truce, because it was a maxim "that the king of Spain must keep himself in action to vent his Neapolitans: an idle, seditious and redundant people."[1] It was, in short, a cold-war situation, in which religious animosities or secular rivalries might well produce a flare-up at any one of several places.

In circumstances like these it was highly necessary that the Protestant states of Europe not quarrel among themselves. Thus the wisdom of the English decision in May, 1609, to issue a proclamation on the subject of fishing aimed chiefly at the Dutch was questionable, to say the least. Hitherto, said King James, he had allowed his allies to fish gratis in British waters to the ultimate hurt of his own subjects; now this was to stop. After August 1 every alien who wished to fish had to obtain a license—in London for England and Ireland, in Edinburgh for Scotland—listing the number of his ships

[1] B.M. Stowe Mss. 171, f. 43.

142

and their tonnage.[2] Cecil, in sending copies of the proclamation to his ambassadors abroad, instructed them to stress the fact that this was the mildest course England could adopt, given the phenomenal increase in the number of foreigners engaged in the fishery. Fifty or sixty years before, there had been only one or two hundred sail a year working in British waters from Scotland to Suffolk; now there were two or three thousand. The king's sovereignty extended one hundred miles out to sea, and the sovereignty of the Channel had been England's "time out of mind"; so there could be no doubt of James's right to regulate the trade as he wished. No rates had as yet been set for the purchase of the licenses; they were subject to negotiation —which made it clear that the real purpose of the proclamation was not to halt the fishing completely, but to control it and make money out of selling the licenses.[3]

Even before the proclamation was issued Boderie expressed concern about it, and suggested that his government might forbid Frenchmen to fish off the English coasts in order to avoid trouble. Cecil explained to him that the order was aimed principally at the Dutch and the Dunkirkers; Boderie believed this, but replied that the English action might well be in violation of French treaty rights, and asked his government for evidence on this point.[4] King Henri was not pleased. His fishermen, especially those of Dieppe, were complaining of the hardship this order would cause, and Boderie was instructed to hint at possible retaliation. Brulart was inclined to let the Dutch and the Archduke take the lead in the matter of the protests, but he instructed Boderie to try to get the proclamation suspended at least for the current year—it was due to become operative right in the middle of the season.[5]

[2] R. Steele, *Tudor and Stuart Proclamations 1485–1714*, I (Oxford, 1910), 127.

[3] See, e.g., May 17, 1609, Cecil to Edmondes, B.M. Stowe Mss. 171, ff. 58–59.

[4] Mar. 30/Apr. 9, May 17/27, May 24/June 3, 1609, Boderie to Brulart, *Boderie* IV, 290–93, 328–34, 342–49.

[5] May 24/June 3, 1609, Henri to Boderie; May 24/June 3, June 9/19, Brulart to Boderie, *ibid.*, pp. 349–52, 352–54, 360–63.

As Boderie anticipated, the loudest complaints came from the Dutch. The proclamation, wrote Sir William Browne from Flushing, "gave matter of great discourse and more discontent and murmuring than you can imagine." They might yield "some little recognisance" to the king; "but to come to any great imposition I think they will never accord but by force."[6] The Dutch made it clear that they would go on fishing despite the proclamation. They appealed to ancient treaties; they pointed to the economic disaster which would overtake 60,000 people who made their living from the fishing and its ancillary businesses; and anyway, in their view, a prince controlled the sea only as far as his cannon reached.[7] Oldenbarnevelt was as tactful as possible in his discussions with Winwood, and proposed the sending of an embassy to London to discuss the matter; in the meantime, he hoped, James would not object if the fishing went on as usual.[8] Richardot, in talking to Edmondes, raised the question of freedom of the seas; Edmondes promptly pointed to Spanish claims to monopoly in the Indies, and Richardot backed away, saying that it was really the affair of the Dutch anyhow.[9] Only the Spanish government was pleased by James's action, since it would create friction between England and the Dutch.[10]

On June 19 Jeannin, in writing to the governor of Calais, predicted that the combined pressure which would be applied to James in this question would cause him to back off.[11] In fact, he had already done so. The king and Cecil realized that they had acted too precipitously; they acceded to Boderie's request for a suspension, and assured him that they would be more accommodating to France than to anyone else. It was Boderie's view that the English action was taken out of financial desperation, and that it was not likely to succeed in its principal objective: Caron had told him that the Dutch

[6] June 1, 1609, Browne to Lisle, *De L'Isle* IV, 127–28.
[7] P.R.O., S.P. 84/66, f. 264.
[8] Sept. 6, 1609, Winwood to Cecil, *Winwood* III, 63–64.
[9] May 31, 1609, Edmondes to Cecil, B.M. Stowe Mss. 171, ff. 75–76.
[10] July 12, 1609, Cornwallis to Cecil, P.R.O., S.P. 94/16, f. 134.
[11] *Jeannin* XV, 515–18.

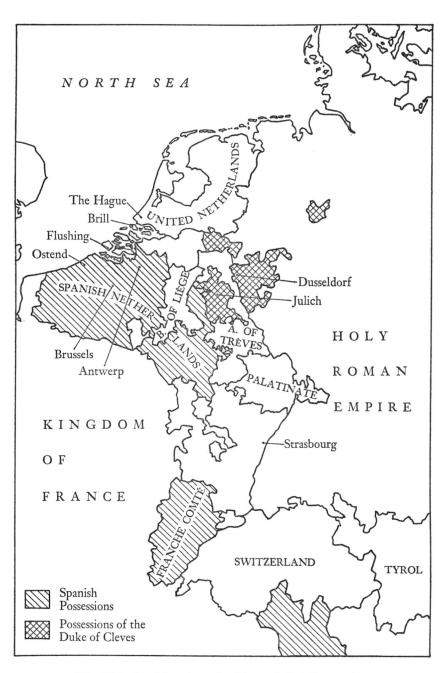

NORTH SEA

The Hague
Brill
Flushing
Ostend

UNITED NETHERLANDS

SPANISH NETHERLANDS

B. OF LIÈGE

Dusseldorf
Julich

A. OF TRÈVES

HOLY

ROMAN

EMPIRE

Brussels
Antwerp

PALATINATE

KINGDOM

OF

FRANCE

Strasbourg

FRANCHE COMTÉ

SWITZERLAND

TYROL

Spanish
Possessions

Possessions of the
Duke of Cleves

The Rhineland in 1609: the Cleves-Julich Succession

would fight rather than yield.[12] Boderie was quite right. In the spring of 1610 the Dutch did indeed send an embassy to England, to discuss the fishing among other things; the negotiations dragged on, and eventually came to nothing. The English action was hasty, ill-considered, quite unenforcible unless King James was prepared to go to war, and profited them nothing. It was also singularly badly timed, as ill-timed as James's current literary controversy with Cardinal Bellarmine, because in the spring of 1609 it was imperative that England, France, and the United Provinces cooperate as closely as possible in the extremely complicated question of the Cleves-Julich succession.

William, Duke of Cleves, died in March, 1609, leaving behind him no male heirs and a tangled succession problem, whose complexity was increased by the fact that the laws of succession in his various territories were far from identical. The two major claimants were the Elector of Brandenburg and the Duke of Neuberg. Brandenburg's claim came through the late duke's eldest daughter, whose daughter he had married; Neuberg's as the husband of the second daughter, in the name of his son, on the theory that his son was a second-generation male while the Electress was a female: the male Neuberg claimant was a generation nearer the parent stock. The Elector of Saxony also had a claim, through the duke's eldest sister. All these three were Protestants; the late duke was a Catholic. If a Protestant claim, any Protestant claim, were made good, the religious balance inside the Holy Roman Empire would be altered; and the lines of religious division there were now hardening.

Under the law of the Empire the territories involved should pass into the hands of the Emperor, who would administer them until a decision on the conflicting claims could be reached—which, in view of the way in which the mechanism of Imperial administration functioned, might take years if not decades. Owing to the geographical

---

[12] June 10/20, 1609, Boderie to Henri, and to Brulart, *Boderie* IV, 364–68, 369–74. Carew was relieved at the decision to backtrack; P.R.O., S.P. 78/55, ff. 116–17.

location of the duchies, their administration by the Habsburgs would be extremely dangerous to the Dutch, who simply could not afford to have them in Habsburg hands when the truce with Spain expired. "Habsburg hands" at this point meant, in effect, Spanish hands. The old, mad Emperor Rudolf was slipping slowly into his grave; his brother Matthias had taken over most of his powers, but Matthias's position was somewhat anomalous as long as Rudolf lived. If the Cleves territories fell into Habsburg hands, it would be the Archduke and Spinola who would control them—far worse, from the Dutch point of view, than control by Rudolf or Matthias.

Henri IV had foreseen the complications which were likely to arise from the duke's death, and had tried to get an agreement between Brandenburg and Neuberg beforehand. He had failed, partly because of the recent death of the Elector's father; the new Elector was naturally concerned first with establishing himself in his own territories. Henri did not much care who acquired the duchies, as long as the Habsburgs did not; after the duke's death his first concern was to immobilize the Archduke.[13] The most interested party, the government of the United Provinces, was not so impartial; it favored the Brandenburg claim, chiefly because Brandenburg was far stronger than Neuberg, whose religious leanings and friendliness to the Habsburgs made him already suspect.[14] Prince Maurice, for his part, was anxious to move at once, and to occupy the duchies; Oldenbarnevelt prevented this, fearing that Maurice might be using this as a device to renew the war. Jeannin suggested that the authorities in the territories of the late duke might ask officially for French protection.[15] It was his opinion that if the Elector had moved quickly, asserted his claim and occupied the duchies at once, he might well have settled the question immediately, for all practical purposes, since in addition to Dutch support he had powerful

[13] Mar. 24/Apr. 3, 1609, Henri to Jeannin et al., *Jeannin* XV, 325–31. Apr. 5, Carew to Cecil, P.R.O., S.P. 78/55, ff. 64–67.

[14] See May 20, 1609, Winwood and Spencer to Cecil, *Winwood* III, 41–42.

[15] Mar. 28/Apr. 7, Mar. 29/Apr. 8, 1609, Jeannin et al. to Henri, *Jeannin* XV, 350–55, 358–60.

friends in Germany and the king of Denmark was his brother-in-law.[16] But he let the favorable moment pass—he was, in fact, in far-off Prussia when the crisis broke—and gave his rivals a chance to assert themselves. The upshot was the Treaty of Dortmund, an agreement reached late in May, 1609, between the two major claimants, represented by the Elector's brother and Neuberg's son, to the effect that they would jointly administer the late duke's territories until their claims could be adjudicated by a group of friendly princes (unnamed). They also agreed to resist the claims of any third party to any share in the territories.[17]

The Dortmund agreement was welcomed in London, Paris, and The Hague. Oldenbarnevelt and his associates, who were hardly anxious for the war to resume while the ink on the Truce of Antwerp was still wet, assured the Archduke that they wanted a peaceful settlement.[18] King James's sympathies lay with Brandenburg, partly for religious reasons, partly on account of his Danish brother-in-law; but, as always in cases of this kind, he was concerned with legal right. At all events, he felt that it was none of his business, and he would not meddle with it.[19] The French government was also pleased. Carew's opinion was that the French, if anything, had favored Neuberg at first, but not very strongly. Their chief fear was of what might happen if Brandenburg, in whose behalf the Dutch asked their support, and Neuberg both proved obstinate and the Habsburgs were able to exploit that obstinacy. They disapproved of Maurice's bellicosity and were anxious for an amicable settlement, which they might well mediate.[20] Carew also was very pleased by the Treaty of Dortmund. He felt that the crisis was over,

[16] Apr. 28/May 8, 1609, Jeannin et al. to Henri, May 30/June 9, Jeannin to Villeroy, *ibid.*, pp. 403–14, 461–69.

[17] *Winwood* III, 43–44.

[18] May 29/June 8, 1609, Jeannin to Richardot, *Jeannin* XV, 444–48.

[19] Apr. 13/23, 1609, Boderie to Brulart, *Boderie* IV, 298–307.

[20] Apr. 5, 1609, Carew to Cecil, P.R.O., S.P. 78/55, ff. 64–67. May 10, May 22, Carew to Edmondes, B.M. Stowe Mss. 171, ff. 57, 61. Apr. 15/25, May 8/18, Henri to Jeannin et al., *Jeannin* XV, 394–99, 432–40.

and that therefore the French could not use it as an excuse to stall on an arrangement about the debt.[21]

The ambassador's rejoicings were premature. The Dortmund agreement was far from welcome to the Habsburgs, who were well aware of the divisions in the other camp—a few weeks before the treaty Edmondes reported that Neuberg, who had sought Dutch support in vain, had now approached the Archduke to ask for his backing.[22] So, in July, the Archduke Leopold, bishop of Strasburg, acting, as he said, in the name of his Imperial brother, whose rights the claimants had egregiously flouted, collected about eighteen hundred men and seized the city of Juliers. At the same time the Emperor summoned all the claimants to his court to have their rights examined. Anyone who upheld the claims of Brandenburg and/or Neuberg before the Emperor made his decision was to be put under the ban of the Empire.[23] The Habsburg counterattack had begun.

These moves were bound to produce a severe reaction, especially from France and the Dutch; Henri had made it clear from the beginning that he would not tolerate Habsburg occupation of any part of the disputed territories.[24] He therefore reacted noisily to Leopold's action—"great bravadoes," said Winwood. He asked the Dutch to send the French regiments in their service to a station near Cleves, promised to intervene if necessary, and urged the States-General to a "manly resolution." Carew believed, as did Winwood, that Henri hoped and expected to frighten Leopold out of Juliers without fighting, which, in Winwood's opinion, he was determined to avoid.[25] And, indeed, it looked as if there would be no large-scale

[21] Apr. 24, June 20, 1609, Carew to Cecil, P.R.O., S.P. 78/55, ff. 73–78, 116–17.

[22] May 10, 1609, Edmondes to Cecil, P.R.O., S.P. 77/9, ff. 254–55. Apr. 28/May 8, Jeannin et al. to Henri, *Jeannin* XV, 403–14.

[23] July 19, 1609, Edmondes to Cecil, B.M. Stowe Mss. 171, ff. 120–21. July 28/Aug. 7, Maurice to Cecil, P.R.O., S.P. 84/66, f. 248.

[24] Mar. 27/Apr. 6, 1609, Villeroy to Jeannin, *Jeannin* XV, 341–46. July 3, Carew to Cecil, P.R.O., S.P. 78/55, ff. 122–24.

[25] July 21, 1609, Carew to Edmondes, B.M. Stowe Mss. 171, f. 124. Aug. 5, Carew to Cecil, P.R.O., S.P. 78/55, ff. 152–54. Aug. 9, John Dickinson to

fighting, simply because neither Spain nor the Archduke was prepared to support Leopold by other than diplomatic means. In Spain the century-long problem of the unassimilated Morisco minority had come to a head, and the tragedy of the expulsion was under way, with all of the economic and demographic loss which it entailed.[26] From Brussels Edmondes reported that both Spinola and the Spanish ambassador had denied to him any foreknowledge of Leopold's move on the part of their governments. The Archduke was very much afraid of the possibility of war, given the vigorous French reaction, since he was in no condition to do anything. All France had to do was to hold firm, said Edmondes, and the Archduke would give way.[27]

Henri, when the nuncio and the Archduke's ambassador asked him not to intervene by force in Juliers, replied that he would do so only if others did, and he talked confidently of getting English support.[28] He was equally firm with Richardot when the Archduke's veteran negotiator came to Paris to assure him that Spain and the Archduke would not meddle in the affair.[29] He had some reason for his expectation regarding England. After the Treaty of Dortmund, but before the news of Leopold's coup had reached England, James issued a sort of manifesto which instructed Winwood to notify the agents of Brandenburg and Neuberg at The Hague that he heartily approved of their agreement, and that Winwood would be empowered to go to Dusseldorf or anywhere else to aid in the process of arbitration. James also promised that if any ill-intentioned person

Cecil, P.R.O., S.P. 84/66, ff. 250–51. Aug. 15, Winwood to Cecil, *Winwood* III, 58–60. Dickinson was Winwood's secretary.

[26] On this subject see Sept. 17, 1609, Cornwallis to the Privy Council, B.M. Cott. Mss. Vesp. C XI, ff. 399–400.

[27] July 26, Aug. 2, 1609, Edmondes to Cecil, P.R.O., S.P. 77/9, ff. 275–76, 277–78. Aug. 3/13, Marc Antonio Correr to the Doge and Senate, *C.S.P. Venetian 1607–1610*, pp. 316–17. Aug. 15, Edmondes to Carew, B.M. Stowe Mss. 171, f. 151. Correr replaced Giustinian in England late in 1608.

[28] Aug. 5, 1609, Carew to Cecil, P.R.O., S.P. 78/55, ff. 152–54.

[29] Aug. 2, 1609, Edmondes to Cecil, P.R.O., S.P. 77/9, ff. 277–78. Aug. 16, Carew to Cecil, P.R.O., S.P. 78/55, ff. 156–59.

attempted to disrupt this accord by violence, he would help Brandenburg and Neuberg.[30] Now that such an attempt had been made, the
English government had to consider carefully what to do about it.
It was difficult to fathom Henri's intentions, wrote Cecil; "he is one
of the greatest Polliticks of a king for managing causes of this nature that liveth at this day." For the moment, therefore, Winwood
was to temporize and to hold to the terms of James's previous
declaration.[31]

Winwood followed his instructions, though he was afraid of the
possibility of dissension between Brandenburg and Neuberg. Both
rejected any discussion of partition, which, they claimed, was for-
bidden by the fundamental law of the duchies, and neither was willing to permit the other to buy him out. So Winwood made a great
parade of James's impartiality, concealing England's leaning toward
Brandenburg.[32] This was probably a mistake; firm and unanimous
support for Brandenburg on the part of the anti-Habsburg governments might well have persuaded Neuberg to allow himself to be
bought off. But James, having publicly adopted the pose of defender
of the right, wherever it might lie, would not permit himself to allow the right to take second place to English national interest. The
Spanish government did what it could to encourage James to maintain this stance, and even to support the Habsburg contention that
the Emperor was the rightful judge in this cause. James was not prepared to go this far, but he wanted more information before he
would commit himself as to who had best right, "being no way disposed to create any title, though he be resolved to defend the rights
of his friends." He was also insistent that Brandenburg and Neuberg
settle their own differences peaceably.[33]

---

[30] The manifesto is dated July 15, 1609; *Winwood* III, 53–54.
[31] Aug. 14, 1609, Cecil to Winwood, *ibid.*, pp. 57–58.
[32] Aug. 24, 1609, Winwood to Cecil, P.R.O., S.P. 84/66, ff. 256–57. Christian of Denmark was urging James to support Brandenburg. See his letter of
July 5, P.R.O., S.P. 75/4, ff. 136–38.
[33] Oct. 4, 1609, the Privy Council to Winwood, *Winwood* III, 75–77. Nov.
24/Dec. 4, Francis Cottington to Cornwallis, P.R.O., S.P. 94/16, f. 244. Cot-

The upshot was that, as in the negotiations for the Dutch-Spanish treaty, the English temporized, delayed, offered support in general terms to French policy, would commit themselves to nothing specific in the way of aid on the ground that the situation was still too nebulous for them to do so, and sat back to see what King Henri would do. They did their best to disguise the fact that they were following in the wake of the French; declarations were sent to Brandenburg so that he would know, as Cecil said, that English decisions were their own and "fetch not their roots from other men's soils."[34] Henri told Carew that he was pleased at James's offer of support, but he put on a show of impatience to the ambassador when he remarked that Leopold should have been driven out at once, without allowing him time to entrench himself. Now, with winter and the end of the campaigning season coming on, he would be that much more difficult to expel in the spring.[35] Winwood also was impatient; Leopold was energetically doing all that he could to improve his situation, while the claimants and their friends were dawdling and showing a lamentable lack of resolution. Brandenburg and Neuberg were, however, applying pressure on him to go to Dusseldorf, as James had promised he would, and he wanted instructions, especially as to what aid the king was prepared to give in ousting Leopold. If the allies delayed their public stand in favor of the claimants too long, the Habsburgs would win Neuberg over. Winwood wanted action, and as promptly as possible. "It is pity so fair an occasion with one blow to beat down the Pope and the House of Austria should be let slip," he wrote Edmondes.[36]

One of the curious features of this situation was that when Winwood wrote this letter, in mid-October, he was the only English

tington was left in charge of the Madrid embassy when Cornwallis returned home.

[34] Aug. 3, 1609, Cecil to Lake, P.R.O., S.P. 81/9, f. 222.

[35] Sept. 4, 1609, Carew to Cecil, P.R.O., S.P. 78/55, ff. 166–69.

[36] Oct. 20, 1609, Winwood to Edmondes, B.M. Stowe Mss. 171, ff. 177–78. See also his letters of Sept. 25, Oct. 7, and Oct. 20 to Cecil, P.R.O., S.P. 84/66, ff. 285–88, 290–92, 294–96.

ambassador to the countries concerned who was at his post. Edmondes, Carew, and Cornwallis were all on their way to London, or already there, as part of a normal diplomatic reshuffle. Edmondes was slated to succeed Carew in Paris; no decision had been made as to Brussels and Madrid. In addition there was no French ambassador in London, Boderie having returned to France earlier in the summer. This state of affairs was accidental, but it hardly contributed to rapidity of decision on anyone's part.

The diplomatic initiative therefore lay with Paris, since the Dutch government had adopted essentially the same line as the English. They would intervene, they said, if the English and French did, but they would not act alone.[37] It seems likely that Henri made up his mind shortly after Leopold's occupation of Juliers as to the line he would take. The Venetian ambassador reported before the end of July that both Sully and Jeannin advocated war over Juliers, and in September it was rumored that Boderie would be sent back to London to discuss the situation and a possible marriage alliance.[38]

The French king was very slow to reveal his intentions, however. For one thing, the Archduke's government, which was weakened by the death, late in August, of Richardot, its best diplomatic brain, was evidently not inclined to support Leopold openly. More important, however, was Henri's realization that haste on his part would spoil his plans, which were, very simply, to launch a grand attack upon Spain with as many allies as possible. He had learned from experience that he would get nowhere with King James by a straightforward appeal to make war on Spain, and he was doubtful of the Dutch, in view of the ascendancy of Oldenbarnevelt and the general war-weariness, which was causing some towns in the United Provinces to balk at contributing to the national army. Therefore the only way for Henri to bring his allies into a general war with Spain was to conceal from them until it was too late for them to with-

[37] Oct. 20, 1609, Winwood to Edmondes, B.M. Stowe Mss. 171, ff. 177–78.
[38] July 23/Aug. 2, 1609, Foscarini to the Doge and Senate; Sept. 16/26, Correr to the Doge and Senate, *C.S.P. Venetian 1607–1610*, pp. 310, 357–58.

draw that this was what he was doing. From this point of view, Leopold's being in Juliers was a godsend, and the longer he stayed there, fortifying himself and adding to his garrison, the more men Henri could reasonably expect from his allies as an initial commitment, to get Leopold out. So there was no hurry. There must also be no suggestion of French leadership—the quarrel in the first instance was Brandenburg's and Neuberg's, after all, not Henri's. Therefore, before the king's plans could be set in motion, the two claimants had to commit themselves specifically to the provision of a certain number of men to attack Leopold when making their request for aid; Henri would go to war as their auxiliary.

By August the king was fretting over the claimants' failure to make such a request to him; he thought that perhaps they feared that he would attach religious conditions to his help. But in September it looked as if the wheels might at last be ready to turn: Count Albert von Solms, an important official at the court of the Elector of the Palatinate, arrived in Paris as the claimants' envoy. It turned out, however, that he had nothing to promise the king; his mission was to ask Henri's permission for the claimants to use the two French regiments in Dutch service, and to request the king to ask the Dutch to supply them with artillery and munitions. The Dutch were uneasy about this, unless Henri was prepared to give them an ironclad promise of intervention, which he would not do until the claimants had committed their own forces more fully. So the king held his hand—he was, so Solms's son later told Prince Maurice, "nothing so warm at their departure as . . . at their first arrival." Boderie's return to England was delayed, and Henri contemplated sending an agent to the claimants to induce them to do better than this.[39] He denied to the ecclesiastical Electors that he had any intention of invading Cleves or Julich, and informed the Pope that the

[39] Aug. 16, 1609, Carew to Cecil; Oct. 10, William Becher to Carew; Nov. 3, Nov. 16, Becher to Cecil, P.R.O., S.P. 78/55, ff. 156–59, 206–208, 217–19, 223–25. Nov. 25, Winwood to the Privy Council, *Winwood* III, 89–91. Becher, Carew's secretary, was left in charge of the Paris embassy after Carew's departure late in September.

issue was one of right rather than religion—after all, the Imperialists were pushing the claims of the Elector of Saxony, claims which Henri refused to countenance.[40]

All this delay served its purpose: it helped to convince Henri's potential allies that he was not aggressive, and thus made them more willing to follow his lead. Cecil reiterated in November that James's policy was to cooperate with others whose interest was more nearly concerned. At the same time he repeated his bewilderment at Henri's vacillations.[41] Winwood also professed bafflement at Henri's tactics. His support of the Protestant cause Winwood found astonishing; so, too, was Henri's energetic promotion of a meeting of the claimants, the princes of the Protestant Union (the league of German princes formed in the wake of the Catholic coup in the city of Donauwerth in 1607), and the representatives of England, France, and the Netherlands: this would take time, and meanwhile Leopold would act.[42] There were straws in the wind, however. Henri was negotiating with Savoy. There were reports of a marriage alliance which rather alarmed the English, and of an aggressive war in Italy.[43]

At last, in December, Henri got what he wanted from Brandenburg and Neuberg. The claimants were understandably cautious; Henri's tactics could easily be interpreted as suggesting that his policy was to embroil them with Leopold and then offer them aid on terms they might find unpalatable.[44] Finally, however, the rep-

---

[40] P.R.O., S.P. 81/9, f. 252, S.P. 78/55, ff. 200–202. Oct. 25/Nov. 4, 1609, Foscarini to the Doge and Senate, *C.S.P. Venetian 1607–1610*, p. 377. James too was not inclined at this stage to pay any heed to the Saxon claim. Nov. 9/19, Nov. 23/Dec. 3, Correr to the Doge and Senate, *ibid.*, pp. 386–87, 392–93.

[41] Nov. 19, 1609, Cecil to Becher, P.R.O., S.P. 78/55, ff. 232–33.

[42] Nov. 2, 1609, Winwood to Cecil, P.R.O., S.P. 84/66, ff. 300–302. See also Nov. 7/17, Foscarini to the Doge and Senate, *C.S.P. Venetian 1607–1610*, p. 384.

[43] Sept. 27/Oct. 7, Oct. 25/Nov. 4, 1609, Foscarini to the Doge and Senate, Nov. 16/26, Correr to the Doge and Senate, *C.S.P. Venetian 1607–1610*, pp. 365, 378, 389–90. Nov. 21, Becher to Cecil, P.R.O., S.P. 78/55, ff. 235–37.

[44] On this point see Becher's letters of Oct. 10 and Nov. 3, 1609, P.R.O., S.P. 78/55, ff. 206–208, 217–19.

resentatives of the claimants and of the other princes of the Protestant Union met in Heidelberg and agreed that the claimants
would raise 4,500 foot and 1,200 horse, and the other princes 4,000
foot and 1,000 horse, to attack Juliers. The ambitious and aggressive Prince of Anhalt hastened to Paris with the news; the delighted
king agreed at once to match their numbers as long as they produced
at least 8,000 foot and 2,000 horse. He would also send a delegate,
Jean de Thumery, seigneur de Boissise, to their assembly, and would
consult at once with the English and Dutch.[45]

At the same time King Henri had another small piece of good
fortune, though no doubt he regarded it as at best a blessing in disguise. He had lately been paying court in his own unambiguous way
to the Princess of Condé, a ripe charmer of fifteen, who panicked at
the attentions of this aging but vigorous Lothario and fled to Brussels, followed by her husband. The king professed to believe that the
Archduke had foreknowledge of Condé's flight.[46] Condé was a
prince of the blood; if the Archduke gave him and his wife asylum,
Henri could always pick a quarrel over this, at whatever expense to
his personal dignity. Henri hated to be frustrated; it may well be that
the princess's decision to decamp added a certain urgency to his desire to come to grips with his Habsburg foes.

The arrival of Condé in his territories caught the Archduke by
surprise, and Spinola wrote to Spain to ask Philip what he wanted
to do. The answer came back with surprising speed—in less than a
month—that the king would protect Condé.[47] Henri clamored for
the extradition of the fugitives, ostensibly because Condé might
attempt to jeopardize the succession of Henri's son if the king
should die.[48] There were reports, from time to time, of French plots

[45] *Winwood* III, 96–97.
[46] Dec. 1, 1609, Becher to William Trumbull, *ibid.*, p. 92. Trumbull was in
charge of the Brussels embassy.
[47] Dec. 19/29, 1609, Spinola to Philip, Jan. 17/27, 1610, Philip to Spinola,
Pays-Bas I, 343–44, 345.
[48] Feb. 24/Mar. 6, 1610, Boderie to Henri, *Boderie* V, 104–23.

to kidnap the princess and murder her husband.[49] The Spaniards found the whole affair amusing; the Archduchess Isabella remarked that she could not help laughing whenever she thought of Henri's face.[50] Henri was not above laughing too. When he was told that the princess was having a gay time in Brussels, and being kissed by the Archduke's courtiers, he remarked, "She will kiss the Spaniards so long, that at length she will gain the escrouelles [scrofula], and then she must be fain to come to me to be cured."[51]

More serious business was afoot across the Channel. On December 23 Boderie departed for London. He was to tell James that Henri supported Brandenburg and Neuberg, that he wanted to oust Leopold from Juliers, peacefully if possible, by force if necessary. Henri wanted to act jointly with England, which would mean, also, action with the Dutch, who would follow the Anglo-French lead. To make James less reluctant to take action which might well result in war, Boderie was to stress the religious nature of the confrontation at Juliers—a line the exact opposite of which Boissise was to use with the ecclesiastical Electors of Germany, in order to keep them neutral.[52] Henri believed that James was likely to go along, if only to prevent too great an increase in French influence; so Boderie was to find out if an alliance could be negotiated, preferably an offensive alliance. To make such a proposal more attractive, Boderie was instructed to agree that a settlement of the French debt be included in the league. He could also tell James, if asked, that a league with Savoy would be concluded in February.[53] At the same time Boissise was sent off to Germany, the pace of the French negotiations with Savoy quickened, and the process of contracting for Swiss mer-

---

[49] Feb. 13/23, 1610, Foscarini to the Doge and Senate, *C.S.P. Venetian 1607–1610*, p. 429. Feb. 12, Throckmorton to Lisle, *De L'Isle* IV, 180–81.

[50] Apr. 12/22, 1610, Isabella to Lerma, *Pays-Bas* VI, 154.

[51] Jan. 18, 1610, Becher to Trumbull, *Winwood* III, 106.

[52] Feb. 22/Mar. 4, 1610, Contarini and Correr to the Doge and Senate, *C.S.P. Venetian 1607–1610*, pp. 438–40.

[53] The instructions are dated Dec. 18/28, 1609. *Boderie* V, 1–29.

cenaries began.[54] Anhalt, meanwhile, moved on to The Hague, to ask the Dutch for three regiments of foot, which, in the view of Sir John Throckmorton, he was apt to get.[55] The wheels were turning.

Boderie had considerable success, in spite of the suspicions which occasionally cropped up in London that the real object of the French was to embroil England with Spain.[56] Henri's hot-and-cold tactics of the past few months had convinced the English that he did not want a major war, that what he had in mind was just what he said he wanted: to get Leopold out of Juliers.[57] James dared not allow the French to act alone, and thus become the sole leader of anti-Habsburg Europe by default. So, by the end of January, the fundamental decision was made: England also would join in the expedition, to the extent of 4,000 men. Boderie and Caron were delighted.[58]

The king's decision to join in the military action against Leopold was not an easy one for a ruler who prided himself above all on his reputation as a peacemaker. According to the Venetian ambassador his great hope was that Leopold would be frightened or coaxed into getting out of Juliers, so that there would be no need to fight at all.[59] Until that happened, however, England, having committed herself, had to prepare to implement the commitment at minimum cost to her embarrassed treasury. On February 8 Winwood was instructed to ask the Dutch for the use of 4,000 men from the ranks of the English regiments in Dutch service; England would take over the payment of their wages for the duration of the campaign.

[54] Dec. 21, 1609, Becher to Trumbull, *Winwood* III, 99. Dec. 28, Becher to Cecil, P.R.O., S.P. 78/56, ff. 10–13.

[55] Dec. 28, 1609, Throckmorton (see Chapter II, n. 63) to Trumbull, *Downshire* II, 202–203.

[56] See, e.g., Mar. 22/Apr. 1, 1610, Boderie to Henri, *Boderie* V, 160–73.

[57] See, e.g., Dec. 28, 1609, Edmondes to Trumbull, *Downshire* II, 210–11.

[58] P.R.O., S.P. 84/67, ff. 24–31. Jan. 29, 1610, Cecil to Becher, P.R.O., S.P. 78/56, ff. 16–18. Feb. 8/18, Contarini and Correr to the Doge and Senate, *C.S.P. Venetian 1607–1610*, pp. 426–27.

[59] Apr. 16/26, Apr. 26/May 6, 1610, Correr to the Doge and Senate, *C.S.P. Venetian 1607–1610*, pp. 470–72, 479–81.

The charges were calculated at over £6,000 a month; the English hoped the Dutch would agree to find the actual cash and deduct their expenditures from their debt to England. If they did not agree to this, it would be necessary to ask Parliament for money, and Cecil did so in February.[60]

Winwood was further instructed to urge the Dutch to make their own separate contribution to the expedition, and to point out that the English contingent, though numerically smaller than that of France, represented about the same amount in terms of additional costs, since Henri was planning to use the French regiments in Dutch service, which he already paid, as part of his commitment. Winwood was to go to Dusseldorf to notify the claimants and their allies of the English decision, and to urge them to stick together and settle the question of rightful ownership judicially or by arbitration. England took no sides in this matter; her purpose was to prevent war, since God had committed the general peace of Christendom especially to England.[61] Here spoke James the peacemaker, and there is no question of his sincerity. He informed a Saxon agent who had come in search of support for the Elector's tenuous claim that his master should join with Brandenburg and Neuberg either in working out a compromise or in agreeing to a judicial proceding which would be compatible with the Imperial constitution.[62]

Winwood had no difficulty in getting the States-General to agree to the loan of the men, who would return to Dutch service after the campaign. There was to be a separate English commander. Sir Edward Cecil, the secretary's nephew and an experienced if hardly gifted soldier, was chosen; his only superior was to be the commander-in-chief of the combined armies, a post first slated for Anhalt but later taken over by Prince Maurice. The French request that

[60] P.R.O., S.P. 81/10, f. 42. Feb. 1/11, Feb. 22/Mar. 4, 1610, Contarini and Correr to the Doge and Senate, *C.S.P. Venetian 1607–1610*, pp. 419–21, 438–40. Feb. 9, Edmondes to Trumbull, *Downshire* II, 236–37.

[61] P.R.O., S.P. 84/67, ff. 24–31.

[62] Feb. 8, 1610, Cecil to Winwood, *ibid.*, ff. 22–23.

Maurice take command, which Winwood reported on May 3, was one more indication of the scope of Henri's plans.[63] Winwood in fact had been getting nervous about the situation for some time, not only about Henri's ambitions, but also about the domestic confusion in the Republic, where the city of Utrecht was in a virtual state of rebellion against the financial demands of the government. He delayed his departure for Dusseldorf on account of the situation in Utrecht, and asked his government for specific instructions to the effect that the English troops were to be used only for the purpose of ousting Leopold from Juliers and putting the claimants in possession.[64] The Dutch were nervous too, especially over Henri's ultimatum to the Archduke demanding that the latter allow the French army to pass through his territories. Oldenbarnevelt would not commit the Dutch to support this move as fully as Henri wished, and expressed the hope that Henri would go through the territories of the archbishop of Trier instead; as Winwood said, they remembered Vervins.[65]

Winwood also wanted instructions in the matter of a possible English alliance with the Protestant Union, which was urging James to join it, perhaps even become its head. The idea was attractive to James, but not so attractive that he was willing to become entangled in a large-scale war in consequence, and he evidently feared that such a move on his part would arouse the Catholics of Germany and lead them to support Leopold. The Union sent the Prince of Wurttemberg to London in mid-April to persuade the king to join, and to ask for greater military aid. The Prince was to stress that the Union's survival was a necessity, in order to provide protection to its members from the encroachments of the Emperor, whose regime was "Espagnolisé et corrumpu par les Jésuites, Janizaires du Pape." Such language was apt to appeal to the king, but by then Henri's plans were becoming apparent, and James's caution reasserted itself.

[63] *Ibid.*, ff. 121–22.
[64] Mar. 31, 1610, Winwood to Cecil, *ibid.*, ff. 69–72.
[65] See Winwood's dispatches of May 3, 1610, *Winwood* III, 155–57.

At the end of April he betook himself to Royston and Newmarket to hunt, and to avoid having to give the Prince a direct answer—or so the Venetian ambassador believed. It was the general opinion in London that James would join the Union eventually, but that he would keep this alliance separate from the projected league with France.[66]

Once the English decision to join in the expedition against Juliers was made, the negotiations for an Anglo-French alliance took on a new urgency and importance. Cecil, in his discussions with Boderie, asked what would happen if Spain intervened. The ambassador replied that France would go ahead anyway, and that this possibility made an Anglo-French defensive league all the more necessary. Cecil rejoined that that was all very well, but that France's attitude on the debt had not been conducive to persuading the English to negotiate.[67] Here was the sticking-point: France would have to make some firm agreement on the debt, or there would be no alliance. The financial situation of the English government was very bad, and worried Cecil greatly: this was the year of the abortive Great Contract.

Henri, as always, was unwilling to pay, and justified his unwillingness by his belief that England was an unreliable ally, and would be more unreliable than usual if a breach with Spain occurred. Since Henri was determined to force such a breach, the league with England was necessary, if only to prevent her from siding with Spain in the event of a French victory. So Henri agreed to what he expected would be a fictitious concession: if there were no war with Spain, Henri would pay James 600,000 livres (£60,000) over a four-year period in total settlement of all his claims. If war with Spain broke out, there would be no payments. Since, according to

[66] Apr. 16/26, Apr. 26/May 6, May 2/12, 1610, Correr to the Doge and Senate, *C.S.P. Venetian 1607–1610*, pp. 470–72, 479–81, 481–83. May 2, Edmondes to Trumbull; May 3, John More to Trumbull, *Downshire* II, 284–86, 287–88. The Union's appeal to James is in P.R.O., S.P. 81/10, ff. 34–39.
[67] Jan. 29/Feb. 8, 1610, Boderie to Henri, *Boderie* V, 37–46.

the English figures, France owed about six times that amount, this was hardly a princely offer. Another problem, in Henri's view, was the English decision to provide their 4,000 men from their regiments in Dutch service; he was afraid that the Dutch defenses would be too much weakened—another clear indication that he anticipated a general war.[68]

Boderie transmitted the king's offer to Cecil as if it were his own idea, in order to give himself and his government as much room for maneuver as possible. Cecil was not happy with the slow rate of payment, and expressed a preference that France assign a specific branch of the revenue to the repayment, but Boderie was hopeful that he would accept the French offer. The ambassador was himself in the dark as to the scope of his master's plans. He did not believe that a general war would break out; he wanted the English alliance, and, in a well-meant effort to bring agreement nearer, he suggested that Henri might cut down on his military commitment to the claimants and apply the savings to payment of the debt. He told the king that the only way England could practically supply her 4,000 men was by using the men in Dutch service, on account of her financial difficulties, and that if he expressed any concern to them for the security of the Dutch frontiers, they would think that Henri was anticipating a general war.[69] Henri saw the force of this last argument and dropped the matter. He unhesitatingly rejected Boderie's suggestion that he cut down on his military commitment, but he was willing to pay the 600,000 livres in three years rather than four, if the rest of the treaty was satisfactory. The agreement on the debt was to be kept separate from the treaty of alliance, however, so that England would not be able to renege on her military commitments by alleging French welshing on the debt payment.

[68] Feb. 12/22, Feb. 17/27, 1610, Henri to Boderie, *ibid.*, pp. 58–73, 89–96. See also Historical Manuscripts Commission, *Mss. of the Duke of Buccleuch and Queensberry* (London, 1899), I, 46.

[69] Feb. 24/Mar. 6, Mar. 3/13, 1610, Boderie to Henri, *Boderie* V, 104–23, 124–27.

As for the alliance itself, the essential questions, in the French king's view, were the commercial clauses, the spelling-out of the conditions under which the *casus foederis* would obtain, and the amount of aid to be provided. Henri was willing that the Scots be included in the treaty, but not that English merchants have the commercial privileges in France of their Scottish counterparts. He was also eager to have the mutual assistance clauses become operative in the event of rebellion as well as war. The king was thinking perhaps of the possibility of disturbances in France over the succession after his death, or of a rising on the part of unreconstructed Leaguers when he launched his attack on Spain in alliance with the Protestant powers.[70] At all events the inclusion of rebellion was calculated to please James, who continued to be nervous over the situation in Ireland. Henri clearly wanted the alliance; he even went so far as to use polite language about James and Cecil in public, which for him was most unusual; this persuaded the Venetian ambassador that the alliance would indeed be made.[71]

The English were still not satisfied on the question of the debt; "we are not so honorably used as I could wish," wrote Cecil's secretary Levinus Munck to Winwood on March 3.[72] Cecil insisted that the payments be made in two years. He also wanted the Dutch to assume, as part of their debt to England, those payments which France had made them after Sully's treaty which the French had defalked from their indebtedness. There would be no league, Cecil warned, if this question were not settled. As before, Boderie was sympathetic; the English, he said, were insisting on payment in two years out of sheer necessity.[73] Henri stalled a bit longer; Boderie was

---

[70] Mar. 10/20, 1610, Henri to Boderie; Mar. 14/24, Brulart to Boderie, *ibid.*, pp. 128–50, 155–60.

[71] Mar. 14/24, 1610, Foscarini to the Doge and Senate, *C.S.P. Venetian 1607–1610*, pp. 448–49.

[72] *Winwood* III, 127–28.

[73] Mar. 22/Apr. 1, 1610, Boderie to Henri; Mar. 26/Apr. 5, Boderie to Villeroy, *Boderie* V, 160–73, 179–80.

instructed to discuss the question of renewal of earlier treaties, which Cecil was willing to do.[74] The Venetian ambassador in England reported that opinion in government circles was pro-French: there was greater fear of Spanish resurgence than of possible French gains.[75] Then, in mid-April, with the time for the launching of the great campaign rapidly approaching, and perhaps encouraged by Boderie's report of the strength of anti-Spanish feeling in England,[76] the king instructed Boderie to make the concession on the timing of the debt payments, and to tell Cecil that he would do everything he could to get the Dutch to agree to assume that part of the English debt which was comprised in French payments to the Dutch—all payments, a total of some three and a quarter million livres by French calculation, including those made after the Anglo-Spanish peace, the legitimacy of the defalcation of which from the French debt England had never admitted.[77] If the Dutch in fact assumed the payment of this amount, this, taken together with the 600,000 livres Henri agreed to pay directly, would satisfy the English claims according to England's own reckoning.

Henri made a great parade of having yielded to English importunity in order to be sure of her friendship,[78] but as far as the alliance was concerned, the concession came too late. William Becher's reports from France indicated that Henri was levying troops on a far larger scale than had been indicated in his original commitment to Anhalt, that he would command the army himself, and that Spinola was himself mobilizing to contest any French attempt to enter the

[74] Apr. 6/16, 1610, Villeroy to Boderie; Apr. 17/27, Boderie to Villeroy, *ibid.*, pp. 180–85, 192–200.

[75] Mar. 8/18, 1610, Correr to the Doge and Senate, *C.S.P. Venetian 1607–1610*, pp. 446–47.

[76] Apr. 10/20, 1610, Boderie to Brulart, *Boderie* V, 186–92.

[77] Apr. 18/28, 1610, Henri to Boderie, *ibid.*, pp. 200–209. See also Apr. 18/28, Villeroy to Boderie, *ibid.*, pp. 210–16. The French figures are in P.R.O., S.P. 84/66, f. 338.

[78] See, for instance, May 8, 1610, Browne to Trumbull, *Downshire* II, 288–90.

territories of the Archduke.[79] The English at last saw that Henri was planning a major war, and they were growing cautious. Agreement had been reached quickly enough on the commercial articles, and on the use of the treaty of 1572 as a model for the new agreement, and England was willing to accept a clause including rebellion as a justification for asking for aid, as long as it was loosely enough drawn to avoid committing them to helping suppress a religious re- volt on the part of the Huguenots. But they haggled over the word- ing of the agreement on the debt, though ultimately they accepted in principle the French proposal that the Dutch should pay the amount the French had defalked on their debt to England on account of their payments to the Dutch, since Henri had promised to get the Dutch to agree to this.[80] The English purpose obviously was to evade commitment at this stage, since if Henri was going to war with Spain they would not be paid anyway. Boderie bewailed the lost opportunity: if the concession on the debt had been made at once, the treaty would now be an accomplished fact. Boderie wrote thus on May 2;[81] three days later his king was dead, and his grandiose schemes with him.

On May 4, the eve of Henri's death, Cecil sent a long dispatch to Winwood which indicated the uncertain stance of English policy. A special embassy from The Hague had arrived in London to ask James to increase his contingent destined for Juliers, accept a Dutch commander for it, and negotiate a tighter alliance with them, the French, and the Union. They also wanted an Anglo-Dutch trade treaty, exemption from the edict on fishing, and English support in their various controversies with the Archduke. Cecil either rejected or sidestepped all of these requests, though he was carefully polite and announced his readiness to talk about most of them. Delay was

[79] See Becher's letters of Mar. 1, Mar. 19, Mar. 28, 1610, P.R.O., S.P. 78/56, ff. 36–38, 42–44, 50–51.
[80] May 4, 1610, Cecil to Winwood, P.R.O., S.P. 81/10, ff. 43–51.
[81] *Boderie* V, 233–48.

clearly the English object, until they discovered whether there would be a major war.[82]

The English government, remembering the belated French enthusiasm for the Spanish-Dutch truce of the year before, was rather slow to credit the evidence of Henri's new aggressiveness. The indications were there, however. On March 1 Throckmorton reported the rumors circulating in The Hague that a Franco-Dutch scheme was afoot to attack Spain, and that Henri was preparing a second front by subsidizing Savoy.[83] From Spain Cottington reported that Franco-Spanish relations were very bad, that the Spanish government was nervous and upset, in no condition to take action, and wishfully hopeful that Henri's great levies did not mean what they obviously did mean.[84] From England's Italian listening-post in Venice Wotton reported the rumors of a plot between France and Savoy and the prominent part played by the French ambassador in Venice in blocking a Spanish request that Venice permit 6,000 German troops to cross her territory from the Tyrol to reinforce Milan.[85] By early April the report from The Hague was that Henri's army would be in the neighborhood of 25,000 to 30,000 men,[86] far more than was necessary to reduce Leopold's little garrison. The Catholic camp in Germany was in obvious disarray, and would be unable to provide Leopold with any real assistance. The reports from Becher in France of the scope of Henri's preparations, of the decision, despite some misgivings in the French Council, to ally with Savoy and to attempt, unsuccessfully as it turned out, to include

[82] P.R.O., S.P. 81/10, ff. 43–51.

[83] *Downshire* II, 175–76. See also Apr. 22, 1610, Winwood to Cecil, P.R.O., S.P. 84/67, ff. 90–94. Becher had voiced these suspicions as early as January. P.R.O., S.P. 78/56, ff. 7–9.

[84] See his letters of Mar. 21, Apr. 15, May 11, 1610, in P.R.O., S.P. 94/17, ff. 53, 65, 84–86.

[85] See Wotton's letters of Jan. 11/21, Mar. 3/13, Apr. 27/May 7, and May 4/14, 1610, in P.R.O., S.P. 99/6, ff. 1–3, 25–27, 36–37, 38–41.

[86] *Downshire* II, 273–74. On Apr. 9/19, 1610, Anhalt informed James that Henri would send more than the 10,000 men he had promised. P.R.O., S.P. 81/10, f. 33.

Venice in the anti-Spanish combination as well, of the king's plan to take command of the army himself, of the ultimatum to the Archduke demanding permission to cross his territory—all this pointed inescapably in one direction.[87] The last-minute acceptance of the ultimatum by the Archduke, who was as unprepared as his Spanish brother-in-law, after some feverish efforts to raise sufficient forces to defend himself and a suggestion that he might return the Princess of Condé,[88] was not likely to conjure the storm. But then Ravaillac's little pin bore through Henri's castle wall, and farewell king!

The murder of Henri IV saved the peace-loving James from an entirely unlooked-for and unwelcome involvement in a major war. It had taken the French government a long time to fathom the somewhat foggy diplomatic world in which the Scottish Solomon moved, the combination of benevolence and passivity and talk and belief in the right, all complicated by financial necessity, which were its central characteristics. James did not share the anti-Spanish temper of his people. He did not believe in rebellion, or in war, even to serve the English national interest. But he could be led, if an appeal could be made to his vanity and to his desire for diplomatic success on the cheap, because he was timid and feared isolation. Henri's tactics in this final crisis were supremely skillful, and he carefully led James, step by step, to the brink of the abyss. Even his one tactical error, in his handling of the problem of the debt, cost him very little. By May, 1610, it was impossible for James to pull back without sacrificing all his friends in Europe and becoming utterly dependent on the unlikely possibility that he could make a friend of the Habsburg colossus. English unwillingness to make policy for herself had led her almost to the war which James, above all things, wished to avoid.

[87] See Becher's dispatches from Feb. 2, 1610, on, P.R.O., S.P. 78/56, ff. 19ff.
[88] Apr. 27, 1610, Becher to Trumbull, *Downshire* II, 283.

CHAPTER VIII

❊ ❊

After Henri IV

IN THE *State Papers, France*, in the Public Record Office in London there is an anonymous document attributing to Henri IV all sorts of ambitious territorial designs in Italy, the Empire, and the Low Countries: "But these designs Machiavell, the Devil, and the Jesuits taught the Spaniards to disaffect, by a poor knife in the hand of a resolute knave."[1] No evidence connects Spain with Ravaillac, though there is no doubt that the Habsburgs were both pleased and relieved at his deed—the Archduchess Isabella, for example, wrote to Lerma that God looks after His own.[2] They had good cause for rejoicing; their most implacable enemy in Europe was no more. The government of Philip III was the great gainer by the assassination; England, where opinion was profoundly shocked, was ultimately to be the principal loser.[3]

The removal of Henri IV at this particular moment was almost certain to lead to a revolution in French foreign policy. His son and heir, now Louis XIII, was a boy of nine, and although his father's fears that his succession might be challenged proved groundless, he

[1] P.R.O., S.P. 78/56, ff. 429–30.
[2] *Pays-Bas* VI, 155. See also May 16, 1610, Cottington to Cecil, P.R.O., S.P. 94/17, f. 91.
[3] Not all Englishmen regretted Henri's death. Wotton, for one, was not too sorrowful, since Henri, after all, was a renegade Protestant. May 18/28, 1610, Wotton to Cecil, P.R.O., S.P. 99/6, ff. 42–43.

obviously could not govern for himself. His mother, Marie de Medici, became regent—a timid, cautious, pious, and rather stupid woman whose principal objective was to keep everything as quiet as possible for as long as possible. Everyone in France remembered all too well the disasters which had befallen the country during the years of power of the other Medici queen. The aristocratic pressure groups which the late king had kept in check inevitably revived, but they were no more anxious for a return to civil war than was the Queen Regent. They made demands on her, for money and power and office, but they did not push her too far. Marie, in her turn, granted as much as she could, and sometimes more than she should, and, inevitably, jealousies arose. She came more and more to rely on one of her countrymen, an ambitious and unintelligent adventurer named Concini, on whom she showered titles and offices, and who was eventually assassinated with the young king's connivance—he too was jealous of Concini—in 1617.

Foreign observers also remembered the days of Catherine de Medici, and wondered whether France was to undergo a similar agony. Every indication that this might happen was duly noted and carefully reported to their governments. The letters of Sir Thomas Edmondes, whom James had designated to succeed Carew and who arrived in Paris to take up his post within a month of the assassination, are full of such reports and speculations. At one point shortly after his arrival Edmondes spoke to the Regent in a way which suggested that he was offering to mediate between her and her nobility, an attitude which Marie naturally resented. James hastily disclaimed any desire to meddle in French domestic affairs, but added that he did not want to see his friends and relatives badly treated.[4] France, Edmondes felt, was hovering on the brink of civil catastrophe—a catastrophe which never quite arrived, but which for years appeared to be imminent. In such circumstances the value of alliance with

---

[4] July 5/15, 1610, Villeroy to Boderie; July 13/23, Boderie to Villeroy, *Boderie* V, 330–38, 358–66. July 8, Edmondes to Cecil, P.R.O., S.P. 78/56, ff. 208–11.

France markedly diminished in the eyes of the government in London.

Nor was this all. France was henceforth an unreliable friend—but was it certain that, reliable or not, she would even remain a friend? The Queen Regent was far more apt to be influenced by the agents of the Roman Church than her ex-Huguenot husband had been; Edmondes took careful note of the waning influence of Sully, owing not only to his religion but also to his opposition to the Regent's generosity with the state's money.[5] From the beginning King James and his advisers were afraid that Marie might turn into a heresy-hunter. Sully's decline and Bouillon's lack of influence alarmed them; it was their steady policy to urge the Huguenot leaders to stick together and not to quarrel amongst themselves. The French government, in its turn, was suspicious of James's dealings with the Huguenots, protested against his unconcealed view that France was slipping into the hands of the Jesuits, and resented his occasional warnings that he could not allow any persecution of the Huguenots on religious grounds to pass unchallenged.

Marie's religious proclivities, coupled with her desire to avoid any sort of domestic or foreign crisis during her son's minority, pointed in one direction: rapprochement with Spain. France would no longer be the leader of anti-Habsburg Europe. Instead, she would adopt the policy which James had been following for the past seven years, a policy of peace and neutrality and friendship with everyone. The new direction in French policy became gradually apparent in the months which followed the death of the king. After some initial hesitation the Regent decided to honor Henri's treaty commitments to the German Protestants, and to send the promised forces to oust Leopold from Juliers. The Archduke's last-minute capitulation to Henri's demand that he be allowed to cross the Archduke's territory made it easier for Marie to do this, since she could, and did, avoid

[5] See, e.g., June 27, Nov. 20, 1610, Jan. 19, 1611, Edmondes to Cecil, P.R.O., S.P. 78/56, ff. 196–97, 354–55, S.P. 78/57, ff. 12–14. Aug. 18, 1610, Edmondes to Winwood, *Winwood* III, 208–209.

the large-scale war which Henri had envisaged. But the delay in the arrival of the French forces, the underhand maneuvering which was designed to persuade Leopold's commander in Juliers to surrender to the French alone and not to the combined force, the effort to have a neutral Catholic named as administrator of Juliers instead of the representatives of Brandenburg and Neuberg—all this was indicative of the new policy, and gave rise to very deep suspicions among the Protestant powers. Marie also abandoned Henri's forward policy in Italy; the alliance with Savoy was dropped, and the duke left to fend for himself, to placate the angry Spanish government as best he could. Among the duke's maneuvers was a vain attempt to arrange a marriage alliance with England.

As seen from London, then, French policy abroad as well as at home took on an increasingly anti-Protestant coloration. France was suspected of wanting to disrupt the alliances and friendships which existed among the Protestant states, of reverting to the policy of a Catholic league. In one of his letters to Edmondes King James raised the specter of St. Bartholomew's Day and spoke of "this alliance and popish cabal" between France and Spain which he was anxious to break up.[6] The Regent had no intention of cutting all her ties with the anti-Habsburg world, however. She continued to pay the French regiments in Dutch service, though she did so only on condition that the Dutch assume payment of the bulk of the French debt to England. The Dutch yielded to this blackmail, albeit with a very bad grace, calculating that James's financial embarrassments would lead him in the end to accept a small proportion of the debt in cash rather than wait forever for the whole, and that in this way they could regain control of their cautionary towns, a calculation which ultimately proved correct. Marie also authorized the conclusion of the league with England, which was signed on August 19, 1610. It was, essentially, a defensive alliance; if either party was attacked it could call on the other for a certain specified amount of aid. The

[6] Aug. 27, 1612, James to Edmondes, B.M. Stowe Mss. 173, ff. 79–81.

commercial treaty of 1606 was renewed, with some additional clauses which dealt with problems inadequately covered in that treaty. The endless question of the debt produced prolonged haggling, was only partially settled, and finally was omitted save in the most general way from the treaty.[7]

The English willingness to sign this treaty, even though the question of the debt was not settled, marked a considerable shift in their attitude and reflected the uncertainties of the post-Henrician diplomatic scene. In part, certainly, the willingness stemmed from a realization that France would not now precipitate a major war. James and his advisers saw how perilously close they had come to being lured into such a war, and their chief anxiety now was to finish the dangerous business at Juliers as expeditiously as possible. "I only wish that I may handsomely wind myself out of this quarrel, wherein the principal parties do so little for themselves," James wrote to Cecil after the fall of Juliers.[8] But there was more to the English decision to sign the treaty than the fact that it was not likely now to plunge them into war. The new tendencies in French policy were already apparent; an English alliance might bind France to the Protestant camp, might make the feared Franco-Spanish rapprochement more difficult to achieve, might, in fact, make it possible for England to achieve the leadership of the coalition which Henri IV had put together, and use it for pacific purposes. To this end James and Cecil pushed ahead with the negotiations for a similar defensive alliance with the princes of the Protestant Union, an alliance which was signed in March, 1612, and which James hoped would help to blunt the dangerous rivalries among the various claimants to the Cleves-Julich inheritance and thus minimize the possibility of English involvement.[9] James urged both France and the Dutch to make

[7] The treaty is in P.R.O., S.P. 103/9, ff. 175–82. The negotiations can be followed in *Boderie* V, 252 ff.

[8] Quoted in S. R. Gardiner, *History of England from the Accession of James I to the Outbreak of the Civil War* II, 100.

[9] See, e.g., James's instructions for John Dickinson in December, 1610, P.R.O., S.P. 84/67, ff. 212–15, and his letter to the princes of the Union in

similar alliances with the Union; the French would not, but the United Provinces did so, in May, 1613.

The death of Henri IV thus gradually caused the English government to adopt what appeared to be a new line in foreign policy, a line which, if logically followed, would put England at the head of anti-Habsburg Europe. Yet it was not really a new line; it was the same old line, with all of its many contradictions gradually becoming more and more exposed. James's major preoccupation was still to keep the peace and to live on good terms with everybody. It was a policy which made sense only if James was free to mediate between two fairly clearly defined opposing camps, free to throw his weight in whatever direction would keep (or restore) the peace, and, when he was compelled to take sides, to do so as an auxiliary rather than as a principal. It was not a policy which was compatible with the leadership of one of the major parties, unless that party was incontestably the stronger. James's party would be so only if France were a member of it, and if France remained strong. France was no longer as strong as she once was. Nor, for that matter, was England: all of Europe knew of the king's financial difficulties and the steadily increasing weakness of his armed forces, and of the domestic divisions within the country.[10] Furthermore, France was no longer a reliable member of the anti-Habsburg coalition. Her new policy of friendship with everyone was made dramatically clear by the double marriage treaty with Spain, which was negotiated in 1611, and which was followed, during the next two years, by prolonged negotiations with England for a French bride for James's heir, first Prince Henry, then, after his death, Prince Charles.

If Marie de Medici was going to play the role which James had

---

November of that year, P.R.O., S.P. 81/10, ff. 227–29. The text of the treaty is in T. Rymer, *Foedera* XVI, 714–18.

[10] In November, 1610, Boderie spoke of the possibility of a Sicilian Vespers directed against the Scots, "tant ils continuent à être détestés et abhorrés." *Boderie* V, 506–13. See also June 22/July 2, June 30/July 10, 1612, Pedro de Zúñiga to Philip III, P.R.O., S.P. 94/19, ff. 107, 109. Zúñiga, formerly the Spanish ambassador in England, was on a special mission to England in 1612.

been playing during the lifetime of Henri IV, then there were really only two options open to James: he himself really did have to play Henri IV and actively take upon himself the leadership of anti-Habsburg Europe, or else he would have to adopt a policy of isolation and withdraw altogether from the affairs of the Continent. His financial condition, for which he was largely responsible and which Cecil did not effectively improve,[11] dictated a policy of isolation, since the alternative required military and financial preparedness on a scale which was beyond the abilities of James and Cecil to provide with the crown's regular resources and which Parliament in its current mood would not supply.[12] James did not understand this, and Cecil, who might have, lost considerable influence with the failure of the Great Contract. Cecil's health began to break under the immense burden of his accumulated offices, and he died in May, 1612, unmourned by most of his colleagues. The years which followed his death were disastrous. Cecil's gifts as an administrator and statesman have perhaps been overrated, but in comparison with the mediocrities who succeeded him he was a positive genius. Worse still, the cohesion which he, in his unique position, had been able to impose on the formulation and conduct of foreign policy evaporated. Winwood, who became secretary of state in 1614, was a competent enough diplomatist, but he never possessed the king's full confidence; in addition he was irascible, difficult to deal with, and thoroughly unimaginative. He was also Puritan-minded and anti-Spanish; so he supported James's conception of himself as the leader of European Protestantism.

The leader of a party, of course, has to lead; James's failure to do so was an additional handicap to him in the stance which Winwood wished him to adopt after Henri's death.[13] In this new situation

[11] See the damning account of Cecil's stewardship in M. Prestwich, *Cranfield, Politics and Profits under the Early Stuarts* (Oxford, 1966), ch. 1.

[12] Parliament was "much distasted already ... with the King's excessive demands," wrote one observer a few days after Henri's death. *Winwood* III, 159–61.

[13] See, e.g., Aug. 4, 1610, Winwood to Cecil, P.R.O., S.P. 81/10, ff. 105–107.

James's tactics remained the same as before: to eschew the initiative, to wait on events rather than to anticipate them, and then, once he was faced with a given situation, cope with it as best he could, just as he had during the negotiation of the Truce of Antwerp. The king's passivity was unpopular with his diplomatists. "It hath always been our custom," wrote Edmondes in 1611, "to seek still to put off the time and never to endeavour the preventing of mischiefs till they be fallen upon us, which maketh that afterwards they are not either at all to be remedied, or at the least not without great difficulty."[14] James's attitude was particularly dangerous with respect to Spain. "We . . . are contented through the charms of our fatal security to neglect our own welfare, and to believe either that Spain will do us no harm, or God miraculously without secondary means will deliver us from danger."[15] But James's ways were set. His attitude was still very much that of the king of Scots, the ruler of a small, weak state facing a powerful neighbor, save that the microcosm of Britain had been exchanged for the macrocosm of Europe: the place which England had occupied in his thinking before 1603 was now taken by Spain. And, of course a king of Scots had to wait upon events, since he had no power to influence them. In this field, as in so many others, the king held to attitudes which circumstances had made obsolete.

James may have been the most prominent of the Protestant rulers of Europe, but there was hardly such a thing as a Protestant party. James did exert himself, and with some success, to keep the peace among the Protestant powers. His mediation helped to end a war between Sweden and Denmark in 1613, and he was instrumental in preventing an eruption over the Cleves-Julich problem. This question constituted one area in which England and France were able to cooperate, since Marie de Medici was no more anxious than James to see a war break out over the disputed provinces. But James could

[14] *Downshire* III, 128–29.
[15] Nov. 6, 1612, Trumbull to Sir John Digby, English ambassador in Spain, Historical Manuscripts Commission, 10th Report, App. 1, pp. 612–13.

not bring about a settlement of this immensely complicated matter, and as the years went by, his relations with the Dutch grew steady worse as the commercial rivalry between the two nations mounted, both in Europe and overseas. England's decision to sell the cautionary towns in 1616 removed one potentially serious check on Dutch aggressiveness. ("Ever since the restoring of those cautionary towns the Hollander hath much neglected us and forgotten who were his protectors and supporters," wrote Bishop Goodman.)[16] This situation was partially counterbalanced by the Dutch awareness that the truce with Spain had but five years to run. James was aware of the fragility of the diplomatic structure he had built; he was aware of the unreliability of France and of her seeming weakness; and so he turned to the policy which seemed to him the most likely means of keeping the peace: he sought the friendship of Spain.

A great deal of nonsense has been written about James's policy toward Spain, largely because that policy collapsed so disastrously in the 1620s. By then, it is true, the policy made very little sense, but this does not mean that prior to the outbreak of the Thirty Years War it was altogether foolish. What James sought from Spain was not the same sort of agreement as that which he might have made with Henri IV. A league with Henri would have had an anti-Spanish thrust, and might well have led to war. What James wanted from Spain was not an arrangement directed *against* anybody, but rather one which would preserve peace. Those contemporaries who disapproved of James's attitude laid most of the blame on the Spanish ambassador, Count Gondomar, who served in England, with one two-year break, from 1613 to 1622. Gondomar was depicted as devilish and Machiavellian, a Jesuit in courtier's clothing, who obtained an unparalleled and sinister influence over the king, and until recently most historians of the period have followed this line.[17] In

---

[16] G. Goodman, *The Court of King James the First* I, 49.

[17] A more accurate assessment of Gondomar began with the brilliant sketch by G. Mattingly, *Renaissance Diplomacy* (Boston, 1955), pp. 255–68. Mat-

fact Gondomar was neither as influential nor as sinister as has been commonly believed. Nor, indeed, as clever: in a country where anti-Spanish feeling was strong and openly expressed, he made far too much of a parade of his influence with the king. Gondomar genuinely believed in the desirability of Anglo-Spanish friendship; it was, therefore, most unwise of him as well as of James to allow it to appear that James was following such a policy, not because it was in the interest of England, but because of the ambassador's personal influence.

James never undertook to explain his foreign policy to his people: this, after all, was a matter for the king to decide. Law and precedent were on the king's side in this matter, but hardly wisdom, especially when a shift in policy was involved which ran directly counter to the most deeply felt national prejudices. James's policy of coexistence with Spain was not necessarily foolish or detrimental to the English national interest, given the soundness of the premise on which it was based, namely, that the Spanish government was itself weak and therefore anxious for peace. There was plenty of evidence to support such a view: the truce with her rebels in the Netherlands, her passivity in the Cleves-Julich crisis, the problem of the Moriscos, the corrupt and indolent regime of the Duke of Lerma. These weaknesses were stressed by the new ambassador in Spain, Sir John Digby, a very able man, who managed to create an intelligence network which supplied James not only with a list of those Englishmen receiving Spanish pensions but also with copies of Gondomar's dispatches from London.[18] It was the general belief, to be sure, that Spain had great potential strength, and that a long breathing-space might allow her to build up her resources and once again become a

---

tingly's suggestions have been followed up by his student, C. H. Carter, in various articles and in his *The Secret Diplomacy of the Habsburgs 1598–1625.* Professor Carter is at work on a full-scale study of Gondomar.

[18] Carter, *Secret Diplomacy*, p. 129. Mattingly, *Renaissance Diplomacy*, pp. 260–61.

menace to the other states of Europe. Henri IV thought so: hence his plan to renew the war. James, however, utterly rejected the philosophy of preventive war. He was under no illusions as to the genuineness of Spanish goodwill toward him; all his life, both before and after 1603, he had had to cope with Spanish and Catholic plots. But if Spain, for whatever reason, was now anxious for peace, then it only made sense to extend the hand of friendship to her, because, given the condition of France, only Spain could plunge Europe into a major war.

James, like most other dynasts, believed firmly in the value and potential permanency of royal marriage alliances. Prior to the death of Henri IV James had dabbled in marriage diplomacy; after 1610, with two of his children, Henry and Elizabeth, of marriageable age, he took it up seriously—he never had any enthusiasm for cradle contracts. His policy in this regard was a clear reflection of his view of the European diplomatic scene and of England's place in it. In his capacity as the leading Protestant ruler in Europe he married his daughter Elizabeth to the young Elector of the Palatinate, who might be expected in due course to become the leading Protestant prince in the Empire. There was never any serious consideration given to a Catholic husband for Elizabeth; apart from everything else, such a marriage might lead the Catholics to attempt to restore England to the ancient faith by the simple expedient of assassinating James and his male progeny.[19] For his son and heir he sought a Catholic wife, and he came to believe that the most useful bride would be a daughter of Spain. There were only two alternatives, really, Spain

[19] So wrote Dudley Carleton from Venice in July, 1611, ostensibly quoting the opinion of the Venetian government, but actually reflecting his own, since he talked of the "treacherous and bloody practices of Romanists and Spaniards." P.R.O., S.P. 99/7, ff. 372–75. In 1610 the Swedish government wanted to discuss the possibility of Elizabeth's marrying Gustavus Adolphus. James rejected the overture because he wanted to marry his daughter to a prince whose state was "less subject to opposition and unquietness." P.R.O., S.P. 75/4, ff. 191–95. It is interesting if inconclusive to speculate on how history might have been changed if this marriage had taken place.

or France, since it was not simply a matter of a Catholic wife—there were Italian princesses aplenty, some with sizeable dowries, if it came to that—but rather, of a Catholic wife who would further England's diplomatic objectives.

As between Spain and France, Spain appeared to be the better choice. The long negotiations over the debt did not inspire anyone in England with confidence that France would be willing to pay whatever dowry might be agreed on, even though the French were far more accommodating about the debt after Henri's death than they ever had been before; furthermore, Marie de Medici's largesse to her grasping aristocrats raised serious questions as to her ability to pay. James's need of ready cash to mitigate his financial woes was great, and increased after the fiasco of the Addled Parliament in 1614. In the second place the shift in French policy after 1610, the pro-Spanish outlook of the Regent, made a French match much less desirable. There seemed not much more to be gained from a French princess than from a daughter of Savoy, and it seems likely that the sporadic marriage negotiations with France were undertaken principally with an eye to disrupting the Franco-Spanish marriage arrangements. These arrangements were both distasteful and alarming to the English government, which became more mistrustful than ever of Marie de Medici's regime. Furthermore, a bargain with France might well involve England in pledges respecting the Huguenots. James had no desire to become involved in any active way in their behalf, but any commitment respecting them which he might make to the government of Marie de Medici might well be interpreted as a betrayal, and seriously damage James's pretentions to the leadership of continental Protestantism.

In a sense, however, all the preceding were secondary considerations. The crux of the matter was this: if the policy of peace was truly to be furthered, only a match with Spain would help. Spain, having neutralized France by the marriage treaty with her, might become aggressive again; after the treaty was announced, even the peace-loving Archduke contemplated measures against the English cloth trade.[20] James's convictions as to the desirability of friendship with Spain for the sake of peace were strengthened by Gondomar, who believed firmly in the necessity of good relations, whatever Spain's continental objectives might be, whether peace or war, and who sincerely wanted the marriage to take place. The king's convictions were also the stronger because Cecil was no longer there. Cecil had never liked the idea of a marriage alliance with Spain. "Our brave Prince may find roses elsewhere instead of this olive there," he wrote in the last year of his life.[21] But it was the olive that his master came to seek.

James's error—apart from the blunder of making no attempt to explain his policy to his subjects—lay in his failure to understand that there were limits to the problems which a dynastic marriage could solve. Such a marriage could cement and solidify a pre-existing friendship, as had James's own to a Danish princess. It could add further to a tentative friendship between two states who had no major conflicting ambitions and some interests in common, as did the marriage alliance negotiated in the time of Henry VII and Ferdinand and Isabella. The situation in the second decade of the seventeenth century bore very little resemblance to that of the 1490s, however. In addition to the religious gulf between the two countries, there were at least two major causes of friction, in the colonial world and in the Netherlands. Either James would have to abandon his commercial and territorial designs in the overseas world—or rather, compel his subjects to do so—or Spain would have to accept the English view, which James upheld as vigorously as had Elizabeth, that only effective occupation allowed a power to claim a monopoly, and that the sea (except, of course, the British sea) was free to all. As for the Dutch, either James would have to abandon them, or Spain would have to make a genuine peace with them and acknowledge their independence without reservation. In this period there were rumors

[20] May 23, 1612, Digby to Trumbull, *Downshire* III, 300–301.
[21] Sept. 5, 1611, Cecil to Carleton, P.R.O., S.P. 99/8, ff. 63–64.

that some of these things might happen, but they were most unlikely, and in fact never did occur.

Even so, an Anglo-Spanish marriage alliance might prevent these potential sore spots from erupting and leading to a major clash, if both sides were willing to work to see to it that this happened, and there was a major counterbalancing factor here, in the growing Dutch aggressiveness in the colonial world, which worked to the disadvantage of both England and Spain. What a marriage alliance could not do, what it was futile to expect a marriage alliance to do, was to settle an immediate crisis which arose because the parties had a major conflict of interest, as James might have learned from the failure of Don Pedro de Toledo's mission to France in 1608.[22] An infanta for Prince Charles could not resolve the complication over the Palatinate in the 1620s; James was right when he expressed his unwillingness to marry his son with a portion of his daughter's tears. He should never have tried, because by the 1620s it was obvious that Spain no longer shared any of his objectives. She was no longer pacific; her interest was no longer in the maintenance of the European status quo, but rather in its alteration.

Had James been a younger and more resilient man when the great diplomatic crisis of his reign came upon him with the Thirty Years War, he might have been able to adjust and devise a policy to meet it. The king's neglect of business had long been apparent; but in his last decade the difficulty went deeper than mere neglect. In 1616 the Venetian agent in London commented on "the daily increasing abhorrence which he feels for the toils and cares involved in government. In order to escape them, he lives almost entirely in the country, accompanied by a few of his favourites, whose counsels, conceived in their own interests, are very remote from decisions involving expense and trouble."[23] James's behavior in the years after 1618 is a

---

[22] See above, pp. 120–22.
[23] *C.S.P. Venetian 1615–1617*, pp. 314–15. It has been suggested that James suffered from porphyria. See I. Macalpine and R. Hunter, "Porphyria and King George III," *Scientific American* CCXXI, 1 (July, 1969), 46.

classic example of the truth of Machiavelli's remarks about the disaster which overtakes a prince who is unable or unwilling to adapt his conduct to meet changed circumstances. A policy which made perfectly good sense at a time when it appeared that the only major power capable of disturbing the peace of Europe did not wish to do so, no longer made sense when that power, for whatever reason, became involved in a major effort to alter the status quo.

James's inadaptability went deeper, however. He was too wedded to his policy of peace and friendship with everyone. The policy had worked, and worked well, for James for thirty years. It had brought great results while he was still only James VI; when he became James VI and I it still worked, first because of the character and policy of Henri IV, as this study has tried to make clear, and then, delusively, for a few years more owing to the temporary exhaustion of Spain. Given the dangerous situation in the decaying Holy Roman Empire, however, a situation which was clearly growing worse year by year, when crises like that over the Cleves-Julich succession could not be solved but only prevented from erupting because all the potential fishers in those muddy and dangerous waters were simultaneously and temporarily willing to hold their hands, peace was at the mercy of an incident.

The turning point of James's reign was the Truce of Antwerp. It was in the English interest that the war between Spain and the Dutch should go on as long as possible, exhausting both sides, while James and—to a lesser degree, because he supported the Dutch more substantially—Henri IV stood by and profited from that exhaustion. Had there been a real understanding between England and France when the peace negotiations began, it seems probable that they could have kept the war going, as Henri very much wanted to do. Because there was no such understanding, because each suspected that the other was anxious somehow to profit from the situation at his expense, each government came to the conclusion that the safest way out was to allow the war to end. The majority of the onus for this disaster must fall upon James; his penchant for playing *tertius gau-*

dens had given him a reputation for unreliability which his irresolute behavior in the opening months of the negotiation did nothing to dispel—though, to be sure, as seen from London, the reliability and benevolence of Henri IV were certainly open to question. Henri came to see quickly enough that the truce spelt potential disaster for France, and he moved to renew the pressure on Spain, only to die before he could launch his war. The truce and the great king's death, taken together, changed the whole aspect of European diplomacy and set the stage for the Thirty Years War—not, indeed, for the eruption in Bohemia, which was likely in any event, but for the invasion of the Palatinate, which would have been far less likely without the truce and the change in French policy which occurred after 1610. And it was the invasion of the Palatinate which made the war into an European war, and which brought James's diplomatic house crashing in ruins around his head.

Possibly the fact that the truce was a truce, and would expire in twelve years unless, in the meantime, it was converted into a permanent peace, lulled James into a false sense of security. The Spanish-Dutch conflict was not really ended; when it resumed, England would regain the advantage she enjoyed before 1609. None of the tentative efforts made after 1609 to convert the truce into a permanent peace came within measurable distance of success. What produced the disaster for England was the unfortunate coincidence that the crisis in Bohemia which gave Spain the excuse to invade the Palatinate broke out just before the truce was due to expire, when such a military gamble, if successful, would pay maximum dividends. To occupy Juliers with eleven years of the truce unexpired would be foolhardy; so Leopold's little army met its fate. To occupy the Palatinate with only one year unexpired made far better sense, and James's daughter and son-in-law, and James himself, suffered the consequences.

The actions of murderous fanatics are always unpredictable, and it is unlikely that a different diplomatic constellation in the spring of 1610 would have deterred Ravaillac. It is quite possible, however, that the policy of Marie de Medici's government would have been different if the Spanish-Dutch war had still been going on. There might, of course, have been a shift in French policy in any case, given the domestic circumstances of the country, but the fact of general peace made it much easier for the regent to bring about the change. So it is not too much to say that for the foreign policy of James I the Truce of Antwerp was a misfortune which brought all the failures of the later years of the reign in its wake, and the disaster was owing in large measure to the failure of England and France to arrive at a diplomatic understanding which would have prevented it. The government of Henri IV would have welcomed such an understanding, in spite of the hostility to England which pervaded official circles in Paris, because it would have furthered the anti-Spanish policy which France so steadily pursued during his reign. James, however, failed to see that his apparent freedom of choice as between France and Spain was illusory, and he was most reluctant to enter any sort of political agreement, bilateral or multilateral, with Henri IV. The French interpretation of Sully's treaty made him thoroughly distrustful of Henri, and his vanity made him unwilling to play second fiddle to the French king in a general alliance. The personal animosity between the kings, which colored all their dealings with each other, was crucially important in their inability to come to an agreement. In the years between 1603 and 1610 James's government was occasionally fearful that English failure to make a league with Henri might lead to a Franco-Spanish rapprochement, but such qualms usually passed quickly enough. Enmity between Spain and France was taken to be a permanent fact of life, and so no serious attempt was made to arrive at an understanding with France until it was too late.

Too often we have heard of the failures which were owing to the deficiencies of King James—his arrogance, his laziness, his penchant for favorites. In this case, at least, his failure was owing in some degree to his virtues. He believed in peace. Peace for England: hence there must be no entangling commitments which might lead to war. Peace for others, too, even if such a peace damaged English interests, if the only alternative was English participation in a war. Peace is a blessing, to be sure, but not every peace. It was to prove tragic for England and for himself that King James did not see this truth more clearly.

INDEX

❖ ❖

Aerssens, François van, Dutch agent in Paris, 62, 74, 77–78, 102, 107

Albert, Archduke, ruler of the Netherlands: sends Aremberg to England, 20; besieges Ostend, 21; and Anglo-Spanish peace, 36, 37; relations with England after peace, 45–46; and negotiations for end of war with Dutch, 68–69, 72, 77, 82, 104–108, 119, 128–33; and Tyrone, 91–93; and Anglo-Dutch league, 114–15; sends Giron to England, 127; and English Catholic exiles, 138; and Cleves crisis, 147–50, 153; gives asylum to Condés, 156–57; Henri's ultimatum to, 160, 165, 167; mentioned, 7, 41, 44, 63, 65, 143, 180. *See also* Isabella, Archduchess

Anhalt, Christian, Prince of, 156, 158, 159, 164

Anne, Queen, wife of James I, 26, 34, 103

Antwerp: Dutch refuse to allow reopening to trade, 49; and Spanish-Dutch peace negotiations, 108; decay of trade in, 134; mentioned, 46, 47

Antwerp, Truce of: signed, 133; effect of, 134–37, 140; Venetian opinion of, 142; significance for James, 182; mentioned, 71

Aremberg, count of, Archduke's ambassador in England, 20, 22, 28, 29

Baldwin, Father, Jesuit: and Gunpowder Plot, 46, 65

Beaumont, Christophe de Harlay, count of, French ambassador in England: irritates James, 22; and Anglo-French commercial negotiations, 54, 55; return to France, 58; mentioned, 20, 29, 38, 51, 52, 57

Becher, William, English agent in France, 164

Bellarmine, Robert, Cardinal: James's controversy with, 137–39, 146

Bingley, George, 111

Boderie, Antoine le Fèvre de la, French ambassador in England: instructions to, 63-64; and James, 64–67, 78–79, 95; and Cecil, 65, 76, 78; attitude to Spain, 66; on Anglo-Spanish relations, 76-77; and Tyrone affair, 93; and alliance with England, 111–12, 123, 157, 158, 161–66; and debt negotiations, 111–12, 125; and English proclamation on fishing, 143–44; mentioned, 61, 91

Boissise, Jean de Thumery, seigneur de: mission to Germany, 156, 157

Bouillon, Henri de la Tour d'Auvergne, duke of, 32, 63, 65, 170

Boulogne: peace negotiations at, 7, 9

Brandenburg, John Sigismund, Elector of: and Cleves-Julich crisis, 142–67 *passim*, 171

Brizuela, Inigo, 130

Browne, Sir William, English commander at Flushing, 67, 144

Brulart, Pierre, French secretary of state, 85, 102, 140–41

Buzenval, Paul Chouart, seigneur de, French agent in the United Provinces, 68

Camerino, bishop of, Papal nuncio in France, 33–34

Carew, Sir George, English ambassador in France: and Franco-Spanish relations, 50; to replace Parry, 56; Villeroy's opinion of, 67; and French debt, 73–74, 102–103, 124–25; and Tyrone affair, 92–93; view of French, 110; account of condition of France, 140; welcomes Treaty of Dortmund, 148; mentioned, 59, 60, 63, 85, 101, 120, 121, 131, 134, 137, 149, 153

Carleton, Dudley, 38, 57, 87, 96
Caron, Noel, Dutch agent in England: Boderie instructed to cooperate with, 64; and Anglo-French marriage alliance, 112; and English proclamation on fishing, 144–46; and English decision to intervene in Cleves crisis, 158; mentioned, 49, 69, 72, 85
Cautionary towns: and Anglo-Spanish peace, 36; payment of garrisons, 100, 102; and Anglo-Dutch league, 114; Dutch buy back, 171, 176; mentioned, 37, 46–47, 60, 101, 104, 127
Cecil, Sir Edward: to command English contingent at Juliers, 159
Cecil, Robert, English secretary of state: and James, 13, 18; political outlook, 17; and Spain, 18–19, 44–45, 51, 66, 91, 115, 136–37, 180; and Dutch, 20, 21, 47–49, 99–101, 109–10, 165–66; and Turkey, 31; and nuncio in Paris, 33–34; rewarded for Spanish peace, 38–39; and Anglo-Flemish trade, 41–42; and France, 51–52, 53–58, 65, 73, 76, 78, 79, 81, 85, 103, 109–10, 111, 113, 122–24, 125, 161–66; and Dutch-Spanish truce negotiations, 105–109, 129; and Don Pedro de Toledo's mission, 121; and proclamation on fishing, 143; and Henri's tactics in Cleves crisis, 155; death, 174; mentioned, 6, 69, 72, 87, 94, 151
Charles, Prince, 181
Christian IV, King of Denmark, 21, 148
Clement VIII, Pope, 8, 33
Cleves, William, Duke of: death, 146
Cleves-Julich crisis, 116, 142–67 passim, 175–76, 182
Concini, Concino, 169
Condé, Prince of: flees to Brussels, 156–57
Condé, Princess of: flees to Brussels, 156–57; mentioned, 167
Cornwallis, Sir Charles, English ambassador in Spain: opinion of Anglo-Spanish peace, 42; and problems of trade, 42–44; and Franco-Spanish relations, 50; on chances of Dutch-Spanish peace, 108–109; and Don Pedro de Toledo's mission, 121; involvement in sovereignty question, 128–29; mentioned, 46, 76, 97, 100, 115, 122, 136, 138, 153

Coton, Pierre, Jesuit, 32
Cottington, Francis, English agent in Spain, 166

Debt, Dutch, to England, 44, 47–49, 100, 102, 113, 163
Debt, French, to England, 9, 24, 27, 39, 51–52, 68, 72–74, 100–103, 111, 124–25, 161–62, 171
Denmark, 21, 135, 175
Digby, Sir John, English ambassador in Spain, 177
Dortmund, Treaty of, 148, 149
Droit d'aubaine, 55, 56, 58

Edmondes, Sir Thomas: English ambassador in Flanders, 50; and Tyrone affair, 91–93; to succeed Carew in Paris, 153; on French situation, 169; opinion of English policy, 175; mentioned, 13, 62, 87, 100, 129, 138, 150
Elizabeth I: policy toward Scotland, 5; and succession question, 6; and Henri IV, 9; mentioned, 4, 12, 39
Elizabeth, Princess, 123, 178
England: Catholics in, 8, 138; political relations with France, 8, 15, 50–53, 59–60, 67, 72–74, 74–76, 109–10, 122–24, 137, 161–66, 168–72; commercial relations with France, 9, 24, 29–30, 53–59, 74, 110–11; and balance of power, 13; relations with the Dutch, 14, 46–49, 59–60, 68, 97–102, 109–10, 113–16, 176; relations with Spain, 15, 27, 34–40, 42–44, 53, 76–77, 180–81; change in policy anticipated 1603, 17; relations with Turkey, 30–31; and Franco-Spanish commercial relations, 31–32; relations with Archduke Albert, 41, 45–46, 127–30; pacifism of, 61, 82; and Spanish-Dutch negotiations, 69–70, 71, 72, 74–75, 77–79, 81, 94–96, 97–102, 106, 109, 113–16, 127–30, 136–37; irresolution of, 85; financial position of, 100, 139, 174; and Don Pedro de Toledo's mission, 120; nature of policy assumptions, 137; military unpreparedness, 139; pro-Spanish faction in, 140; proclamation on fishing, 142–46; policy after Treaty of Dortmund, 150–51; and Protestant Union, 160–61, 172; anti-Spanish opinion in, 164; post-

Henrician policy of, *passim. See also* Cecil; James I
English Channel: proposal to demilitarize, 45–46
Essex, Robert Devereux, earl of, 6, 17

Fishing: English proclamation on, 142–46
France: relations with Spain, 9, 14, 31–32, 34, 53–54, 121–22, 140, 170–72, 173, 179; commercial relations with England, 9, 24, 29–30, 53–59, 74, 110–11, 143; privileges of Scottish merchants in, 10; growing strength of, 13; relations with the Dutch, 14, 60–62, 68, 97–102, 104; political relations with England, 15, 19, 60–62, 67, 74–75, 76–77, 96, 122–24, 127, 137, 161–66, 170–72, 179; Cecil's view of, 18; and Anglo-Spanish peace, 27–29, 34–37, 39–40; and Anglo-Turkish relations, 30–31; policy wavers, 66; naval preparations, 69; and Spanish-Dutch relations, 69–72, 74–75, 77–79, 96, 97–102, 105, 109, 134–36; Italian policy of, 74–76; Carew's view of, 110, 140; condition of, 1609, 135–36; pro-Spanish faction in, 140; welcomes Treaty of Dortmund, 148; reaction to seizure of Juliers, 149; evidence of aggressiveness of, 166; effect of Henri IV's death on, 168–71; shift in foreign policy, 170–72; and Protestant Union, 172–73. *See also* Debt, French; Henri IV

Geneva, 22
Giron, Don Fernando: mission to England, 127, 129, 131
Giustinian, Georgio, Venetian ambassador to England: on Anglo-Spanish relations, 45; on English policy toward Dutch, 48; on English pacifism, 61; on English and French policy in Italy, 75; on Dutch-Spanish peace, 87–88
Gondomar, Don Diego Sarmiento, count of, Spanish ambassador in England, 139, 176, 177, 180
Goodman, Godfrey, bishop of Gloucester, 3, 176
Gunpowder Plot, 44, 46, 48, 51, 62, 138

Hampton Court, Treaty of: negotiated, 26–27; English interpretation of after Anglo-Spanish peace, 51–52, 62; French view of, 73
Hay, James, Lord, 35
Henri III, King of France, 5, 77
Henri IV: opinion of James, 7, 9–10, 15, 29, 69–70, 80, 84, 129–30, 138, 153, 184; and English succession, 8, 10; attitude to Spain, 13, 121–22, 134, 178; and Papacy, 14, 75; attitude to England, 19–20, 22, 34–35, 50, 52–53, 54–55, 59, 62–63, 90, 99, 103, 123, 125, 161–66, 182–83; instructions to Sully in 1603, 23–24; illness in 1603, 24–25; and Anglo-Spanish peace negotiations, 28, 38, 39; religious policy of, 32–33, 51; and James's religious policy, 33; attitude to Dutch, 53, 86, 98–99, 102, 103; Italian policy of, 60, 74–76; change in policy 1605, 62–63; disciplines Bouillon, 63; instructions for Boderie, 63–64; instructions for Jeannin, 79–80; hostility to Cecil, 84; suspicion of Oldenbarnevelt, 84; and Tyrone affair, 92–93; sends ostriches to James, 110; and Richardot's letter on truce, 127–28; Carew praises, 140; and Cleves-Julich crisis, 147, 150, 152–58, 160; and flight of Condés, 156–57; levying troops, 164; death, 165, 167; significance of death of, 168ff.
Henry VIII: and English succession, 6
Henry, Prince of Wales, 44, 74
Holland, 74, 107, 108
Holy Roman Empire: and Cleves succession, 142–67 *passim*
Huguenots, 22, 35, 170

Ibarra, Don Diego de: mission to Flanders, 82–83
Indies: and Anglo-Spanish peace, 36; and Dutch-Spanish negotiations, 106–108, 131–34
Inquisition, 36, 43
Ireland: Spain's failure in, 7; and Anglo-Dutch league, 114; mentioned, 91, 139, 163
Isabella, Archduchess, wife of Archduke Albert: Spanish candidate to succeed Elizabeth, 7; favors peace with Dutch, 82; and flight of Condés, 157; reaction to Henri's death, 168
Italy: French policy in, 60, 74–76

James I: historians' views of, 3; as King of Scotland, 3–16 *passim;* character, 5, 184–85; opinion of Henri IV, 10, 15, 69–70, 95, 184; ideas on foreign policy, 11–16; views known, 1603, 17; and Cecil, 18; attitude to Dutch, 19, 48, 78–79, 81, 87, 91, 106, 109–10, 129–30; and siege of Ostend, 21; and peace with Spain, 23, 38–39; attitude to Spain, 25–26, 49–52, 81, 91, 139, 176–78; attitude to France, 25–26, 31–33, 49–52, 59, 68, 69, 75, 109–10, 182; and Sully's mission, 26; religious policy of, 33; laziness, 61; and Englishmen in Archduke's service, 62; and Bouillon episode, 65; sends deer to Henri, 110; Maurice insults, 132; pacifism, 136; controversy with Bellarmine, 137–39; weaknesses in policy of, 139–41; and Treaty of Dortmund, 148, 150–51; and Cleves crisis, 158–61, 172; and Protestant Union, 160–61; and Ireland, 91, 163; Henri's death saves from war, 167; and Marie de Medici, 169–72; financial difficulties, 173; character of policy, 173–76, 181–85; marriage diplomacy of, 178–81

Jeannin, Pierre, French diplomatist: heads commission to advise Dutch, 72, 79; instructions to, 79–80; analyzes Dutch opinion, 83–84; and Dutch-Spanish negotiations, 84, 86, 90, 108, 119, 126, 128–29, 132–33; and Winwood, 84, 89, 110, 125–26; and toleration for Catholics in United Provinces, 90, 134; and treaty of guarantee with Dutch, 97–99, 103–104, 131; attitude toward England, 104, 111–12, 123, 134; Maurice's view of, 135; and English proclamation on fishing, 144; and Cleves question, 147

Jesuits: English dislike of, 32, 34, 51, 160

Joyeuse, Cardinal: mediates Italian crisis, 76

Juliers: seizure by Leopold, 149, 150, 153, 154, 157, 158, 160, 161, 183; surrender of, 171

Lake, Thomas, 19, 94

Lennox, Ludovick Stuart, duke of: mission to France, 54

Leopold, Archduke: seizure of Juliers, 149, 150, 152, 153, 154, 155, 158, 160, 166, 170, 183

Lerma, duke of, 44, 130, 134, 136, 168, 177

Lesieur, Sir Stephen, English agent, 32, 136

Locks, Richard, English merchant in Spain, 42–43

Louis XIII, King of France, 26, 123, 168

Marseilles: plot to betray to Spain, 58, 62

Matthias, brother of Rudolf II, 147

Maurice, Prince: opposes peace with Spain, 71, 72, 116; reconciliation with Oldenbarnevelt, 126; insults James, 132; view of French government, 135; and Cleves question, 147; to command army against Leopold, 159–60; mentioned, 104, 109, 154

Medici, Marie de, wife of Henri IV: becomes regent, 169; policy of, 169–72, 175–76

Melville, Andrew, 5

Merchant Adventurers, 47

More, John, 120

Munck, Levinus, Cecil's secretary, 163

Neuberg, Philip Louis, duke of: and Cleves crisis, 142–67 *passim,* 171

Neville, Sir Henry: opinion of English policy in 1608, 121

Neyen, Jean, Archduke's agent, 83, 108, 109

Northampton, Henry Howard, earl of, 23, 42

Oldenbarnevelt, Johan van, Dutch statesman: mission to England in 1603, 21, 23; and Dutch debt to England, 47, 49; view of English policy, 68; leader of peace party, 72, 116, 117, 119; French opinion of, 84; and treaties of guarantee, 98, 99; and renewal of Dutch-Spanish truce, 109; reconciliation with Maurice, 126; and English proclamation on fishing, 144–46; and Cleves question, 147, 148, 160; mentioned, 65, 90, 153

Ostend: siege of, 21, 26

Owen, Hugh: England demands extradition of, 46, 65

Palatinate, Frederick, Elector of: marries Princess Elizabeth, 178

Papacy: quarrel with Venice, 60, 74–76; reaction to James's book, 138

Parliament, 4, 43, 67

Parry, Sir Thomas, English ambassador in France: on Sully's mission, 22; commercial negotiations with France, 29–30, 54–58; and Papal nuncio, 33–34; and Franco-Spanish relations, 49–50; and French debt, 51–52; Carew to replace, 56; mentioned, 37

Persons, Robert, Jesuit, 6, 34

Philip II, King of Spain, 7, 13, 15, 134

Philip III, King of Spain: government of, 7; and toleration for English Catholics, 8; and English succession, 8, 11; and peace negotiations with Dutch, 71, 91, 118–19, 131; Henri's view of, 134; and English Catholic exiles, 138; to protect Condés, 156; gains from Henri's death, 168; mentioned, 15, 50, 116, 130

Préaux, Charles de l'Aubespine, abbé de: mission to Archduke, 128

Protestant Union: and forces to attack Juliers, 156; and league with England, 160–61, 172; and league with Dutch, 172–73; mentioned, 155

Puritanism: impact on English policy, 139

Ravaillac, François, murderer of Henri IV, 167, 168, 183

Richardot, Jean, Flemish diplomatist: on Anglo-Flemish trade, 42; interprets Spanish ratification, 91; letter on truce without sovereignty, 127–30; and Indies trade, 131–32; and English proclamation on fishing, 144; death, 153; mentioned, 119, 150

Rudolf II, Holy Roman Emperor, 7, 136, 147, 149

Salisbury, earl of. *See* Cecil, Robert

Savoy, Charles Emanuel I, duke of: quarrel with Geneva, 22; relations with France, 135, 155, 157, 166, 171

Saxony, Christian II, Elector of: claim to Cleves inheritance, 146, 155; seeks English support, 159

Scaramelli, Giovanni, Venetian agent in England, 19, 23

Scotland: James as king of, 3–16 *passim*

Solms, Albert von: mission to Paris, 154

Spain: difficulties before 1603, 7; war with Dutch, 12, 13; weakness of, 13; relations with France, 14, 31–32, 34, 53–54, 153, 161, 163, 166, 173, 179; Cecil's view of, 17, 66; peace with England, 27, 34–40; commercial relations with England, 43–44, 76–77; and Dutch debt to England, 47; pensions English officials, 60–61, 136–37; suggests English mediation of Dutch war, 63–64; revival of power feared, 71; peace negotiations with Dutch, 72, 79, 82, 86, 90, 105–109, 118–19, 120, 125–26, 131–33, 135; and Italian situation, 75–76; war party in, 108; financial condition of, 108–109; and Anglo-Dutch league, 114–15; England potential ally, 136–37; and English proclamation on fishing, 144; and Cleves crisis, 150, 151, 166; gains by death of Henri IV, 168; James's policy toward, 176–81

Spencer, Sir Richard: commission to mediate between Spain and Dutch, 82; instructions to, 88–89, 94

Spinola, Ambrogio, Spanish commander in Flanders: favors end of war, 82; on question of Dutch sovereignty, 106; on religious question, 108; mobilizing in 1610, 164; mentioned, 75, 119, 130, 147, 150, 156

Stuart, Arabella, 22

Sully, Maximilien de Béthune, duke of: mission to England in 1603, 19, 22–28; on Anglo-French relations, 61, 137; proposals on Low Countries, 66, 68; and Treaty of Hampton Court, 73; and debt negotiations, 102–103, 111, 124–25; waning influence of, 170

Sweden, 135, 175

Throckmorton, Sir John, 158, 166

Toledo, Don Pedro de: mission to France, 120, 128, 129, 181

Turkey: relations with England, 30–31

Tyrone, Hugh O'Neill, earl of, 91–93, 107

United Provinces: war with Spain, 12, 13; England and France support, 14; commercial challenge of, 14–15, 71; Cecil's view of, 18; special missions to England, 19, 82, 86, 165–66; and Ostend, 21; and Sully's mission to England, 26; and Anglo-Spanish peace, 34, 35, 37–40; and Anglo-Flemish trade, 41, 45–46; relations with England after Anglo-Spanish peace, 46–49, 59, 65, 68; aid to, 51–53; and peace with Spain, 61–62, 72, 83–84; and Henri's move against Bouillon, 63; and truce with Archduke, 68–69, 77, 83, 93–95, 104–105, 109; war-weariness in, 74, 135–36; suspicion of England and France, 83; aid if war resumed, 89; Catholics in, 90; treaties of guarantee, 97–117 *passim*; issues in negotiations with Spain and Archduke, 105–108, 118–19; and Anglo-French marriage alliance, 112; independent policy of, 116; war party revives, 119; settlement with Spain imminent, 125–26; potential disunity of, 126; and final stage of truce negotiations, 127, 130–33; and English proclamation on fishing, 142–46; and Cleves-Julich crisis, 147, 148, 153, 154, 159, 160; assume French debt to England, 171; relations with England worsen, 176. *See also* Cautionary towns; Debt, Dutch

Venice: quarrel with Papacy, 60, 74–76; and French policy, 1610, 166–67

Verreyken, Louis, Flemish diplomatist, 83

Vervins, peace of, 9, 20, 76

Villa Mediana, count of, Spanish ambassador in England, 20

Villeroy, Nicholas de Neufville, seigneur de: and Anglo-Spanish peace negotiations, 27–28; instructions to Boderie, 64, 80; and England, 67, 103, 110–12, 123, 140; opinion of Carew, 67; opinion of Oldenbarnevelt, 84; and Dutch, 86, 102; and Tyrone affair, 92; and Richardot's letter on truce, 127–28; mentioned, 59, 77, 98, 102, 107

Virginia, 15, 139

Vitry, M. de, 29

Wilson, Thomas, 30

Winwood, Sir Ralph, English representative in the United Provinces: and Dutch-Spanish truce, 72, 74, 77–78, 82, 86–89, 90, 91, 93–94, 98–99, 100–102, 107–108, 119, 126, 128–29, 131–33; and Jeannin, 84, 110, 125–26; and triple league, 104; and Anglo-French marriage alliance, 112; friends' political views, 120–21; and Cleves-Julich crisis, 151, 152, 155, 158–61; becomes secretary of state, 174; mentioned, 37, 45, 47, 60, 65, 69

Wotton, Sir Henry, English ambassador in Venice, 75, 142, 166

Wurttemberg, Prince of: mission to London, 160–61

Zealand, 74, 107, 108

A note on the author

MAURICE LEE, JR., is professor of history and chairman of the history department at Douglass College, Rutgers University. Born in Buffalo, New York, he received his A.B., M.A., and Ph.D. degrees from Princeton University. His many honors include a Woodrow Wilson Fellowship, a Guggenheim Fellowship, and the David Berry Prize from the Royal Historical Society of London for his book *John Maitland of Thirlestane and the Foundation of the Stewart Despotism in Scotland* (1959). He is a member of the American Historical Association, the Conference on British Studies, and the Scottish History Society, and is a Fellow of the Royal Historical Society, London. Other books by Mr. Lee include: *Selections from Bayle's Dictionary*, with Elmer A. Beller (1952), *James Stewart, Earl of Moray* (1953), and *The Cabal* (1965).

UNIVERSITY OF ILLINOIS PRESS